GCSE
WORLD HISTORY
1870 to the Present Day

Peter Lane
Christopher Lane

Letts
EDUCATIONAL

Letts Educational
Aldine Place
London W12 8AW
Tel: 0208-740 2266
Fax: 0208-743 8451
e-mail: mail@lettsed.co.uk

First published 1984
Revised 1987, 1989, 1992, 1994, 1997
Reprinted 1992, 1995, 1996, 1999, 2000

Text: © P. Lane and C. Lane 1997
Design and illustrations: © Letts Educational Ltd 1984, 1992, 1995, 1996, 1997

British Library Cataloguing in Publication Data

A CIP record for this book is available from the British Library.

ISBN 1 85805 444 3

ACKNOWLEDGEMENTS

Thanks go to the following Examination Groups for their permission to use GCSE examination
material:
Edexcel Foundation (incorporating London Examinations)
Midland Examining Group
Northern Examinations and Assessment Board
Southern Examining Group

The answers supplied to Exam Board questions are solely the responsibility of the authors, and are not
supplied or approved by the Exam Boards.

The authors would also like to thank their wives and children for their encouragement during the
writing of this book. They also pay tribute to their teaching colleagues, fellow examiners and students
for the insights they have received over many years.
Christopher Lane would particularly like to thank colleagues and former students at Our Lady's
Catholic High School, Lancaster, for their encouragement in his career as a teacher.

Photographs and prints by permission of BBC Hulton Picture Library, Punch Ltd, the *Evening
Standard*, Camera Press Ltd.

Printed in Great Britain by Bath Press Colourbooks, Glasgow

Letts Educational Limited, a division of Granada Learning Limited. Part of the Granada Media Group

Contents

Starting points

Introduction 1
How to use this book 1
Introduction to GCSEs 1
Coursework 2
A revision programme 4
Advice and guidance on types of exam question 6

Syllabus analysis 8

History Topics

1 Russia, 1900–14 15
1.1 National and local government 15
1.2 The Russian People 15
1.3 Growing opposition to Tsardom 16
1.4 'A short, victorious war' with Japan 16
1.5 The danger of revolution 17
1.6 The October Manifesto, 1905 17
1.7 Weakening the Duma, 1906–14 17
1.8 Stolypin's reforms, 1907–11 18
Summary 18
Quick questions 19

2 International Relations, 1870–1914 20
2.1 A new German Empire 20
2.2 The Balkans, 1877–79 20
2.3 Keeping France isolated 21
2.4 The scramble for Africa 21
2.5 The Balkans, 1885–88 22
2.6 Kaiser Wilhelm (William) II, 1888–1918 22
2.7 New alliances and friendships, 1892–1907 23
2.8 The outbreak of war 23
2.9 Britain goes to war 24
Summary 24
Quick questions 25

3 The First World War, 1914–18 26
3.1 Great expectations dashed 26
3.2 Trench warfare 27
3.3 New weapons 27
3.4 The Russian front 28
3.5 The British and the Turkish front 28
3.6 The Arab revolt 28
3.7 The war at sea 29
3.8 The USA enters the war, April 1917 29
3.9 The Germans defeated 30
Summary 30
Quick questions 31

4 Peacemaking, 1919–23 32
4.1 The Conference at Versailles, 1919 33
4.2 The Treaty of Versailles, 22 June 1919 33
4.3 German humiliation and anger 34
4.4 The Treaty of St. Germain with Austria 34
4.5 Some criticisms of the Treaties 35
4.6 The Treaties of Sèvres (1920) and Lausanne (1923) 35

4.7 Mandated territories 36
Summary 36
Quick questions 37

5 The League of Nations 38
5.1 The Covenant 38
5.2 The organisation of the League 38
5.3 How did the nations judge the League? 40
5.4 Some early successes and failures 40
5.5 Failing major tests, 1931–39 41
5.6 The Disarmament Commission and Conference 41
Summary 41
Quick questions 42

6 Russia, 1914–53 43
6.1 Growing threats of revolution in Russia 43
6.2 The March 1917 Revolution and the fall of the Tsar 43
6.3 The failures of the Provisional Government 44
6.4 The November 1917 Bolshevik Revolution 44
6.5 The Treaty of Brest Litovsk, March 1918 44
6.6 The Russian Civil War, 1918–22 45
6.7 War Communism and the New Economic Policy 45
6.8 Lenin is succeeded by Stalin 46
6.9 Stalin eliminates his enemies 46
6.10 Stalin's modernisation of industry 47
6.11 Stalin's modernisation of agriculture 47
6.12 How World War Two affected the USSR 47
6.13 Stalin and society in the USSR 48
Summary 49
Quick questions 50

7 China, 1911–49 51
7.1 The land, people and government, 1900–1908 51
7.2 China and the western world 51
7.3 The 1911 Revolution 52
7.4 Chinese war lords 53
7.5 Sun in power, 1917–25 53
7.6 Chiang Kai-shek and Mao Tse-tung 53
7.7 Mao Tse-tung and the Kiangsi Soviet 54
7.8 The Long March, 1934–35 55
7.9 Chiang and the Japanese, 1931–37 55
7.10 The Civil war, 1945–49 56
Summary 56
Quick questions 57

8 Germany, 1919–30 58
8.1 Germany in 1918 after defeat in World War One 58
8.2 German attitudes to the Treaty of Versailles 58
8.3 The Weimar Constitution 58
8.4 Growing disorders in Germany, 1919–23 59
8.5 Reparations and hyper-inflation in 1923 59

8.6	Recovery under Gustav Stresemann, 1924–29	59
8.7	Weaknesses in the Weimar Republic's recovery	60
8.8	The Nazi Party, 1920–1928	60
8.9	The collapse of the Weimar Republic and Hitler's coming to power, 1929–33	60
8.10	Hitler's consolidation of power, 1933–34	61
8.11	The Totalitarian State	61
8.12	Why many Germans supported Hitler	62
Summary		63
Quick questions		63

9	The United States of America, 1919–39	64
9.1	Causes of the 1920's economic boom, 1919–1929	64
9.2	The effects of the boom: prosperity of the 'Roaring Twenties'	64
9.3	The economic problems hidden behind the boom	65
9.4	A violent society	65
9.5	The end of prosperity – The October 1929 Wall Street Crash	66
9.6	The Great Depression	66
9.7	Franklin Delano Roosevelt's New Deal, 1933–39	67
9.8	Opposition to, and failures of, the New Deal	67
9.9	Foreign policy	68
Summary		68
Quick questions		69

10	International Relations, 1919–39	70
10.1	Collective security	70
10.2	Acting outside the League	70
10.3	Japan, the League and Manchuria: Case Study 1	71
10.4	Italy, the League and Abyssinia: Case Study 2	71
10.5	Hitler's aggressive foreign policy, 1933–35	72
10.6	Three steps towards war, 1935–38	73
10.7	Czechoslovakia, 1938–39: Case Study 3	73
10.8	And so to war	74
Summary		75
Quick questions		75

11	India, 1900–49	76
11.1	Government and people, 1901	76
11.2	Wealthy Indians and the demand for change	76
11.3	Political reforms, 1909–19	76
11.4	Ghandi and politics, 1914–19	77
11.5	Ghandi and politics, 1920–35	78
11.6	The Government of India Act, 1935	78
11.7	India and the War, 1939–45	78
11.8	The last days of the Raj, 1946–47	79
11.9	A partitioned India	79
Summary		80
Quick questions		80

12	The Second World War, 1939–45	81
12.1	Poland partitioned, and the 'Phoney War'	81
12.2	Blitzkrieg in the west	81
12.3	The Battle of Britain	82
12.4	The Battle of the Atlantic	82
12.5	The Balkans and the Middle East	83
12.6	Russia, 1941–44	84
12.7	Italy, 1943–44	85
12.8	The Japanese War	85
12.9	The defeat of Germany	86
12.10	Wartime conferences between Allied leaders	86
Summary		87
Quick questions		87

13	The British Home Front, 1914–18 and 1939–45	88
1914–18		
13.1	'Over by Christmas'	88
13.2	The Liberal Government's attitude to war, 1914	88
13.3	The new reality, 1914–16	89
13.4	Soldiers versus civilians	89
13.5	Women and war	89
13.6	Air raids	90
13.7	The effects of the submarine campaign	90
13.8	Working people and the war	90
1939–45		
13.9	Early preparations	90
13.10	Government powers increased	91
13.11	Evacuees	91
13.12	Rationing	91
13.13	The Blitzes	92
13.14	Towards a new Britain	92
Summary		93
Quick questions		93

14	The United Nations Organisation	95
14.1	How the United Nations began	95
14.2	The aims of the United Nations Organisation	95
14.3	The organisation of the United Nations	96
14.4	Attempts of the UNO to keep the peace	96
14.5	The agencies of the United Nations Organisation	97
14.6	Peacekeeping by the UNO in the 1990s	98
14.7	Problems caused by the United Nations Aid policies	98
14.8	Comparison between the UNO and the League of Nations	99
Summary		99
Quick questions		100

15	International relations, 1945–64	101
15.1	Uneasy Allies: February–August 1945	101
15.2	The Cold War	101
15.3	1947: a critical year	102
15.4	The Cold War becomes even cooler, 1948–49	102
15.5	Two new alliances	103
15.6	A new attitude? 1953–56	103
15.7	Crises and conferences, 1960–61	104
15.8	The fall of Khrushchev, 1964	104

Summary		104
Quick questions		105

16	**Towards détente, 1964–95**	**106**
16.1	Russian expansionism, 1964–82	106
16.2	The arms race, 1960–70	106
16.3	Nixon's new foreign policy, 1968–73	106
16.4	Détente defined	107
16.5	A more peaceful Europe, 1972–75	107
16.6	SALT 2 and human rights	107
16.7	Reagan and the USSR, 1980–84	108
16.8	Reagan and Gorbachev, 1985–88	108
16.9	More arms reductions, 1989–95	109
Summary		109
Quick questions		110

17	**Three international case studies**	**111**
17.1	The Berlin Wall, 1961–89	111
17.2	The Berlin Wall – a case study	112
17.3	The Cuban Crisis, 1962	114
17.4	The Cuban Crisis – a case study	114
17.5	Vietnam, 1960–75	116
17.6	Vietnam – a case study	117

18	**Russia, 1964–95**	**120**
18.1	Khrushchev succeeds Stalin	120
18.2	De-Stalinisation	120
18.3	Modernisation of industry and agriculture	120
18.4	The fall of Khrushchev	121
18.5	The decline of Communism in the USSR, 1964–85	121
18.6	Mikhail Gorbachev and the collapse of Communism, 1985–90	122
18.7	The fall of Gorbachev	122
Summary		123
Quick questions		124

19	**Eastern Europe, 1945–95**	**125**
19.1	Stalin's European Empire	125
19.2	1948: Stalin's gains and losses	125
19.3	Extending Stalinist Power	126
19.4	Anti-Soviet movements, 1953–56	126
19.5	Czechoslovakia, 1968	127
19.6	Poland, 1970–80	127
Summary		128
Quick questions		128

20	**Western European Integration, 1945–95**	**129**
20.1	Why the European nations came closer together after 1945	129
20.2	The beginning of European co-operation	129
20.3	The European Coal and Steel Community (ECSC)	130
20.4	The European Economic Community (EEC), 1957	130
20.5	The EEC grows and becomes the EC	131
20.6	The development of the European Union	132
20.7	The Treaty of Maastricht, November 1993	132
20.8	Britain and the EEC	132
Summary		133
Quick questions		134

21	**The USA, 1945–95**	**135**
21.1	The effect of World War Two on the USA	135
21.2	McCarthyism	136
21.3	The campaign for civil rights before 1960	136
21.4	Civil rights under Kennedy and Johnson, 1960–68	137
21.5	From Nixon to Clinton	138
21.6	The development of youth culture	139
Summary		139
Quick questions		140

22	**China, 1949–95**	**141**
22.1	How Mao Tse-tung faced the problems of China in 1949	141
22.2	Agricultural reform	141
22.3	'The Hundred Flowers Campaign', 1957	141
22.4	The Great Leap Forward, 1958	142
22.5	Retreat from the Great Leap Forward	142
22.6	Industrialisation: the five-year plans	142
22.7	The impact of industrial and agricultural modernisation	143
22.8	The Cultural Revolution, 1966–71	143
22.9	Communist China and the USSR	144
22.10	Communist China and the USA	144
22.11	Communist China and her neighbours	145
22.12	The modernisation of China after Mao	145
22.13	Opposition to the 'modernising' Deng Xiaoping	145
22.14	Tiananmen Square	146
Summary		146
Quick questions		147

23	**South Africa, 1945–95**	**148**
23.1	The origins of apartheid	148
23.2	How the apartheid system worked	148
23.3	How apartheid was enforced	149
23.4	The impact of apartheid on the Africans and the whites	149
23.5	Opposition to apartheid within South Africa	149
23.6	Opposition to apartheid outside South Africa	150
23.7	The movement to majority rule	150
23.8	Nelson Mandela becomes President of the new South Africa	151
Summary		151
Quick questions		152

24	**The Middle East**	**153**
24.1	Important features of this region	153
24.2	Palestine and the Middle East	153
24.3	Palestine, 1945–47	154
24.4	The first Arab-Israeli War, 1948–49	154
24.5	An uneasy peace, 1949–56	154
24.6	An uneasy peace, 1956–57	155
24.7	The third (Six Day) Arab-Israeli War, 1967	156
24.8	Tension and terrorism, 1967–73	156
24.9	The fourth Arab-Israeli War, 1973	156
24.10	1974–76: more crises	157
24.11	Egyptian-Israeli peace, 1977–79	157
24.12	Israel and Lebanon, 1976–82	157
24.13	Israel and the Arab uprising, 1987–89	158

24.14 The USA peace plan, 1991–93   158
Summary   159
Quick questions   159

25   The Suez Crisis: a case study   160
25.1   The background to the crisis   160
25.2   The course of the crisis   160
25.3   The results of the war   161
25.4   Interpreting and evaluating sources 161

Questions and answers

Examination questions   165
Answers to examination questions   185
Answers to quick questions   203
Abbreviations and glossary   207
Index   215

Introduction

How to use this book

This book has been written to help you prepare for GCSE and Scottish Standard Grade Examinations. It provides:
- Information about GCSE in England, Wales and Northern Ireland, and Standard Grade in Scotland, with explanations of the Assessment Objectives to be tested (pages 1–2) and Examining Boards' explanations of how Grades are awarded;
- Guidance on the types of questions set, and how to tackle them;
- Guidance on coursework (pages 2–4);
- Notes on your syllabus, showing the papers you have to take, the coursework you have to write and the link between these and the Assessment Objectives ('Syllabus analysis' pages 8–14);
- Tables showing which of the Chapters in the main text you have to study ('Syllabus analysis' pages 8–14);
- Twenty five chapters of text where you will find the information you need for your written papers and, in many cases, for your coursework;
- A summary at the end of each chapter, picking out the key facts;
- A 'quick' test at the end of each chapter;
- A glossary of some words and abbreviations used in the text. Boards often ask for definitions of such words and abbreviations;
- Answers to the 'Quick questions' set in each chapter (in the 'Question and answer' section at the back of the book);
- Examples of examination questions with suggested answers (in the 'Question and answer' section at the back of the book).

Introduction to GCSEs

Assessment Objectives (AO)

You have to show ability to:
AO 1   recall, select, organise and deploy knowledge of the syllabus content;
AO 2   describe, analyse and explain the events, changes and issues studied, and the key features and characteristics of the periods or societies studied;
AO 3   in relation to the historical context:
      (i) comprehend, analyse and evaluate representations and interpretations of the events, people and issues studied;
      (ii) comprehend, interpret, evaluate and use a range of sources of information of different types.

In the notes on your syllabus (pages 8–14) you will see how the Board tests those Objectives in its papers and through coursework. You will see that, in most cases, the Boards put Objectives 1 and 2 together.

Grade Descriptions (taken with permission from the NEAB syllabus)

Grade descriptions are provided to give a general indication of the standards of achievement likely to have been shown by candidates awarded particular grades. The descriptions must be interpreted in relation to the content specified by the syllabus; they are not designed to define that content. The grade awarded will depend in practice upon the extent to which the candidate has met the assessment objectives overall. Shortcomings in some aspects of the examination may be balanced by better performances in others.

Grade F

Candidates recall and deploy some relevant knowledge of the syllabus content.

Candidates identify and describe some reasons, results and changes in relation to the events, personalities and developments studied. They describe a few features of an event, issue or period, including characteristic ideas, beliefs and attitudes.

Candidates identify some differences between ways in which events, people or issues have been represented and interpreted. They comprehend sources of information and, taking them at their face value, begin to consider their usefulness for investigating historical issues and draw simple conclusions.

Grade C

Candidates recall, select, organise and deploy historical knowledge of the syllabus content to support, generally with accuracy and relevance, the descriptions and explanations of the events, periods and societies studied.

Candidates produce structured descriptions and explanations of the events, people, changes and issues studied. Their descriptions and explanations show understanding of relevant causes, consequences and changes. They also consider and analyse key features and characteristics of the situations, periods and societies studied, including the variety of ideas, attitudes and beliefs held by people at the time.

Candidates recognise and comment on how interpretations of events, people and issues have been produced. They evaluate and use critically a range of sources of information to investigate issues and draw relevant conclusions.

Grade A

Candidates recall, select, organise and deploy historical knowledge of the syllabus content accurately, effectively and with consistency to substantiate arguments and reach historical judgements.

Candidates produce developed, reasoned and well-substantiated analyses and explanations which consider the events, changes and issues studied in their wider historical context. They also consider the diversity and interrelationship of the features and ideas, attitudes and beliefs in the periods, societies and situations studied.

Candidates analyse how and why interpretations have been produced and consider their value in relation to their historical context. They evaluate and use critically a range of sources of information in their historical context to investigate issues and reach reasoned and substantiated conclusions.

Coursework

Each of the Examining Groups requires candidates for GCSE to submit coursework. In the Syllabus analysis on pages 8–14 you will see the marks assigned to this work by your Board, as well as the Assessment Objectives which this work is meant to examine. Each board has its own requirements concerning this work and it is important that you understand what your particular Board demands. However, there is some practical advice which will help you, no matter which examination you are taking. We are grateful to examiner-teachers for these important suggestions.

Organisation of Coursework

- Jotter – if using a jotter, use a separate one for each unit of work.

- 'Science-type' note books will prove useful as permanent holders of all notes and pupil tasks. However, you may find that it is difficult, if not impossible, to insert new material into such a book.
- Loose-leaf A4 ring-binders have the benefit that you will be able to add new material to previous work, which may also be improved on or discarded at a later date. This updating or improving on your work during the year may well be an important feature of your coursework. Diagrams and/or slides can be inserted into the ring-binder in see-through folders. However, note that you are not allowed to submit your final work in a ring-binder.

The layout of the work

- Headings should be used to differentiate aspects of each topic: you might illustrate these or pick them out in red capital letters.
- Use paragraphs (each separated by a space) for each item of information, detailed at some length.
- Sentences and not a series of notes must be used. Make sure that each sentence is complete and factually accurate.
- Highlighting of important points by underlining of certain words or phrases will improve the appearance of your work.
- Summarise your conclusions with a single page at the end of your work.
- Contents: use a series of headings at the start of your work to show the examiner the logical way in which you have laid out the work which follows.
- Illustrations should be used to enhance your written work. If you are drawing a diagram, make sure you use a ruler when drawing straight lines. If you are using coloured pens or shading, make sure that this work is done neatly. Do not forget to add explanatory notes to photographs or slides and other illustrative material.

Skills to be developed

- You have to develop your ability to write a sustained answer. Examples of such writing should be part of your coursework.
- As well as such written work, examples of slides, videos and computer programmes may be attempted. You may submit tapes of oral reports or photographs of artefacts, with accompanying descriptions and commentary.
- Interviewing skills can be shown by, for example, a taped interview of a person being asked pre-arranged questions intended to provide you with specific information.
- Historical diaries and records of visits should be encouraged. Each item used in such work should be detailed and follow a logical sequence: for example, an account of a visit to a museum should show:
  - what you hoped to gain from the visit;
  - what you saw;
  - how far the experience of the visit was relevant to the topic being pursued.
- Handling of sources: your coursework should show your ability to interpret various types of source material, and to use these as bases for arguments you wish to make. In developing your argument, you will be expected to show an ability to arrange work logically, to explain it fully and to arrive at correct conclusions.

Consult your teacher

Before you decide what work you wish to do consult your teacher and be guided by his or her advice. Teachers will know whether the examiners will accept some work or not (e.g. they will not necessarily accept the 'story' of your local football team, although you may find it interesting). Teachers will know what sources are easily available that will be useful for you. Your teacher will help you to improve your work during the two years. Make sure that you follow any suggestions which may be made.

Doing the work – on time

Make sure that you keep up to date with your coursework by doing the work regularly. Try not to get behind with it. You cannot do good work if you leave most of it until the last few months or weeks. Start it at the beginning of the (one or) two-year period of study for the examination, and make sure that you have each piece completed in good time to be accepted by your teacher. There is a dead line – a date by which the whole of the completed coursework has to be submitted to your examiners. Find out from your teacher what this date is, and aim to have your coursework ready well before that date.

Make your work as good as possible

Do take a great deal of care with your coursework and make it as good as you can. Unlike the examination – where you have a limited time in which to show the examiners what you understand and can do – you can normally take as much time as you like with your coursework. Because the mark for this work is added to the marks you gain in the written examination, your final grade can often be better than it would otherwise have been if you obtain a high mark for your coursework.

Examining groups differ

Make sure that you understand what your Group demands – as to length and number of assignments, the Assessment Objectives being examined in each piece and the total value of coursework. Your teacher will provide this information; if you are a private candidate you can get the information from the syllabus, which is available from the appropriate Group's address shown in the Syllabus analysis.

A revision programme

Why revise?

You may know people who do not seem to do much preparation before examinations, yet who still obtain high marks. You may also know people who spend a great deal of time at revision, some even studying up to the day of the examination. It is impossible to define 'the best method' for all candidates, because people are different and what suits one may not do so for another. But long experience has shown teachers and examiners that most people learn more, gain in confidence and perform better in examinations after they have made suitable preparations by a sensible programme of revision.

Planning your revision

Some people prefer to read a Chapter several times before testing themselves to see whether they can remember the work they have studied. Others prefer to make notes as they read and to use these notes for revision purposes. Almost everyone learns best by tackling small portions of work. Study one Chapter, test yourself on it and then decide whether you have understood the Chapter. By the time you have gone through all the necessary Chapters you should have a list of topics which need further revision to help you overcome your weaknesses.

A revision timetable

A complete revision requires a good deal of time and needs sensible planning. The following timetable is based on the assumptions that the examination will take place in mid-June. If your examination takes place in May, November or January, obviously you will need to change the suggested dates.

End of March
- Check how well you did in the mock examination so that you can see which topics you need to study carefully.
- Make up a timetable using the Chapters in this book and any other topics which you need to study.
- The timetable should cover April and May and you should plan to do extra work during the Easter holidays.
- The timetable should be drawn up to allow you to finish your revision by the end of May. This will give you two weeks for further revision of your weaker points and a final revision of the main points in the days before the examination.

April and May
- Allow yourself about one hour every day for history revision.

June
- Revise the main points, using the examination questions at the back of this book. Make a list of the main points needed to answer any of the questions in that section.

Examination day
- Make sure that you arrive at the examination in time and that you have with you all the things you might need – pens, pencils, ruler, crayons and eraser.

Taking the examination

Read the paper carefully
Almost every Report made by examiners complains that candidates did not understand the questions asked or failed to use the information supplied in the examination paper. If the examiners ask you to 'Give an account of Gladstone's domestic policies', they expect less analysis than they expect from answers to 'Account for Gladstone's defeat in the Election of 1874'. If you are asked to 'Give an account of Disraeli's domestic policy in his ministry of 1847–80', do not waste time by offering accounts of his foreign and imperial policies.

Tick off the questions you intend to do
As you read through the paper tick off the questions which you think you could answer. Then check the instructions at the head of your examination paper to see how many questions you have to do, and from which sections, if the paper is sub-divided into sections.

Having ticked off a number of questions, go back through the paper and choose those which you intend to do. As you do this, number the questions – 1, 2 and so on – to remind yourself which question you intend to tackle first, which next and so on to the end. Always do first the question which you think you can answer best; this will give you confidence to go on with the rest of the paper.

Plan each answer before you start
This refers to those questions which require you to write either an essay or a brief note on some item. It does not refer to the fixed-response questions.

Time yourself
If you only answer half the questions asked for, you cannot expect to get more than 50% even if you get full marks for each answer. It is important to attempt to answer the required number of questions. To help you do this:
- **Before the examination**, practice doing questions in the time allocated. This is important because you have to find out how much you can write in the 25 or 30 minutes which you can spend on a question in the examination.
- **In the examination room**, make a note of the time which you will allow for each question. If, for example, you have to do four questions in two hours you will have 100 minutes in which to write your answers (if you have spent 20 minutes on planning). This means that each answer should take 25 minutes. So if you start

writing at 2.00 pm you should finish your answer to the first question at 2.25 pm, your second answer should be finished at 2.50 pm and so on.

- **When answering the paper**, keep an eye on your proposed timing and so on the clock. When you get to the end of the time allocated to an answer, stop writing, even if you have not completed the answer. Leave a space and, if you have time, complete the answer later. It is better to have answered all five questions (if that is the number required), even if the answers are incomplete, than to answer only three – which you might do if you take five minutes more for this answer and a further five minutes for another.

Answering the questions

You should remember that examiners have to mark a large number of papers. They will appreciate it if your work is neat, although they will not object if you have crossed out such things as plans for answers. They will object to a sort of shorthand which some candidates use, such as 'Pam' for Palmerston or 'Dizzie' for Disraeli. They will not give you any credit for the use of 'etc.' since they will think that this means you do not know any more. If you really do know more, then you should write it down so that the examiners can award the marks you deserve.

Advice and guidance on types of exam question

Different boards use different types of question, all designed to test your mastery of the Assessment Objectives. During your course you should become aware of these objectives (listed on page 1); during the examination you must make sure that you address them in your answers.

All questions consist of a varying number of sub-questions, and the examination paper will show how many marks can be earned by each sub-question. If only 1 or 2 marks are given for one sub-question, you will gain no extra points for writing a long essay as your answer. If, on the other hand, half the total mark is given for one sub-question, clearly that sub-question calls for an extended (maybe essay-type) answer. There are *three* types of question:

Type 1

These are structured essay questions based on three or four sub-questions. The different marks awarded to the various sub-questions indicate whether you should give a shorter or a longer answer. These questions, often based on one or more pieces of stimulus or source material, may call for some evaluation (AO 3), but are generally testing Assessment Objectives 1 and 2.

Type 2

These consist of:
- a number of sub-questions requiring brief (maybe one word) answers;
- one or two sub-questions calling for more extended answers; and
- a structured essay question calling for an even longer answer.

As with Type 1, these questions may be based on stimulus or source material, and may call for some source evaluation.

When writing extended answers:
- read the question carefully;
- make a plan of your proposed answer and make sure that you have put the facts in the correct order, and that you are not going to repeat yourself;
- make sure that you have covered all the points needed to answer the question and, just as important, check that you have not included things that are irrelevant.

Type 3

All boards set questions based on a set of pieces of evidence. These are meant mainly to test Assessment Objective 3, but also test Assessment Objectives 1 and 2.

It is essential that you study both the pieces of evidence and the sub-questions very carefully. In particular note that:

- if you are told to 'use Source A to explain your answer', make sure that you do just that, quoting words/sentences from a written piece, or pointing out features in an illustration;
- if you are told to 'compare the evidence in A with the evidence in B', make sure that you make comparisons, for example by pointing out similarities and/or differences;
- if you are told to 'use your own knowledge' to answer a question, do this and win marks by being aware of Assessment Objectives 1 and 2;
- you should not be afraid to challenge the evidence in a source: is it one-sided (biased)? Does it deal with only one place/event so that it cannot tell us much, if anything, about a general situation? Is it contemporary or produced with the benefit of hindsight (when we are often, but not always, wiser)?

You will find examples of each of the different types of question, and advice on answering all three types of question in the 'Question and answer' section at the back of the book.

Syllabus analysis

Midland Examining group (MEG)

Address: 1 Hills Road, Cambridge, CB1 2EU.   Tel: 01223 553311

Syllabus B (1607) Modern World

Compulsory Core: International Relations, 1900–c.1989	Covered in Chapters	✔
1919–1939	4, 5, 10	
1945–c.1989	14, 15, 17, 19	
Depth Studies		
A. Germany, 1918–1945	4, 8	
B. Russia, 1905–1941	1, 6	
C. The USA, 1919–1941	9	
D. China, 1945–c.1990	7, 22	
E. Britain and the First World War, 1914–1918	3, 13	
F. South Africa, 1945–1994	23	
G. Israel and the Arab-Israeli Conflict, 1945–1994	24, 25	
Coursework		
On 2 Depth Studies; see analysis below		

Paper analysis

Paper 1   *2 hours – 45%*

A: 2 source-based questions on Core: 1 to be answered. Part 1 tests Assessment Objective 3 (5%) and Part 2 tests Assessment Objectives 1–2.

B: 1 of 4 structured questions on Core. Testing Assessment Objectives 1–2.

C: 3 structural questions on *each* Depth Study: 2 to be answered. Testing Assessment Objectives 1–2. Overall, Paper 1 tests Assessment Objectives 1–2 for 40%.

Paper 2   *1½ hours – 30%*   Several compulsory questions on a range of sources on an issue taken from the Core. For 1998 this will be taken from *The Cold War in Europe, 1945–49*. Testing Assessment Objectives 1–2 (7½%) and 3 (22½%).

Coursework *25%*   Two assignments on *two* Depth Studies different from the one chosen for answers in Paper 1C. 1 testing Assessment Objectives 1–2 (12½%) and one testing Assessment Objective 3 (12½%).

Northern Examinations and Assessment Council (NEAB)

Address: 12 Harter Street, Manchester, M1 6HL.   Tel: 0161 953 1180

Syllabus B The Modern World

1 Thematic Study: Conflict in the Modern World	Covered in Chapters	✔
c.1900–c.1963	2–4, 10, 12, 14–17	
2 Depth Studies		
A: 1 Russia, 1900–56	1, 6	
2 Germany, 1918–39	4, 8	
B: 3 USA, 1919–41	5, 9	
4 Britain, 1905–51		
3 Coursework/Alternative Paper 3 units		
1. International Co-operation	5, 7, 10, 14, 25	
2. The Arab-Israeli Conflict	24, 25	
3. Vietnam	17	
4. Modern Europe, Post 1945	15, 16, 19, 20	
5. Human Rights	9, 18, 21, 22, 23	
6. Colonialism	11, 17	

Paper analysis

Paper 1	*1¼ hours – 35%*	Compulsory structured multi-source based questions on the Theme. Sub-questions testing Assessment Objective 3 (25%) and Assessment Objectives 1 and 2 (10%).
Paper 2	*1¼ hours – 40%*	1 question of 2 from *each* section. Multi-source based questions testing Assessment Objective 3 (5%) and Assessment Objectives 1–2 (35%). One sub-question calls for extended answer.
Paper 3	*1½ hours – 25%*	An alternative to coursework 1 compulsory question on *each* of options 1–4. 1 to be answered; sub-questions calling for short and extended answers. Testing Assessment Objectives 1 and 2 (15%) and 3 (10%).
Coursework (alternative to Paper 3)		2 assignments totalling 2500–3000 words based on options 1–6. Testing Assessment Objectives 1–2 (15%) and 3 (10%).

Syllabus D (2142) – Short Course
Paper 1 follows the pattern of Paper 2 above, and Coursework follows the pattern of Coursework above.

Northern Ireland Council for the Curriculum, Examinations and Assessment (NICCEA)

Address: Beechill House, 42 Beechill Road, Belfast BT8 4RS   Tel: 01232 704666

Depth Study	Covered in Chapters	✔
Section A. *One* from:		
1. Germany, 3. 1918–c. 1939	4, 8, 10	
2. Russia, c. 1914–c. 1941	1, 6	
3. USA, c. 1918–c. 1941	9, 12	
Section B: Britain, Northern Ireland and Ireland		
Outline Study: Superpower relations c. 1945–c. 1985		
Key issues		
1. Superpower Rivalry in Europe	15, 16, 17, 18	
2. Flashpoints of the Cold War: Korea/Vietnam	14, 16, 17	
3. From Arms Race to Arms Limitation	16, 17	
Coursework (extending Depth and Outline Studies)		
1. Germany, c. 1918–c. 1939	2, 4, 8, 10	
2. Russia, c. 1914–c. 1941	1, 6, 7, 19	
3. USA, c. 1918–c. 1941	9, 12, 21	
4. Superpower Relations, c. 19145–c. 1985	15,16,17,18,21,24,25	

Paper analysis (note tiering in examination papers)

Paper 1   *2⅔ hours – 40%*   Section A: 2 from 4 questions on chosen Depth Study. Short answer and structured type.
Assessment Objectives 1 and 2 for 40%.
Section B: not covered in this book.

Paper 2   *1½ hours – 35%*   1 question based on source material: 1 of the structured type, 1 of extended writing type.
Assessment Objectives 1–2 (20%) and 3 (15%).

Coursework *25%*   2 source-based assignments based on studies chosen for Papers 1 and 2, but extending those studies before or after the period shown in the syllabus.
Total length maximum 2500 words.
Assessment Objective 3 (25%).

Scottish Qualifications Authority (formerly SEB)

Address: Ironmills Road, Dalkeith, Midlothian, EH22 1LE.   Tel: 0131 663 6601

Final Paper based on 3 units of study

	Covered in Chapters	✔
Unit 1: Changing Life in Scotland and Britain	Companion volume, *History 1750–Present Day*	
Unit 2: International Co-operation and Conflict		
1890s–1920s	2, 3, 4, 5, 13	
or		
1930s–1960s	10, 12, 13, 14, 15, 17	
Unit 3: People and Power. *One* from:		
India, 1917–47	11	
Russia, 1914–41	1, 6	
Germany, 1918–39	4, 8	
Coursework 400–12000 words long		
Compulsory for all Levels of Grading.		

Paper analysis

Foundation Level		*1 hour* Based on any *one* of units 1–3.
		Questions testing all Assessment Objectives.
General	*1½ hours*	Based on Units 1–3.
		Testing all Assessment Objectives.
Credit	*1¾ hours*	Based on Units 1–3.
		Testing all Assessment Objectives.

Southern Examining Group (SEG)

Address: Stag Hill House, Guildford, GU2 5XJ.   Tel: 01483 506506

Syllabus B (2120) Modern World History

Coursework. *One* from:	Covered in Chapters	✔
1. Social and economic developments in Britain, 1900–39	Companion volume, *History 1750–Present Day*	
2. The First World War, 1914–18	3, 13	
3. The USA, 1918–41	9	
4. The Second World War, 1939–45	10, 13	
5. Race relations in the USA and South Africa since 1945	21, 23	
6. The centre's own choice		
Optional Study Units. *Two* from:		
1. Peace to War, 1919–39	4, 5, 10	
2. The USA and the USSR as World Superpowers, 1945–63	14, 15, 17, 19	
3. The USA and the USSR as World Superpowers, 1963–91	16, 17, 19	
Depth Studies		
1. Russia, 1917–41	1, 6	
2. Germany, 1918–39	4, 8	

Paper analysis

Paper 1	*Coursework – 25%*	2 assignments on *one* unit.
		1 testing Assessment Objectives 1–2 (12½%) and 1 testing Assessment Objective 3 (12½%).
		Overall length 2000–2500 words.
Paper 2	*1¾ hours – 37½%*	2 structured questions on *each* optional unit.
		Any 3 to be answered.
		Single-source based: number of sub-questions.
		Assessment Objectives 1–2 (30%) and 3 (7½%).
Paper 3	*1¾ hours – 37½%*	Section A: 1 structured question on each depth study; answer any 1.
		Based on a set of sources to test mainly Assessment Objective 3 (17½%) and also Assessment Objectives 1–2 (5%).
		Sections B and C: 2 questions on *each* depth study.
		Must answer 1 on *each*, testing Assessment Objectives 1–2 (15%).

University of London Examinations and Assessment Council (ULEAC) (now the Edexcel Foundation)

Address: Stewart House, 32 Russell Square, London WC1B 5DN.   Tel: 0171 331 4000

Syllabus A (1325) Modern European and World History

A: Outline Studies	Covered in Chapters	✔
1. The emergence of Modern Britain, 1868–1914		
2. The Road to War: Europe, 1870–1914	2	
3. Nationalism and Independence in India, c. 1900–49	11	
4. The Impact of War on Britain, c. 1900–50	13	
5. The Emergence of Modern China, 1911–70	7, 22	
6. The Rise and Fall of the Communist State: The Soviet Union, 1928–91	6, 18	
7. A Divided Union? The USA, 1941–80	21	
8. Britain's Changing Role in the World, 1945–90	9, 20, 23, 25	
9. Superpower Relations, 1945–90	15, 16, 17	
10. Conflict and the Quest for Peace in the Middle East, 1948–92	24, 25	
B: Depth Studies		
1. The Russian Revolution, c. 1910–24	1,6	
2. The War to End Wars, 1914–19	3, 4	
3. Depression and the New Deal: the USA, 1929–41	9	
4. Nazi Germany, c. 1930–39	4, 8	
5. The World at War, 1938–45	10, 12	
6. The End of Apartheid in South Africa, 1928–1944	23	
7. Conflict in Vietnam, c. 1963–75	17	

Paper Analysis

Paper 1   1¼ hours – 40%   Outline Studies
2 questions on *each*: 2 to be answered from *different* topics.
Piece of stimulus material followed by 4/5 short-answer questions, *plus* structured essay.
Assessment Objectives 1–2

Paper 2   1½ hours – 35%   Depth Studies
1 question on *each*: 2 to be answered.
Questions based on a series of type of evidence.
Assessment Objectives 1 (7½%) and 3 (27½%)

Coursework 25%   2 assignments based on *two* topics in syllabus *not* assessed in Papers 1 or 2.
Each to be 1250–2000 words long.
One to test Assessment Objective 2 (12½%) and one to test Assessment Objective 3 (12½%).

Syllabus E Themes of British and World History

The syllabus is divided into thematic studies (Sections A and B), depth studies (Section C) and coursework units (Section D).
    Section A: Britain in the Twentieth Century
    Section B: Reconstruction and Co-operation after the Second World War
    Section C: Modern World Depth Study
    Section D: Coursework units
You are advised to study *three* themes, *one* depth study and *two* coursework units.
The 3 themes may be *either* 2 from Section A and *one* from Section B,
        or 1 from Section A and *two* from Section B
        or 3 from either of Sections A or B.

You will see that you may concentrate on Section A (covered in a companion volume, *History 1750 to the Present Day) or* on Section B (below).

Section B: Reconstruction and Co-operation after the Second World War	Covered in Chapters	✔
1. Old Empires and New Nations	11, 17	
2. Superpower Rivalry in the Nuclear Age	12, 14, 15, 16, 17	
3. The United Nations and Global Issues	14	
4. Europe, Divided and United	15, 20	
Section C: Modern World Depth Study. *One* from:		
1. The United States of America, 1917–70	9, 21	
2. Russia and the USSR, 1917–91	1, 6, 18	
3. China, 1911–70	7, 22	
4. Weimar and Nazi Germany, 1919–45	4, 8	
Section D: Coursework Units		
1. Changing Culture and Communication in the Twentieth Century		
2. A Study in Development (e.g. Medicine, c. 1350–present day)		
3. From colonialism to Independence (*two* different geographical areas)		

Paper analysis

Paper 1	*1½ hours – 35%*	2 questions on *each* topic in Section B. 3 to be answered from *different* topics. Piece of stimulus material followed by 4–5 short-answer questions, *plus* structured essay. Assessment Objectives 1–2.
Paper 2	*1½ hours – 40%*	2 questions to be answered on your chosen option; 1 – a structured essay question from 3 offered, 1 – a compulsory source-based question on a nominated topic from within your chosen unit. Check the topic to be examined in the year of your examination. Assessment Objectives 1 and 2 (12⅛%) and 3 (27½%).
Coursework		2 written assignments each 1250–2000 words long. One testing Assessment Objective 2 (12⅛%) and one testing Assessment Objective 3 (12½%).

Welsh Joint Education Committee (WJEC)

Address: 245 Western Avenue, Cardiff, CF5 2YX.   Tel: 01222 265000

Syllabus A Aspects of Welsh/English and non-British History

	Covered in Chapters	✔
Studies in Depth (Welsh/British options)	Companion volume, *History 1750–Present Day*	
Non-British Outline Studies. *One* from:		
1. China, 1911–90	7, 22	
2. Germany, 1913–90	4, 8, 15, 20	
3. The Middle East, 1919–90	4, 24, 25	
4. The USSR, 1924–90	5, 15, 18	
5. The USA, 1920–90	9, 16, 17, 21	

Paper analysis

Paper 1   Depth studies – see companion volume.

Paper 2   *1½ hours – 30%*   Outline Studies testing Assessment Objectives 1–2.

A: 3 compulsory stimulus questions.

Structured questions asking for responses of varying lengths.

B: 1 structured question from 2.

Stimulus based; varied length of responses.

Coursework *12½%*   2 assignments on any historical period *except* those chosen for answers in Papers 1 and 2.

Each 1200–1500 words long and testing Assessment Objectives 1–2 (5%) and 3 (7½%) in each case.

Syllabus B Aspects of Twentieth Century History

Studies in Depth *Two* from:	Covered in Chapters	✔
1. Lenin and the Russian Revolution, 1917–24	1, 6	
2. The United States of America, 1919–29	9, 10	
3. Hitler's Germany, 1933–45	8, 12	
4. China under Mao Ze Dong, 1949–66	7, 15, 16, 22	
5. South Africa, 1960–94	23	
Optional Study. *One* from:		
1. China, 1911–90	7, 15, 16, 22	
2. Germany, 1919–90	4, 8, 15, 17, 20	
3. The Middle East, 1919–90	4, 24, 25	
4. The USSR, 1924–90	6, 12, 15, 16, 18, 19	
5. The United States of America, 1929–90	9, 15, 16, 17, 21	

Paper analysis

Paper 1   *2 hours – 45%*   On *two* chosen depth studies:

A: 1 compulsory on *each*.

Structured and source-based.

Assessment Objective 3 (10% in each question; 20% overall).

B: 1 structured question from 2 on *each*.

Range of stimulus material with response of varying lengths.

Assessment Objectives 1–2 (25%) overall.

Paper 2   *1½ hours – 30%*   On *one* chosen option:

A: 3 compulsory stimulus questions, responses of varying lengths.

B: 1 structured question from 2.

Stimulus-based with responses of varying lengths.

Testing Assessment Objectives 1–2 (30%).

Coursework *12½%*   2 assignments based on local, Welsh, or Welsh/English history.

Each from 1200–1500 words long.

Each testing Assessment Objectives 1–2 (5%) and 3 (7½%).

Chapter 1
Russia 1900–1914

1.1 National and local government

Nicholas II became Tsar (Emperor) in 1896. He was an **autocrat** and ruled without a Parliament. His three main ministers were:

1. Pobedonostev, the lay controller of the Orthodox Church, who opposed any idea of bringing western democratic institutions to Russia. He controlled the secret police, the education system, the press and the appointment of Land Captains to authority in Russia's local government. He resigned in 1905 when a Parliament was first elected (see 1.6).
2. Plehve, the Minister of the Interior was another anti-westerner who opposed de Witte's policies (below) and was frightened by the growth of workers' political parties.
3. Sergei de Witte, Minister of Finance, 1892–1903, who was responsible for the growth of Russian industry. He obtained loans from France to pay for the building of railways and for industrial development. This helped to create a large working class in some towns and cities where the people came under the influence of left-wingers such as Lenin and Trotsky (see 1.3). He was hated by Plehve who persuaded the Tsar to dismiss him in 1903.

In the 1860's, a reforming Tsar, Alexander II, 'the liberator' (1855–81) had set up three kinds of local councils:

- The **mir** (or commune) was the bottom rung of the ladder of government. There were elections in each commune (or group of villages) to choose leaders; their main job was to allocate land to the peasants (see 1.2).
- The district **zemstvos** were district councils elected by the people of a group of communes: their job was to maintain roads, bridges and the district's schools.
- Provincial zemstvos were elected by members of the district *zemstvos*. They looked after the public health system and chose magistrates for the newly established law courts.

1.2 The Russian people

Most Russians were poor peasants living in small villages. Until 1861 they had been serfs 'owned' by the rich landowners. Alexander II freed them in 1861: they did not have to work for nothing on the nobles land and they could own land. On average a peasant family got about 8 acres. This had to be paid for by instalments over 49 years. In fact, the *mir* became the new owners. Each year the elders of the *mir* divided up the freed land according to the numbers in each family, and the *mir* collected the debt instalment each year.

Before de Witte's industrialisation there had been a small middle class in Russia, made up of doctors, lawyers, journalists, merchants and the like. With industrialisation a new middle class of factory owners, bankers and import and export agents emerged.

Because they were more educated and had money and time to spare they were the ones who got themselves elected to the two kinds of *zemstvos*. Their leaders hoped for the setting up of an elected national assembly or Parliament.

Following industrialisation, there was the growth of the town-based working class. Like workers in Britain's first industrial towns, they were badly paid, over worked, poorly housed and restless.

1.3 Growing opposition to Tsardom

By 1903, when de Witte was dismissed, there were three small but well organised opposition groups whom Plehve saw as 'revolutionaries'.

1. The Social Revolutionary Party (SRP) was founded in 1901. It hoped to incite the peasants to a violent revolution. It carried out terrorist acts against landlords and government officials.
2. The SRP was a successor to the **Narodniki** who, in the 1870's had gone from the universities to convert the peasants to socialism. The Narodniki were rejected by the peasants who followed the advice of the government-controlled priests. Savage government action in 1876 squashed the Narodniki, but terrorists then organised 'gangs' which carried out attacks on ministers, murdered Tsar Alexander II (1881) and kept alive the idea that a Russian revolution should be based on the peasant.
3. The Social Democratic Labour Party (SDLP) was formed in 1898 and had its main support among the industrial workers. It took its ideas from the writing of Karl Marx (1818–83) who believed that the workers (or proletariat) would set up a communist system after a revolution. Under communism there would be no private property since all the means of production, distribution and exchange would be owned by the people. Lenin was one of the leaders of the SDLP. With other leaders he was often arrested, imprisoned and exiled. He and his fellow exiles produced a newspaper, *Iskra*, (*The Spark*) which they smuggled into Russia.

In 1903 at a meeting in London the SDLP split in two. Some, led by Trotsky, wanted the SDLP to become a mass party like the SRP. Others, led by Lenin, wanted it to be a small party, with every member a dedicated revolutionary. The argument ended with a vote. The majority (**Bolsheviks**) agreed with Lenin and the minority (**Mensheviks**) agreed with Trotsky.

1.4 'A short, victorious war' with Japan, 1904

Plehve was one of those who believed in Russian imperialism and conquest of the non-Russian people in the south and east. This brought Russia up against Japan which wanted to expand into Korea and Manchuria.

In 1904 Plehve convinced the Tsar that a war against Japan would gain land for Russia and win the support of its restless people. The war was a disaster for Russia. In May 1905 its fleet was destroyed at Tsushima. A series of defeats on land included the one at Mukden where 90,000 Russians died and 40,000 were captured.

President Roosevelt of the USA called both sides to a peace conference in Portsmouth (USA). Russia had to remove her troops from Manchuria. Japan gained Port Arthur, part of the island of Sakhalin, and Korea was named as 'a Japanese sphere of influence'.

Examiner's tip

'Revolutions are led by the half satisfied.' (George Bernard Shaw)

The Russian middle class had made *economic* progress (jobs and incomes) and *social* progress (housing, education etc). They now wanted *political* progress and a democratic state. This would be the pattern in China (Chapter 7), India (Chapter 11) and South Africa (Chapter 23).

1.5 The danger of revolution

The war increased the unrest inside Russia itself. The transport system could not cope with the need to carry military supplies as well as peacetime goods. There was a shortage of food in the industrial towns.

The SDLP organised a series of strikes among industrial workers. Plehve was assassinated by members of the SRP (1904) and peasants rioted and killed Land Captains and nobles.

On **'Bloody Sunday'** (22 January 1905), troops fired on a peaceful demonstration by workers led by Father Gapon, who came to the Tsar's Winter Palace in St Petersburg to ask the Tsar ('the little Father') to do something about their housing, low wages, long hours and lack of food. One hundred and thirty people were killed and 3000 injured.

Sailors on the battleship *Potemkin* mutinied and bombarded the port of Odessa in the Crimea. Railway workers organised a national strike so that food did not get to the industrial towns. Trotsky formed a number of **soviets** (workers councils) in St Petersburg and Moscow. Non-industrial workers such as teachers, lawyers and doctors supported the soviets and called for the overthrow of the Government.

1.6 The October Manifesto, 1905

E xaminer's tip

Use pages 15–17 to study the *long-term* causes of the fall of the Tsar in February 1917 (see Chapter 6).

De Witte was recalled to become chief Minister (October 1905). He got the Tsar to issue a manifesto in which he promised an elected **Duma** which would have to approve any new laws he might propose. Liberals welcomed this move to democracy. Strikers went back to work hoping the Duma would pass the reforms they wanted. The Marxist-led soviets thought the Tsar's promises were not worth much and peasants continued rioting.

Once the army was back from the war (December 1905) the Tsar showed his true colours. Leaders of the soviets were arrested and the army was called in to suppress the armed rising of Moscow workers (December 1905).

De Witte arranged fresh loans from France and Britain (April 1906) to make the Tsar's position stronger. In May 1906 he issued his Fundamental Law of the Empire in which he outlined his policies: Autocracy, 'God given', could not be subject to a Duma. Control of taxation and government finance could not be left to a Duma which would only have limited rights to bring in new laws.

1.7 Weakening the Duma, 1906–14

The first Duma was elected in May 1906. The Liberal Cadets (from the Russian initials for the Constitutional Democratic Party) won the majority of seats. They reminded the Tsar about his promises in the October Manifesto and asked him for full control of taxation.

In response the Tsar dismissed the Duma and called fresh elections. Leading Liberals fled to Finland and issued an anti-Tsarist manifesto which called on people not to pay taxes or serve in the army.

De Witte was dismissed again and replaced by Stolypin (see below). He wanted to 'carry through effective reforms but resist revolution'. He banned some people from standing for election to the Duma, imprisoned some anti-Tsarist candidates and took many names off the voting lists.

In spite of this, the second Duma (February 1907) was even more radical than the first. The SDLP won 65 seats and moderate Liberals lost seats. This Duma rejected Stolypin's demand that it condemn terrorism, and opposed the Tsar's attempt to arrest some SDLP members. Like the first Duma, the second Duma was dismissed (June 1907).

In 1907 the electoral laws were changed so that SDLP members could not be candidates. Known trouble makers were imprisoned. The third and fourth Dumas (1907–14) were 'loyal' to the Tsar.

1.8 Stolypin's reforms, 1907–11

Examiner's tip

Compare Stolypin's reforms with the reforms of de Witte (see 1.1), and show the examiner that you understand that Stolypin's death was an extra cause of the fall of the Tsar in the first Revolution in 1917.

Peasants remembered Stolypin's reforms rather than his anti-Duma policies. He abolished the *mir* and allowed the peasants to own or rent land without interference from the *mir*. He set up Peasants Banks to make loans to help peasants buy their land outright. Many did so, and these richer peasants (Kulaks) were the more go-ahead, dynamic ones. They made their land more profitable and sold food to the town workers and for export (to pay for foreign loans to Russia's Industry). As they prospered they tended to be loyal to the Tsar and less inclined to support revolutionary movements.

Stolypin was assassinated (1911) in a theatre where he sat with the Tsar. By then, and until 1914, Russia's industry was growing and the influence of the SDLP was falling. The countryside, where most people lived, was peaceful and, as more people owned land, the influence of the SRP was falling.

It was the First World War which was to show how fragile this peace was, and how slender was the hold the Tsar had over his people.

Summary

1 Nicholas II, an autocrat, ruled with the aid of two reactionary ministers, Plehve and Pobedonostev. They controlled the powerful orthodox church, education, the legal system and the press.

2 His grandfather, Alexander II, had allowed elections for village, district and regional councils, but refused to allow a Duma to be elected.

3 Most Russians were peasants, paying for their land through the *mir*. Badly-off industrial workers lived in the large towns and cities.

4 Opposition to Tsarist rule came from three groups. The SRP was a mainly peasant-based movement. The Liberals (Cadets) were mainly from the middle class. The SDLP, a workers' party, was Marxist, and in 1903 it split into the Bolshevik and Menshevik parties.

5 The war with Japan led to great unrest, the murder of Plehve, the October Manifesto (1905), the recall of de Witte, and the election of the first Duma. Trotsky helped to set up the first soviets.

6 The Tsar and his chief minister, Stolypin, 'betrayed' the October Manifesto and severely limited the power of the Duma after 1907.

7 Stolypin's agricultural reforms pleased the peasants and made Russia more prosperous and peaceful. His murder in 1911 prevented him from being able to carry his reforms to full fruition.

8 The First World War showed up Tsarism's weaknesses.

Quick questions

1 Against each of the names below, select the correct letter in the key.

Name	Key
1. de Witte	A. District Councils
2. Duma	B. Advised the Tsar to declare war, 1904
3. Cadets	C. Hoped for a peasants' rising
4. Narodniki	D. A reforming Minister, 1907–11
5. Nicholas II	E. Name of Russian Liberal Party
6. Plehve	F. An assembly first elected in 1906
7. Stolypin	G. 'reforming Tsar liberator'
8. *Zemstvos*	H. Minister of Finance, 1892–1903
9. Alexander II	J. The last of the Tsars

2 What do the following initials stand for:
   i) SDLP,
   ii) SRP?

3 Which Marxists wanted
   i) a small, active party,
   ii) a mass party?

4 Which priest led the workers' march on Bloody Sunday, 1905?

Chapter 2
International relations 1870–1914

2.1 A new German Empire

Examiner's tip

Austria is used as a shortened form for 'Austria-Hungary' as the Empire was known after the Hungarian rising of 1867 and the creation of the Dual Monarchy, in which the Emperor of Austria was the King of Hungary.

In 1870–71, Prussia, the largest of the 39 German states, defeated France in the **Franco-Prussian War**. The other German states then joined Prussia to form a united Germany. The French defeat was followed by the humiliation of the announcement of a new German Empire (under the rule of a Kaiser, or Emperor) in the Hall of Mirrors in the former royal palace at Versailles. In the **Treaty of Frankfurt** (May 1871) France was forced to give Alsace and Lorraine to Germany. These iron and coal bearing provinces played a part in the continuing industrial development of Germany. Bismarck, Chancellor of Germany, knew that France would want her revenge for these humiliations. He feared that she might find an anti-German ally, so he tried to he keep France isolated by persuading her to seek African colonies where she might quarrel with Britain and Italy. He also linked Germany with Austria and Russia in an anti-French **Three Emperors League** (**Dreikaiserbund** (DKB)), formed in 1873.

2.2 The Balkans, 1877–79

The map on the following page shows how many Christian Slav states gained their independence from Turkey in the nineteenth century. Russia backed such a move to independence, hoping to gain influence in the new states and to get an outlet to the Mediterranean. Britain had always feared such Russian ambitions. Austria, having lost power in Italy (1860) and Germany(1866) hoped to gain territory and power in the restless Balkans.

The map shows that Bulgaria, Rumania and Serbia gained their freedom in 1878. This followed the **Russo-Turkish war** (1877–78) in which Russian troops won the **Battle of Plevna** and marched towards Constantinople. Russia and Turkey signed the Treaty of San Stephano (1878) which gave Bulgaria, Rumania and Serbia their freedom and gave Russia some former Turkish territory in the Dobruja area. Both Britain and Austria were alarmed at Russia's success.

Bismarck saw that his DKB might break up if Austria and Russia quarrelled, so he persuaded all the Powers to come to the **Congress of Berlin** (1878), which agreed to give part of Bulgaria back to Turkey, and Cyprus to Britain (so that she could keep an eye on Russian advances southwards). Austria was allowed to control Bosnia-

Fig. 2.1 The Balkans, 1878–1914

Herzegovina which Serbia wanted, although she had played no part in the 1877–78 war.

Bismarck had clearly supported Austria and not Russia in this deal. To confirm this support he signed a secret **Dual Alliance** (1879) with the Germanic Austrians. In this he promised to aid Austria if she were attacked by Russia, while Austria agreed to aid Germany if she were attacked by a combination of two powers: he knew he could defeat France if she were fighting on her own.

2.3 Keeping France isolated

The DKB had merely been a 'friendly understanding' when it was signed in 1873. In 1881 Bismarck persuaded the three Emperors to sign a Treaty in which they promised that none of them would help a fourth country (obviously France) if that country went to war with any of the three. This treaty was re-signed in 1884.

Bismarck persuaded France to seek power in North Africa. In 1881 France occupied Tunis and so angered Italy which had her own African ambitions.

In 1882 Bismarck got Italy to join Austria and Germany in the **Triple Alliance**, although Italy insisted she would not fight Britain.

2.4 The scramble for Africa

Most European countries were trying to get colonies in Africa, then relatively undiscovered. They hoped to gain markets for their own products, raw materials for their industries, high profits on investments in mines and other ventures, and men for their colonial armies. Britain already had a colony in the Cape and looked for a Cape-to-Cairo link running through all British colonies. This clashed with French hopes for a Morocco-Sudan link which almost led to an Anglo-French war in 1898. Germany came late to the colonial race, but in 1884 Bismarck organised a conference in Berlin where the Powers agreed to the division of Africa, with Germany gaining part of south-west Africa (now Namibia) and part of East Africa (now Tanzania). Britain saw Germany as one more colonial rival.

2.5 The Balkans, 1885–88

In 1878, the **Congress of Berlin** had divided Bulgaria into three regions. In 1885 the two northern regions ignored that arrangement and united under a nephew of Tsar Alexander II of Russia. Serbia tried to stop this but was defeated in the 1886 war. The Bulgarians then chose a German prince as their king, which angered the Russians but pleased the Austrians, who were also pleased by the defeat of ambitious Serbia. Bismarck feared a Russo-Austrian war over this. In 1887 he made a secret **Reinsurance Treaty** with Russia in which he promised Germany's support for Russia's claims to influence in Bulgaria. He also promised Germany's neutrality in a Russo-Austrian war, if Austria was the aggressor.

This was against the terms of the Dual Alliance and was dishonest. This became clear in 1888 when there was another row over the choice of a German prince to rule Bulgaria. Bismarck published the terms of the Dual Alliance which showed that Russia would have to fight Germany if she attacked Austria.

2.6 Kaiser Wilhelm (William) II, 1888–1918

1888 was the year of the three Kaisers: William I died; his son Frederick died within three months of gaining the throne, and his 28 year old son William became Emperor (or Kaiser) William II. William II's mother was Queen Victoria's eldest daughter, but he always resented England's influence. He also resented Bismarck's great power. By 1890 he had quarrelled with Bismarck about:
- Bismarck's attempts to crush the large Socialist movement. He wanted to come to terms with the Social Democratic Party.
- Bismarck's reluctance to get more colonies. William II wanted to have a large overseas Empire to rival Britain's.
- Bismarck's refusal to build a large navy. William wanted to rival Britain's.
- Bismarck's complicated foreign policy. He wanted to side more openly with Austria, even if this meant a quarrel with Russia.

In 1890 Bismarck was forced to resign and the young Kaiser, much under the influence of his military staff, took firmer control of policy.
- He refused to renew the 1887 Reinsurance Treaty with Russia.
- He supported the plans to build a Berlin-Baghdad Railway, which would go through Constantinople and increase German influence in the Balkans and the Middle East. This alarmed Russia and Britain.
- In 1895 he sent a congratulatory telegram to Kruger, President of the Boer Republic of the Transvaal who had defeated a British 'raid' from the Cape.
- When Britain fought the second Boer War (1899–1902) he allowed the German press and politicians to adopt an anti-British stance.
- After 1892 he supported Admiral von Tirpitz's plans for the building of a large German navy. This alarmed Britain who feared Germany would attack Britain's

overseas colonies. This led to Britain building a new fleet (1908–12) which increased the sense of crisis.

2.7 New alliances and friendships, 1892–1907

In 1892 the **Franco-Russian Alliance** was signed. With the collapse of the DKB in 1890 Russia, like France, was isolated, while Germany and Austria were closely linked. France and Russia had been enemies for many years, but they were brought together by economics and politics. France arranged the loans to pay for Russia's industrialisation (see 1.1), their navies exchanged visits and the press in both countries wrote friendly articles.

In 1897 the Russo-French alliance was strengthened and each country promised to help the other if attacked by Germany.

In 1902 Britain signed the **Anglo-Japanese alliance** because Britain saw the need for Japanese help against Russia in the Far East.

In 1904 Britain signed the **Entente Cordiale** with France, which was a settlement of past differences. France agreed that Egypt was a 'British sphere of interest', and Britain agreed that Morocco was a French one. Military chiefs began to discuss how they would use their armed forces if war broke out with Germany.

By 1904 Germany was a major threat to Britain in the Balkans and the Middle East. Germany's naval and industrial expansion also threatened Britain, so Britain was forced to end her enmity with France.

In 1905 the Kaiser challenged the entente by promising aid to the Sultan of Morocco against French attempts to control his country. At the 1906 Algeciras Conference Britain backed France, who then gained total control of Morocco. These events strengthened the Entente Cordiale and increased Anglo-German rivalry.

In 1907 **Britain and Russia also signed an entente** which settled past differences over Afghanistan, Persia and the Balkans, but said nothing about military aid in the event of war.

E xaminer's tip

A useful revision method for pages 18–23 is to make a time line showing the key events which occurred in this period.

In 1908 a group of Turkish army officers overthrew the rule of the Sultan and promised to form a democratic country. Austria took advantage of the uprising by annexing Bosnia-Herzegovina (see Fig. 2.1). Russia agreed to this but was angry when Austria did not help her get access to the Mediterranean via the Dardanelles. The Serbs were also angry with Austria because they wanted to control Bosnia. Russia wanted to go to war with Austria, but France refused to back her.

In 1911 there was an uprising against the Sultan of Morocco. The Kaiser sent a gunboat, the *Panther* to the port of Agadir pretending to be defending German traders (though there were none there). Britain saw this as a naval threat to her power and put her navy on war alert. At a conference Germany was forced to back down and France gained a freer hand in Morocco. The crisis led to an **Anglo-French naval agreement** in which France agreed to guard both countries' interests in the Mediterranean, while Britain guarded their interests in the Channel. The entente looked like an alliance.

In 1912–13 Greece, Serbia, Montenegro and Bulgaria formed the **Balkan League** and declared war on Turkey. Under the 1913 Treaty of London Turkey was driven almost completely from Europe. Serbia, Montenegro and Rumania then went to war with Bulgaria in the Second Balkan League War which ended with the Treaty of Bucharest (1913), which gave extra lands to Serbia, Greece and Rumania. A new country, Albania, was created at Austria's insistence, to keep Serbia out of the Adriatic Sea.

2.8 The outbreak of war

Serbia came out of the Balkan League Wars much larger, but angry at not having a sea port. Austria feared Serbia's success might gain her more influence among the seven million **Slavs** inside Hungary.

In 1913 the Kaiser told Austria that he would back her if she went to war with Serbia. The Serbs allowed terrorists to train inside Serbia before going on terrorist raids. In June 1914 the Archduke Franz Ferdinand, heir to the Austrian throne went on a tour of Bosnia-Herzegovina, but was assassinated in Sarajevo, the Bosnian capital, by Gavrilo Princip, a student member of the terrorist Serbian Black Hand Gang. The following events led to the breakout of the War:

- 23 July: Austria used this assassination as an excuse to crush Serbia, and she sent a set of demands to Serbia which, if accepted, would end Serbia's independence.
- 24 July: Serbia accepted most of the demands and asked for time to consider the rest.
- 25 July: Austria refused this request. Russia announced she would have to start the slow process of mobilising her forces.
- 28 July: Austria declared war on Serbia.
- 30 July: Russia ordered partial mobilisation. Germany demanded that this be called off.
- 1 August: Russia refused Germany's request so Germany declared war on Russia, which was followed (3 August) by her declaration of war on France, Russia's ally.

E **xaminer's tip**

Examiners expect you to show that World War One was caused by *several* factors. Be ready to explain which factors were the most important, i.e. problems in the Balkans; rivalry over Africa; the arms race; Wilhem II; the two armed camps; the Schlieffen plan.

2.9 Britain goes to war

Some British Ministers wanted Britain to declare war as soon as France was involved (3 August), but some ministers resigned when Britain did declare war on 4 August 1914.

The British declaration of war came because of Germany's invasion of Belgium (3 August) as part of the German invasion of France under the **Schlieffen Plan** (see 3.1). The neutrality of Belgium was guaranteed by the **Treaty of London** (1839). Britain demanded German withdrawal from Belgium, but when this was refused Britain declared war on Germany on 4 August 1914.

Summary

1 The creation of the German Empire (1871) left France humiliated and eager for revenge. Germany was the strongest country in Europe industrially and militarily.

2 Disputes in the Balkans (1877–78) increased Russo-Austrian hostility, and Bismarck signed the Dual Alliance (1879) with Austria and struggled to keep Russia within the Three Emperors League.

3 In 1890 William II refused to re-sign the Reinsurance Treaty with Russia who signed an alliance with France (1892).

4 Bismarck feared a European war over the 'scramble for Africa' and got the Great Powers to divide up the 'spoils' at the 1884 Conference of Berlin.

5 William II sacked Bismarck in 1890 and adopted an anti-British and anti-French policy over the Balkans, Africa and the navy. This led Britain to sign ententes with France (1904) and Russia (1907).

6 The sending of the *Panther* to Agadir led to Anglo-French talks which made the entente look like an alliance.

7 In the Balkans, Austria made enemies of Serbia by taking over Bosnia. The Serbs grew stronger during the Balkan League wars (1911–13).

8 Germany backed Austria's idea of crushing Serbia where terrorists were training to attack Austrians. The murder of the Archduke at Sarajevo (28 June 1914) led to the declaration of war by Austria on Serbia, followed by Germany attacking France and Russia, and then a British declaration of war on Germany after the attack on Belgium.

Quick questions

1 Which two provinces did Germany take from France in 1871?
2 Which two countries signed a Dual Alliance in i) 1879, ii) 1892?
3 i)   Which territory did Austria annex in the Balkans in 1908?
   ii) Which Slav country was most angered by this annexation?
4 Which three countries were linked in the Dreikaiserbund?
5 With which countries did Britain sign an entente in i) 1904; ii) 1907?
6 Which Treaties ended
   i)   the first Balkan War, 1912–13;
   ii) the second Balkan War, 1913?
7 To which north African port did the *Panther* sail in 1911?
8 What words are missing in the following sentences:
   'After 1911, the French fleet would be stationed in ....A...., and the British
   fleet would guard French interests in ....B....'
9 Why did Germany declare war on Russia on 1 August 1914?
10 Why did Britain declare war on Germany on 4 August 1914?

Chapter 3
The First World War

3.1 Great expectations dashed

Cheering crowds in Berlin, St Petersburg, Vienna, London and many other cities welcomed the start of the War. All would have shared the feelings of the poet Rupert Brooke (1887–1915), who wrote: 'Now, God be thanked Who has matched us with His hour/ And caught our youth, and wakened us from sleeping'

In 1905 Schlieffen, Chief of the German General Staff, drew up a plan to knock France out of the war in a few weeks before turning to fight Russia. The map (Fig. 3.1) shows how German troops were to advance into France through Belgium, swing behind Paris, and link up with troops coming up from the south. As the note on the map shows, it was to follow a timetable.

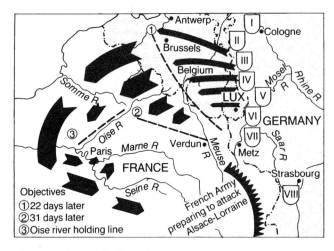

Fig. 3.1 The Schlieffen Plan

The Plan failed because:
- The Russians mobilised more quickly than expected: German troops had to be sent to stop their advance.
- It had not taken British troops into consideration. The small British Expeditionary Force (BEF) met and held the advancing Germans at Mons (23 August) and Ypres (12 October–11 November).
- The slow British retreat from Mons, and German failure to take **Ypres** threw the German timetable off course. The plan was changed and the Germans attacked Paris from the north instead of surrounding it. Joffre commanded the French troops who rallied on the north bank of the Marne.
- They were aided by British troops led by Sir John French. Together they drove the Germans across the River Aisne.

3.2 Trench warfare

By December 1914, the opposing armies were dug in, and trenches ran from Switzerland to the Channel ports. Rain turned these trenches into muddy pathways along which troops moved into position. Men slept where they could, and in their filthy uniforms. Cooking facilities were scarce: armies lived off tinned food. Dead bodies littered the space between the opposing trenches ('No man's Land'). Packs of rats attacked men, dead or alive, and their supplies.

Defending the trenches was fairly easy. Rolls of barbed wire laid in front of the trenches made an enemy advance very difficult. Machine guns allowed defending gunners to wipe out large numbers of attackers. Attacking enemy trenches was difficult and costly. Large guns from the rear bombarded enemy positions (often making the muddy 'no man's land' even muddier, so that troops drowned in the mud), hoping to frighten the enemy and smash the barbed wire. In fact, the artillery attack merely warned the enemy and usually failed to smash the barbed wire.

Generals on both sides tried to break through enemy lines. These attacks rarely worked, but generals insisted on 'another push'.

Major battles took place in 1915 at Ypres, Loos and Vimy Ridge; in 1916 at Verdun (below) and the Somme (below); in 1917 at Ypres (again), Vimy Ridge (again), Cambrai (where the British used massed tanks for the first time), and Messines; in 1918 on the Marne (again) and at Ypres (again) and St Quentin.

Verdun was a fortress built to defend the Rhine (see Fig. 3.1). From 21 February 1916 to the end of June the Germans tried to take it. They lost 281,000 men in these attacks: the French lost 315,000. The French commander, Pétain, became a national hero.

The **Somme** was Britain's most costly battle. It lasted from 1 July 1916 to mid-November. On the first day 60,000 men were killed out of a force of 100,000. More were seriously injured and still more drowned in the sea of mud created by the collapse of the drainage system under artillery bombardment ordered by Haig. By the end of the battle, Britain had suffered 400,000 casualties in this 'graveyard of Kitchener's volunteer army'. German and French losses were equally great and almost nothing was gained.

3.3 New weapons

Examiner's tip

Study carefully the reasons *for* and the *effects of* the stalemate on the Western Front. Questions asking you to explain why the stalemate was not broken are common.

To try to break the deadlock, both sides introduced new weapons.

- Poison gas was first used by the Germans at Ypres in 1915.
- The British invented the tank. When it was first used (too soon) on the Somme in 1916, it went at about 3 miles an hour, got bogged down in the mud and was easily destroyed by enemy artillery or captured by enemy troops because tanks got too far ahead of supporting infantry. Only at Cambrai were tanks used effectively.
- Sappers (the nickname for engineers) made mines beneath enemy trenches where they placed explosives. When these were blown up they destroyed the trenches, but such activities were easily discovered and sappers were often killed before they completed their work.
- Aeroplanes were used by both sides. At first they acted as 'spotters' to guide artillery fire. At Verdun, the Germans used planes to support their troops' attacks, and on the Somme they were used to bomb enemy lines. In 1917 the Germans developed the first two-engined bomber. By 1918 both sides had aircraft industries producing stronger engines: by the end of the war there were four-engined bombers, one of which was to make the first Atlantic crossing in 1919.
- The Germans were the first to develop a machine-gun which could fire through the revolving propeller. The British and French copied this so that the aeroplane became a slightly more efficient machine.
- German airships (Zeppelins) bombed London and some eastern ports.

3.4 The Russian front

In August 1914 Russian troops invaded East Prussia, won small victories and planned to march on Berlin. German troops taken from France (see 3.1) defeated the Russians at the **Battle of Tannenburg**, where 90,000 Russians were captured. The Germans also won the Battle of the Masurian Lakes and drove the Russians from East Prussia.

Russian troops defeated the Austrians at Lemberg, where many Slavs in the Austrian army surrendered without fighting, but in 1915–16 the Germans drove the Russians back. Two million Russians died as they retreated. They lost a million men fighting the Austrians who they did defeat in battle. The defeats helped to bring down the Tsar in 1917 (see 6.1).

3.5 The British and the Turkish front

Turkey entered the war on Germany's side in October 1914. This gave the German-Turkish allies control of the Dardanelles, linking the Mediterranean and the Russian ports in the Black Sea. The western Allies wanted to control the Dardanelles so they could send supplies to Russia.

In March 1915 a fleet of old battleships tried to get through to the Black Sea; several were sunk by mines and the plan was abandoned. The defending Turks had almost run out of munitions and might have given in to another attack or if troops had been used as well as ships.

In April 1915 Sir Ian Hamilton led a small army to try to capture Gallipoli as a step towards an attack from the rear on Constantinople (see Fig. 2.1). He delayed his attack, allowing the Turks time to prepare and enabling them to repulse this attack. British troops, backed by the Australian and New Zealand Army Corps (ANZACS), tried to climb the steep cliffs of the Straits. For eight months they made a series of costly attacks until finally, in December 1915 the remaining troops were withdrawn.

This failure led Bulgaria to enter the war on Germany's side, hoping to gain revenge on Serbia for her 1913 defeat (see 2.7). Serbia was soon defeated.

After the retreat from Gallipoli, the allies sent 600,000 men to the port of Salonika (see Fig. 2.1) to show that they backed the Serbs. This army suffered from lack of food and supplies, and many men died of malaria and other diseases. They failed to save Serbia, but stayed in Salonika from where they attacked Bulgaria until the **armistice** was signed on 30 September 1918.

Examiner's tip

Study carefully the reasons for the British failure on the Turkish front and the effects of this failure.

3.6 The Arab revolt

The Turks threatened an attack on British-controlled Egypt. British troops from India invaded Mesopotamia (modern Iraq – see Fig. 4.3) as part of a plan to defeat Turkey, and to guard British oil interests in the Persian Gulf. However, they were beaten by the Turks at Kut el Amara (April 1916). The city was recaptured (February 1917) and the British went on to take Baghdad.

T.E. Lawrence ('Lawrence of Arabia') helped to bring Arab tribes on to Britain's side against their Turkish overlords. As part of the price for their guerrilla war, Lawrence got Britain to promise that after the war the Arabs would have their independence (see 4.6). In 1917 British and Arab forces defeated the Turks in a series of battles.

General Allenby captured Jerusalem (December 1917) and Damascus (September 1918), which marked the end of the fighting in this area.

3.7 The war at sea

The Royal Navy was meant to ensure a flow of goods and troops to and from Britain, and to stop the enemy receiving food and supplies. Food shortages in Germany (as a result of the naval blockade) played a part in demands for an end to the war. The Royal Navy also guarded the British colonies and helped attacks on enemy colonies.

The German navy had been built to challenge Britain (see 2.6). Small units of that navy fought indecisive battles at Heligoland (1914) and off the Dogger Bank (1915), while another small fleet won a victory at Coronel (1914) off the coast of Chile.

However, Admiral von Spee's fleet was almost wiped out at the Battle of the Falkland Islands (1914). The German High Fleet only sailed once into the North Sea. In one day's fighting, at **Jutland** in May 1916, a British navy led by Admiral Jellicoe had a running battle with the German fleet led by Admiral Scheer.

- Britain claimed a victory as they forced the Germans to retreat to their northern bases and the Fleet never came out again.
- Germany claimed a victory since the British suffered heavier losses.

Germany placed more reliance on the submarine (or 'underwater boat'). In 1915 their **U-Boats** attacked not only Allied ships, but any ship suspected of trading with the Allies. There were also attacks on passenger ships, including the Cunard liner the *Lusitania* which was sunk off the coast of Ireland. As a result 1,198 people died, including 124 Americans. The US Government protested and the Germans called off their 'all out' campaign.

However, attacks on Allied ships continued. Various methods were tried to halt the success of the submarine:

- Echo sounders were fitted to Royal Navy ships protecting merchant ships. It was hoped that this would enable them to find and destroy submarines.
- Naval and merchant ships were fitted with machines to fire depth charges which exploded underwater, and with luck, damaged submarines.
- Q ships were merchant ships manned by Royal Naval crews and carrying hidden guns. These might tempt submarines to attack on the surface and so allow the Naval gunners to sink the submarines.
- In January 1917 a second 'all out' campaign was started. It was very successful and hundreds of ships were sunk in February to April 1917. By then Britain had only six weeks supply of wheat left. Britain was in danger of starvation. Prime Minister Lloyd George forced the Royal Navy to guard merchant ships which were grouped in **convoys**. Fewer British ships were lost after this, and by March 1918 more German U-Boats were being sunk than were being built.

3.8 The USA enters the war, April 1917

President Wilson had been re-elected in 1916 after promising to keep the USA out of the war. The second 'all out' submarine campaign helped to change US opinion in favour of the Allies.

Allied **propaganda** also changed US attitudes. Germans were shown as cruel attackers on 'little Belgium'. Newspapers carried stories about the savage behaviour of German soldiers and the U-Boat campaign. They told of women and children dying at sea.

In April 1917 the US declared war on Germany. The USA's entry into the war ensured reinforcements on the Western Front, and a continuous supply of food and materials. The Allies and the Germans knew that if the war went on there would be a large number of fresh US troops coming on to the Allied side. The Germans realised they could not defeat the USA.

3.9 The Germans defeated

In March 1918 the Germans had forced Russia out of the war, which allowed troops to be transferred from the east to the Western Front. German troops were badly affected by news of starvation and protests at home. The German commander, Ludendorf, decided to make an all out attack on France to end the war quickly before the US troops arrived (see 3.7)

On 21 March 1918 British troops were overrun but managed to regroup. By 31 March they were holding the Germans. In April the attack switched to the north. Again, there were battles in Flanders fields around Ypres. Again the British held the Germans.

In May the Germans attacked the French on the River Aisne. Again they had early victories; the French retreated to the Marne (see Fig. 3.1) and the road to Paris seemed open. This attack was halted with the aid of US troops as well as British, French and ANZAC troops. In July, Foch ordered a series of counter attacks along the front from the Marne to Amiens and broke the German resistance. In August the Germans had what Ludendorf called 'the blackest day in the history of the German army' when the British defeated him at Amiens.

In September the British won victories in Flanders, the US defeated the Germans near Verdun, and the French advanced in the centre.

At roughly the same time Allied forces advanced into Bulgaria from Salonika, and Bulgaria surrendered on 30 September. The Austrians surrendered on 3 November, while the British led by Allenby were victorious in the Middle East.

In Germany there were uprisings, some led by Marxists who hoped for a Russian-style revolution. Others were led by people simply tired of the war. On 4 October Ludendorf asked for a truce on the Western Front. The Allied reply was Wilson's Fourteen Points (see Fig. 4.1). Germany rejected these and continued to fight.

The German Navy mutinied in Kiel, while there were more civilian uprisings by Germans against the Kaiser's Government due to starvation and anger about their defeats in battle. Further Allied victories led to a change of government in Berlin (see 8.1). The Kaiser was forced to **abdicate** on 9 November 1918, and German representatives met the French at Compiègne near Paris to discuss an end to the fighting.

The Germans wanted a peace based on the Fourteen Points, but the Allies said that, because the Germans had rejected them in October, they had to surrender unconditionally. The Germans were told to surrender their fleet and leave the French bank of the Rhine. The naval blockade continued while the talks continued. Some Germans wanted to fight on, but Ludendorf and most generals wanted to avoid further humiliating defeats for the army. The Chancellor, Prince Max of Baden, and most politicians also wanted to save the people from further suffering. Therefore the generals and politicians agreed to accept the harsh terms of the **armistice**. At 11.00 a.m. on 11 November 1918 the War came to an end.

See Chapter 13 to find out how the War affected British civilians.

Examiner's tip

Be ready to explain why the Allies (Britain, France and USA) were victorious in the war. Examiners often ask students to rank the causes of Germany's defeat in order of importance (the Schlieffen plan failure, the war at sea, the USA's role and Germany's collapse).

Summary

1 The Schlieffen plan failed leading to stalemate in the war.
2 The trenches were easier to defend than to attack. Losses were heavy.
3 New technologies (tanks, guns and aircraft) were slow to develop.
4 The Russians had initial successes but then collapsed.
5 Britain disastrously failed to take the Dardanelles even with the aid of the ANZACS and the Salonika campaign also failed.
6 The Royal Navy enforced a blockade on Germany. The German U–Boats did great damage but the convoys overcame the threat. The Battle of Jutland was a stalemate.

7 The USA entered the War in April 1917 to massive effect.

8 Ludendorf's 'all out' campaign (March 1918) failed after some successes.

9 Germany rejected Wilson's Fourteen Points and then were forced to accept unconditional surrender in November 1918.

Quick questions

1 Name the following:
   a) The British Commander on the Somme 1916–17.
   b) The French Commander who led the defence of Verdun in 1916.
   c) The German admiral at the Battle of Jutland 1916.
   d) The Englishman who organised the Arab revolt.
   e) The President who brought the USA into the war in 1917.
   f) The British Commander in the Gallipoli campaign.
   g) The Supreme Commander, Western Front 1918.
   h) The nation which was defeated at Tannenburg.
   i) The port occupied by the Allies to ensure supplies to Serbia.
   j) The British liner carrying American passengers sunk in 1915.
   k) The waterway linking the Black Sea to the Mediterranean.

2 Name the following battles:
   a) the one in which massed tanks were used effectively in 1917;
   b) the only one fought between the main German and British fleets;
   c) the one in which British forces defeated von Spee of Germany.

Chapter 4
Peacemaking 1919–23

Program for Peace of the World
By President Wilson, January 8, 1918

I. Open covenants of peace, openly arrived at, after which there shall be no private international understandings of any kind, but diplomacy shall proceed always frankly and in the public view.

II. Absolute freedom of navigation upon the seas, outside territorial waters, alike in peace and in war, except as the seas may be closed in whole or in part by international action for the enforcement of international covenants.

III. The removal, so far as possible, of all economic barriers and the establishment of an equality of trade conditions among all the nations consenting to the peace and associating themselves for its maintenance.

IV. Adequate guarantees given and taken that national armaments will reduce to the lowest point consistent with domestic safety.

V. Free, open-minded, and absolutely impartial adjustment of all colonial claims, based upon a strict observance of the principle that in determining all such questions of sovereignty the interests of the population concerned must have equal weight with the equitable claims of the government whose title is to be determined.

VI. The evacuation of all Russian territory and such a settlement of all questions affecting Russia as will secure the best and freest cooperation of the other nations of the world in obtaining for her an unhampered and unembarrassed opportunity for the independent determination of her own political development and national policy, and assure her of a sincere welcome into the society of free nations under institutions of her own choosing; and, more than a welcome, assistance also of every kind that she may need and may herself desire. The treatment accorded Russia by her sister nations in the months to come will be the acid test of their goodwill, of their comprehension of her needs as distinguished from their own interests, and of their intelligent and unselfish sympathy.

VII. Belgium, the whole world will agree, must be evacuated and restored, without any attempt to limit the sovereignty which she enjoys in common with all other free nations. No other single act will serve as this will serve to restore confidence among the nations in the law which they have

themselves set and determined for the government of their relations with one another. Without this healing act the whole structure and validity of international law is forever impaired.

VIII. All French territory should be freed and the invaded portions restored, and the wrong done to France by Prussia in 1871 in the matter of Alsace-Lorraine, which has unsettled the peace of the world for nearly fifty years, should be righted, in order that peace may once more be made secure in the interest of all.

IX. A readjustment of the frontiers of Italy should be effected along clearly recognisable lines of nationality.

X. The people of Austria-Hungary, whose place among the nations we wish to see safeguarded and assured, should be accorded the freest opportunity of autonomous development.

XI. Rumania, Serbia and Montenegro should be evacuated; occupied territories restored; Serbia accorded free and secure access to the sea; and the relations of the several Balkan States to one another determined by friendly counsel along historically established lines of allegiance and nationality; and international guarantees of the political and economic independence and territorial integrity of the several Balkan States should be entered into.

XII. The Turkish portions of the present Ottoman Empire should be assured a secure sovereignty, but the other nationalities which are now under Turkish rule should be assured an undoubted security of life and an absolutely unmolested opportunity of autonomous development, and the Dardanelles should be permanently opened as a free passage to the ships and commerce of all nations under international guarantees.

XIII. An independent Polish State should be erected which should include the territories inhabited by indisputably Polish populations, which should be assured a free and secure access to the sea, and whose political and economic independence and territorial integrity should be guaranteed by international covenant.

XIV. A general association of nations must be formed under specific covenants for the purpose of affording mutual guarantees of political independence and territorial integrity to great and small States alike.

Fig. 4.1 Wilson's Fourteen Points

You should study the text in Fig. 4.1. Many people then saw the 'program' (or Points) as a plan for the future of a world free from war, from overseas colonies and of many new, independent and democratic states.

In January 1918 Germany rejected the programme (note the American spelling). In November they hoped that the coming peace would be based on Wilson's plan.

4.1 The Conference at Versailles, 1919

There were 70 delegates from 32 victorious countries, but not one from any of the defeated countries. There were also 60 committees of experts to help the peacemakers, but the Conference was dominated by 'The Big Four' who met secretly to make their decisions.

- Wilson wanted a peace based on his 'program', without any 'punitive damages', and with the people of each nation being allowed to choose or 'determine' (see Points V and X) the way in which they were to be governed in the future.
- Clemenceau of France, wanted to punish the Germans as harshly as possible, to undo the damage done by the 1871 Treaty (see 2.1) and to ensure that Germany would not be able to make any future wars.
- Lloyd George of Britain at first agreed with Wilson. Soon he gave in to pressure from British papers, voters and politicians who wanted to 'make Germany pay' and 'to hang the Kaiser'.
- Orlando of Italy wanted to gain extra territory while also punishing the Austrians, who had defeated Italians during the war. He had little influence, and the 'Big Three' really controlled things. One result of the policies of Clemenceau and Lloyd George was that Wilson was forced to ignore his own 'program'. Look again at Fig. 4.1 and then note the following:

Point 1: the 'Big Four' met in secret, as did the 'Big Three'.
Point 2: Britain insisted on its right to search ships in wartime.
Point 3: tariff barriers were not only maintained but increased.
Point 4: there was no post-war disarmament.
Point 5: Britain and France increased their colonial Empires.
Point 6: the allies sent troops to attack the Bolsheviks (see Chapter 6).
Point 9: the Italian boundary was not settled.
Point 10: the peoples of the old Austro-Hungarian Empire were not given any say in the boundaries of the new states created in 1919.
Point 13: post-war Poland included millions of Germans (see Chapter 10).
Point 14: the League of Nations (see Chapter 5) never worked as Wilson hoped.

4.2 The Treaty of Versailles, 22 June 1919

This only dealt with Germany. Other treaties dealt with Austria, Hungary, Bulgaria and Turkey (see 4.4 and 4.6).

Fig. 4.2 shows the losses suffered by Germany in Europe.

Alsace and Lorraine went back to France; Germany lost three-quarters of her iron deposits. The Saar coal fields were to be ruled by the League for 15 years, with France controlling the mines. West Prussia and Posen with 4 million Germans went to the new state, Poland. Czechoslovakia, a new state, got some German lands and 48,000 Germans. The German port of Danzig, with 300,000 Germans, was to be ruled by the League as a 'Free City'. Memel, another German port with 141,000 German inhabitants, was seized by the new state of Lithuania.

The Rhineland got special treatment. Part (Malmedy and Eupen) went to Belgium. The rest was named a 'demilitarised zone' where the Allies were to keep an army of

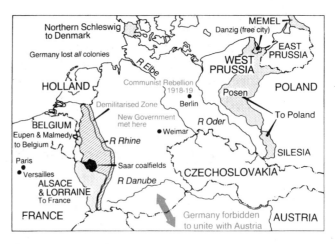

Fig. 4.2 German losses, 1919

occupation for 15 years, while Germany was forbidden to have armies or fortifications in the area after these 15 years.

Germany was also punished in other ways.

- Its colonies were given to the Allies who ran them as **Mandates**. Tanganyika went to Britain, and France took the Cameroons.
- It had to disband its airforce, surrender its navy to the Allies, and had to reduce its army to 100,000 (smaller than the Belgian army).
- It had to pay **reparation** for the damage done by the war – £6,600 million was to be paid in cash. The German merchant fleet was given to Britain. France was to get fixed amounts of coal, and Belgium a fixed number of cattle.

4.3 German humiliation and anger

The Germans had either to accept or reject this 'dictated peace'. The Allies maintained their naval blockade while their armies threatened to resume their attacks on German forces if the German Government refused to accept the terms of the treaty.

In particular the Germans resented Clause 231 of the Treaty which declared that Germany alone was responsible for the losses and damage caused by the war. This 'war guilt' clause was the basis for the reparations to be made by the Germans to the Allies.

When the Kaiser **abdicate**d on 9 November, there was a Marxist revolution in Berlin, so the first post-war Government of defeated Germany left Berlin and met in Weimar (see 8.1). The Weimar Government representatives signed the Treaty in the same Hall of Mirrors in Versailles where Bismarck had proclaimed the German Empire in 1871 (see 2.1 and 28.1). France had got her revenge on Germany.

4.4 The Treaty of St. Germain with Austria

Austria was separated from Hungary (with whom a separate Treaty of Trianon was signed in 1920). Austria became a small landlocked country. From the Austro-Hungarian Empire came:

- A new state for Southern Slavs – Yugoslavia. This was made up of the old Kingdom of Serbia (see Fig. 2.1) and the Southern Slavs who had lived in pre-war Hungary.
- A larger Rumania which got Transylvania from Hungary and Bessarabia from Russia.
- A new state, Czechoslovakia (see Fig. 4.2) was created from the old German

Kingdom of Bohemia and from the northern parts of Austria. A larger Poland which got Galicia.

- A larger Italy which got Trentino, Trieste and part of the South Tyrol. (Even in the 1990's the people still speak German there).

4.5 Some criticisms of the Treaties

Many of the new states created by the Treaties were too small and unable to defend themselves from attacks by major powers. The small states and the larger ones imposed tariff barriers to protect their own industries, contrary to Wilson's 'program'. This led to a fall in world trade and was one of the main reasons for massive unemployment after 1920. Many of the new states included many foreigners. Poland, for example, had millions of Germans inside its new boundaries. This caused unrest in the 1920's and 1930's (see Chapter 10).

Germany had been heavily punished and looked for revenge. Hitler's popularity (see Chapters 8 and 10) was mainly based on his promise to reverse the Versailles Treaty.

The **reparations** imposed on Germany were too high and led to crises in the 1920's because Germany could not afford to pay (see Chapters 8 and 10).

4.6 The Treaties of Sèvres (1920) and Lausanne (1923)

Examiner's tip

i. Prepare for questions comparing the various treaties and the differences between Wilson's Fourteen Points with the actual treaties.
ii. Note that the Peace Treaties were an important long-term cause of the Hitler's rise to power (Chapter 8).
iii. Be ready to write about the different views held about the treaties in Germany, France and Britain.

During the War, the British and French made three separate statements about what was to be done with the Turkish Empire after the War.

- The British promised Hussein, the 'Sheriff' of the Islamic Holy City of Mecca, that he would get some Turkish lands if the Arabs fought the Turks. In section 3.5 we saw how Lawrence of Arabia used this 'promise' to get Arab support for Britain against Turkey.
- In May 1916 Britain and France agreed to divide the Turkish Empire between themselves. France was to get Syria, Lebanon and Mosul (see Fig. 4.3). Britain was to get the areas now known as Jordan, Iraq and northern Palestine. West Palestine was to come under 'an international regime'. An 'Arab State' was also supposed to be set up somewhere.

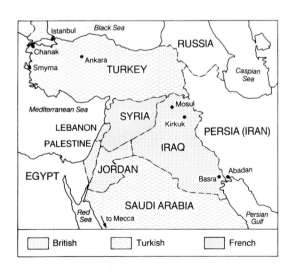

Fig. 4.3 Dividing up the Turkish Empire, 1923

- On 2 November 1917, A.J. Balfour, British Foreign Secretary, published the 'Balfour Declaration' which promised British support for a Jewish 'National Home in Palestine' as long as the rights of the Arabs were safeguarded. This was the main reason for later Arab-Israeli conflict (see Chapter 24).

The **Treaty of Sèvres** (1920) was confirmed by the **Treaty of Lausanne**. Five new states were set up: Syria, Lebanon, Palestine, Jordan and Iraq.

The Treaties gave Syria and Lebanon to France, while Britain got Palestine, Jordan and Iraq from which Britain could look after her oil interests in the Persian Gulf. The Allies were to regard these states as Mandates (see 4.7 below).

Hussein of Mecca hoped that his sons Feisal and Abdullah would each get a 'kingdom', and that he would become the ruler of the southern Arabs. His hopes were dashed by an Arab war. The Arab chief, Ibn Saud defeated Hussein and called his kingdom Saudi Arabia (see Fig. 4.3).

4.7 Mandated territories

The French, who controlled Syria and Lebanon, offered the Syrian crown to Hussein's son, Feisal, but then they drove him out of the Syrian capital, Damascus, when Feisal wanted to rule as an independent King.

France ruled Syria and Lebanon as if they were colonies, and they became independent only after World War Two.

Britain crushed an Arab revolt in Mesopotamia and then created Iraq, the throne of which they gave to Feisal. Britain then created the Kingdom of Transjordan (Jordan in Fig. 4.3). Hussein's son, Abdullah was made King to rule under British control. This control ended in 1956.

Britain also ruled Palestine as a Mandated Territory until 1947, when Palestine was handed to the United Nations (see Chapter 24).

Summary

1 Wilson's Fourteen Points were ignored by the peacemakers.
2 Germany was punished by:
   i)   loss of territory in Europe and overseas,
   ii) demilitarisation, and
   iii) war damages.
3 Germany objected to the 'dictated peace' and France saw the Treaty as 'revenge for 1871'.
4 A number of small states were created in Europe which led to racial and nationalist problems later on.
5 There were three different Allied wartime agreements about the future of the Turkish Empire.
6 The Treaties of Sèvres and Lausanne benefited Britain and France.
7 The Middle Eastern 'Mandates' under the control of Britain and France were difficult to control.

Quick questions

Examine the map of Germany and her neighbours in 1919 (below), and then answer the following questions.

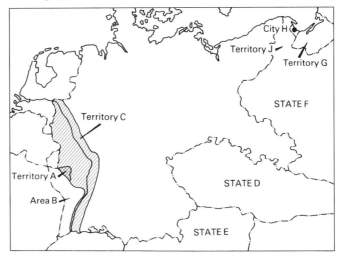

1 Name shaded territory A.
2 State the provisions made in the Treaty of Versailles regarding Territory A.
3 Name the provinces in Area B.
4 State the provisions made in the Treaty of Versailles regarding the provinces in Area B.
5 State the provision made in the Treaty of Versailles concerning shaded Territory C
6 Name State D.
7 Name the state of which most of State D had been part before 1918.
8 Name State E.
9 State the provisions made in the Treaty of Versailles concerning the future of State E.
10 Name the areas marked on the map: i) F; ii) G; and iii) H.
11 Name three states between which State F had been divided before 1918.
12 Name the State which ruled Territory G after 1919.
13 State the provisions of the Treaty of Versailles concerning City H.
14 What purpose was Territory J intended to serve?

Chapter 5
The League of Nations

The 14th Point in Wilson's 'program' (see Fig. 4.1) was a proposal for a 'A general association of nations'. Unlike most of his other Points, this one was adopted by most nations. The League of Nations was set up in 1920, with its headquarters at Geneva in neutral Switzerland.

Its supporters hoped that it would solve the world's problems peacefully and move the world away from the power politics which, in the past, had led to wars.

5.1 The Covenant

This was the constitution (set of rules) of the League. It had 26 articles dealing with such things as arms reduction, control of arms production, the prevention of war, the duty of member states to take all disputes to the League for a decision, the power of the League to impose sanctions on warring nations.

Sanctions could be economic, so that no member state would trade with the warring states, and military, with war being made on the nation which refused to end the fighting (see 10.1)

This Covenant was included in all the peace treaties, 1919–23, so that every nation appeared to accept the idea of a League. The treaties were imposed on the defeated nations (see Chapter 4) so the League was seen as 'an association of victorious states'.

5.2 The organisation of the League

- The **Assembly** was the largest body. Every member state could send three delegates, but only one could vote. It met once a year, but could be called together if needed.

  All member states had one vote so that small states were equal to larger ones. Before a decision could be reached, all members had to vote in favour of what was proposed. Any nation could prevent a decision being reached by the **veto**. In fact, most matters were settled in committees, and members in full meetings of the Assembly preferred to abstain to stop decisions being reached rather than voting against a proposal.
- The **Council of the League of Nations** met at least four times a year and could be called to meet at other times if needed. The permanent members were Britain, France, Japan and Italy. The USA would have been a permanent member if it had joined the League, but the US Senate refused to ratify the Peace Treaty.

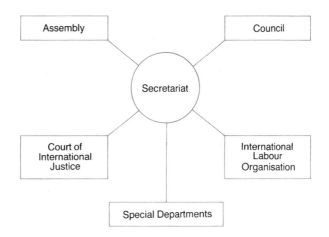

Fig. 5.1 The organisation of the League

There were also non-permanent council members elected from among the smaller nations. in 1920 there were four such members, but by 1939 there were eleven non-permanent members of the Council. Council decisions, like those of the Assembly, had to be unanimous, which led to long arguments and slow progress in times of crisis. The Council also had limited powers to ensure a decision was actually carried out. It had no army under its control, and relied on member states, especially Britain and France to act for it. The Council could not enforce a decision to stop trade with a warring nation; it had to rely on the goodwill of member states to cooperate with it. As a result the Council of the League was really very weak.

- The **Secretariat** was an international civil service that ran the League. Its members were taken from the member states. The first Secretary General was an Englishman, Sir Eric Drummond. His staff had to carry out League decisions and provide the Assembly, Council and the League Commissions with the information they needed on issues being discussed. They also kept the records of all these bodies.

- **League Commissions** (committees) were set up to deal with special problems or issues. There were, for example:
  - The Mandates Commission, which kept an eye on the Mandated States (see 4.7).
  - The World Health Organisation (WHO), which campaigned for such things as attacks on preventable diseases around the world.
  - The Drugs Commission, which informed the world of the dangers of some drugs and suggested ways of controlling the drugs trade.
  - The Minorities Commission, which drew attention to the ill-treatment of some racial minorities, and invited guilty governments to reform.
  - The Commission for the administration of the Saar and Danzig (see Figs 4.2 and 10.6) ensured that these areas were properly governed.
  - The Disarmament Commission got the greatest attention, but also had the least success (see 5.6).

- The **International Labour Organisation** (ILO) was made up of delegates from governments, employers and workers from member states who met at the League's Geneva Headquarters once a year. They aimed at improving the working and living conditions of people everywhere. The ILO proposed new laws to various governments and reported on how governments carried out ILO proposals. The ILO had many successes:
  - Member states agreed that workers should have annual paid holidays. In 1938 all British employers accepted this as part of agreements with trade unions. The ILO declared that workers had a right to form trade unions. This became an important part of workers' campaigns everywhere. Many employers around the world ignored this declaration. In the USA, for example this right was denied by many employers (see 9.8).
  - The ILO decided that no one should be in full time employment before the age of fifteen, and it encouraged governments to act on this. Britain raised the school leaving age to 14 in 1918, but did not raise the school leaving age to 15 until 1947.

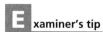
- The ILO published papers on the dangers of using certain materials in manufacturing, and so helped trade unions in arguments with governments and employers as they tried to get dangerous substances banned.
- **The Court of International Justice** had been set up in the Hague in Holland (1900), but few states brought their disputes before its judges. Austria, for example, refused Serbia's plea to take their dispute to the Court in June–July 1914 (see 2.8). In 1922 the Permanent Court of International Justice was set up in the Hague. It had limited powers, unable to force states to accept its judgement, but by 1939, 70 major cases had been settled by the Court. The Court also helped to arrange 400 international agreements.

5.3 How did the nations judge the League?

None of the defeated nations were invited to the first meeting of the League (1922).

- The **USSR** was not invited to the first meeting because the powerful western nations had not recognised the Bolshevik Government (see 6.4). The USSR was allowed to join in 1934, but left after she had invaded Finland (1939).
- The USA did not join the League. Wilson, 'the Father of the League', was prevented by the Republican majority in the US Congress (see 9.9). The Republicans rejected the peace treaties which Wilson signed (1919, 1920)
- France hoped the League would enforce the Treaty of Versailles and ensure her security against Germany. France formed alliances outside the League's control when the League was proved to be weak.
- Britain hoped that the League would solve the world's problems peacefully, but she was unwilling to allow her forces to act for the League because most voters after the war were more **pacifist** than warlike. They remembered the slaughters of the war (see Chapter 3) and did not want another war.
- Germany was allowed into the League in 1926 when Stresemann gained power (see 8.6), but left in 1933 when Hitler failed to get his own way in the Disarmament Conference that year (see 5.6).
- Turkey, one of the defeated states, joined in 1932.
- Japan left the League in 1933 after the League had condemned her invasion of Manchuria (see 10.3).
- Italy left in 1937 after the League condemned the invasion of Abyssinia (see 10.4).

5.4 Some early successes and failures

Danzig was established as an International Free City (See Fig. 4.2) in spite of rivalry between Poles and Germans.

Upper Silesia (see Fig. 4.2), a coal rich area, was peacefully divided between Poland and Germany after the League had organised a **plebiscite** in 1921. Neither country was totally happy with the division, but they accepted it and went on to make a trade treaty.

The **Aaland Islands** were claimed by both Sweden and Finland. The League settled the dispute in favour of Finland (1921) and Sweden accepted the decision.

Austria was on the brink of economic collapse in 1922 when the League stepped in to organise world-wide financial help to save her.

Greek forces invaded **Bulgaria** in 1925. The League persuaded Greece to halt the invasion, withdraw her forces and pay Bulgaria reparations for the damage done.

Vilnius, a Lithuanian city, was attacked by Poland and was made part of Poland in 1922. The League condemned the attack, but Poland ignored it and held on to Vilnius until October 1939.

Corfu, a Greek island, was bombarded by Italian forces in 1923. This was in answer to the murder of an Italian member of a League Commission examining the disputed border between Greece and Albania. Italy did not take this matter to the League, but attacked Corfu instead. The League Council wanted to refer the issue to the Court of Justice. However, a conference of allied ambassadors met and decided that Greece had to pay reparations to Italy to make up for the murder. In this case, a strong permanent member ignored the League, and the other powerful members refused to back the Council.

5.5 Failing major tests, 1931–39

We shall see in Chapter 10 that the League failed to deal with the aggressive policies of:
- Japan in 1931 and 1937 (see 10.3);
- Italy, over the Abyssinian crisis (see 10.4);
- Hitler who, encouraged by Italy's success attacked the territorial and military clauses of the Treaty of Versailles (see 10.5).

5.6 The Disarmament Commission and Conference

The Covenant (see 5.1) called for nations to base their foreign policies on the basis of 'collective security' (Article 10). The authors of the Covenant hoped that nations would give up using their own forces, and rely instead on the united ('collective') power of the League to settle disputes and keep their peace (see 10.1). Therefore, Article 14 of the Covenant called on all nations to disarm. In fact, Britain, France and the other major powers refused to disarm. Plans for a disarmament conference to meet in 1926 collapsed because the planners failed to agree on how armaments were to be defined and counted.

In 1930 Germany asked for a revision of the Treaty of Versailles because she wanted an army and navy as large as those of France and Britain. The French refused to accept these ideas, though Britain was more sympathetic. In June 1932 the Germans threatened to walk out of the Disarmament Conference if they were not given equality of forces with Britain and France. While the Conference was still in session, Hitler came to power in Germany (January 1933). He made himself German dictator (see 8.10), and he withdrew German delegates from the Conference, and from the League. In 1934 the Conference broke up, having failed to reach an agreement.

Summary

1 Woodrow Wilson was the 'Father of the League of Nations'. The League was his 'Fourteenth Point' issued towards the end of World War One.
2 The League's Covenant was included in the Peace Treaties, and expressed the hope for disarmament and peaceful settlement of disputes.
3 The main bodies of the League were the Council, the Assembly, the Court of Justice and the Secretariat.
4 There were specialist organisations such as the ILO and WHO which did valuable work on health matters and working conditions.
5 The USA refused to join the League and Russia, Germany, Italy and Japan were 'in-out' members.

6 The League had successes in some small disputes such as over Danzig, Silesia, and the Aaland Islands, but failed over Corfu and Vilnius.

7 The League failed to stop aggression of Italy, Japan and Germany

8 There was slow progress in the 1932–34 Disarmament Conference, which eventually broke down.

9 Britain and France, though supporters of the League, refused to support the League's decisions with military force.

Quick questions

1 Which statesman may be said to have founded the League of Nations?
2 In which document was the case for a League stated?
3 Where was the League's headquarters?
4 What were the two most important bodies of the League of Nations?
5 Explain the meaning of
  i) ILO, and
  ii) Mandates.
6 What sanctions could be imposed by the League?
7 Which of the major countries:
  i) never joined the League;
  ii) joined the League in 1926 but left in 1933;
  iii) was expelled in 1939?
8 Which crisis involved Japan in 1931?
9 Over what issue did Hitler end Germany's membership of the League of Nations?

Chapter 6
Russia 1914–53

6.1 Growing threats of revolution in Russia 1914–17

Stolypin's reforms (see 1.8) failed to solve the food shortages and to give all the peasants land. This was due mainly to rising population and backward farming methods. Strikes and violent demonstrations in the countryside and cities, often led by **Bolsheviks**, showed many people were angry with the Tsar's Government. Many Liberals were angry that the Tsar had taken power away from the Duma (see 1.7).

The Tsar's Government was weak and was unable to deal with these problems. Nicholas II was indecisive and unsuited to being an **autocrat**, and preferred spending time with his family to ruling the country. He allowed a lot of influence to pass to his German wife Alexandra, whose infatuation with the 'mad monk' Rasputin after the healing of her son, made people think the Government was corrupt. Rasputin got the power to sack and appoint ministers, and Nicholas turned down the Duma's request to send Rasputin away. Nicholas II's Government lost the respect of his supporters.

Failures in the war with Germany made these problems far worse (see 3.4). Early victories were followed by defeats which lowered the Tsar's prestige, especially as he made himself Commander-in-Chief (1915). Food shortages grew due to German capture of corn growing areas and the breakdown of the railway system. Food prices therefore rose and 'Bread Riots' spread throughout Russia's cities. Workers went on strike and soldiers deserted the army, adding to the hungry population. Nicholas was at the war front unable to do anything to end the disorder.

6.2 The March 1917 Revolution and the fall of the Tsar

All the problems outlined above led to the first revolution of 1917. It began spontaneously when soldiers refused to fire on the bread rioters and striking workers. Mobs seized public buildings, released prisoners from jail and took control of police stations and arms stores.

On March 12, two rival groups tried to take control of Russia. The Duma formed an emergency committee, while workers and soldiers formed a Soviet in Petrograd, both meeting in the Tauride Palace. Nicholas, on his way home to Petrograd, was told by his generals to **abdicate** because he had lost control of the army and the people.

On March 15 Nicholas II abdicated in favour of his brother, Grand Duke Michael. When he refused the throne the Duma set up a Provisional Government, and 500 years of Romanov rule came to an end.

6.3 The failures of the Provisional Government

The Provisional Government, led by Prince Lvov until July and by Kerensky until November, failed to overcome the problems of Russia. The decision to continue the war led to mutinies by soldiers and sailors, attacks on noblemen's estates, strikes by workers and continued food shortages. **Soviets** of workers, peasants and soldiers set up rival mini-governments, taking their orders from the Petrograd Soviet.

The Petrograd Soviet issued 'Order No 1' telling the Petrograd soldiers that they must not obey any order from the Provisional Government which the Soviet opposed. This made the Government look weak, so strikes and unrest grew.

6.4 The November 1917 Bolshevik Revolution

Lenin played a crucial role in the Bolshevik Revolution. Germany helped him to return to Russia in April 1917 because Lenin wanted to end the war. He issued the April Theses which promised 'Peace, Bread, Land, Freedom.' These ideas won the support of peasants, who were angry that the Provisional Government delayed land reforms. Soldiers who wanted to stop fighting and hungry workers also supported Lenin's ideas. Lenin's slogan 'All Power to the Soviets' won the support of workers' leaders, and by October the **Bolsheviks** controlled the Moscow and Petrograd Soviets.

The events of July were a setback for Lenin. After more defeats by the German army, Russian soldiers retreated and some **Bolsheviks** tried to take power against Lenin's advice. Kerensky ordered the arrest of leading Bolsheviks, and the newspaper *Pravda* was closed down. Lenin was accused of being a German spy and fled to Finland.

In September 1917 the right-wing general Kornilov tried to replace the Provisional Government with a military dictatorship. Kerensky was forced to arm the Petrograd Soviet and Bolsheviks to defeat Kornilov. This showed that Lenin's Bolsheviks had the real power in Russia.

Leon Trotsky's 'Red Guards' had helped to stop Kornilov, and urged on by Lenin, Trotsky, the chairman of the Petrograd Soviet, drew up plans for taking power. The revolution was signalled by the ship *Aurora* firing on the Winter Palace, and during 6–7 November the Red Guards took over all the key installations in Petrograd and arrested the Provisional Government ministers. On 8 November 1917 the All-Russian Congress of Soviets gave power to the 15 Bolshevik People's Commissars. Lenin was the chairman of the council of People's Commissars.

In the November 1917 General Elections for the National Assembly, the Bolsheviks won only 168 seats out of 700. The SRP (see 1.3) gained 380, so the Red Guards broke up the assembly (January 1918).

Under the new constitution (July 1918) the Bolshevik Party, renamed the Communist Party, was the only legal party in Russia. In 1924 the Russian republics were formed into the **USSR** governed by the **Supreme Soviet**, which in turn was controlled by the **Politburo**, which in turn was controlled by Lenin. This was known as 'democratic centralism'.

E xaminer's tip

When you prepare questions on the causes of the 1917 Revolutions, take care not to be confused between the *March Revolution* when the Tsar fell from power, and the *November Revolution* when the Provisional Government was replaced by Lenin's Bolsheviks.

6.5 The Treaty of Brest Litovsk, March 1918

Lenin agreed an **armistice** with Germany (December 1917). In March 1918 the Treaty of Brest Litovsk was signed. Under the Treaty Russia lost Poland, Finland, Estonia,

Latvia, Lithuania, the Ukraine and Georgia, a third of the population and farming land and three-quarters of the coal mines.

Lenin said that these losses had to be suffered to get peace. He also expected to get these lands back after a communist revolution in Germany

6.6 The Russian Civil War, 1918–22

The anti-communists (the **Whites**) included Social Revolutionaries and Liberals angry about the elections, landlords angry about their loss of land, naval and army officers angry about the Brest Litovsk treaty, as well as ethnic minorities hoping to break away from Russia.

There were also troops from the USA, France, Japan and Britain hoping to destroy the Communist revolution and install a government which would carry on the war against Germany. White Army forces led by Admiral Kolchak came within 200 miles of Moscow, but the Communist forces (the **Reds**) fought back, and by the end of 1920 the Reds had won. The Tsar's family were murdered by the Reds.

The Reds won for a number of reasons:

- They had better supplies of food and war equipment.
- Trotsky, the Commissar for War, organised the Red Army brilliantly.
- The Whites were divided between those who wanted to bring back the Tsar and others who wanted some sort of socialist state.
- The Whites did not have a single leader to organise their armies, and the further they advanced the worse their supply problems became.
- Patriotic Russian peasants hated the White landlords and foreign armies, so they supported the Reds.

6.7 War Communism and the New Economic Policy

In order to win the war Lenin introduced his policy of **War Communism**. All factories and farms were put under State control, and private trade was banned. All food was seized and given to soldiers and town workers. These policies helped to win the civil war, but caused many problems.

The peasants refused to grow any food, causing famine. With the drought in the Volga area this caused 5 million deaths. Industrial production slumped to 15% of the 1913 level. The shortages in food and industrial goods caused inflation. In March 1921 the mutiny by the Krondstadt sailors (who had helped Lenin in 1917) had to be brutally put down by the **CHEKA** (secret police).

Lenin's **New Economic Policy** (NEP) was introduced to try to solve the problems caused by War Communism. Peasants were allowed to sell their surplus food and pay tax on their profits. Private trade was allowed and small firms were privatised, though the State kept control of heavy industry (iron, coal, steel etc). Lenin hoped that these policies would encourage peasants to grow food for exports and to feed the industrial workers, while the small 'capitalist' firms would also increase production. The NEP did succeed. By 1928 grain production and industrial output had reached 1913 levels. Some peasants and businessmen became rich.

6.8 Lenin is succeeded by Stalin

A struggle for who was to succeed Lenin began during his illness (1922–24). In his will Lenin condemned Stalin for being too rough, and said that Stalin should be removed from his position as Communist Party Secretary.

Stalin's main rival, Trotsky, had made many enemies. They were jealous of his brilliance and hated his sarcastic way of speaking. They also disliked Trotsky's belief that the Communist Party should work for World revolution. Stalin cautiously argued for 'Socialism in One Country'.

As Party Secretary, Stalin appointed his friends to the Politburo and they voted to sack Trotsky as Commissar for War (1924), from the Politburo (1926), and finally the Party (1927). He was exiled in 1929 and murdered by Stalin's **KGB** agents in Mexico (1940).

Stalin then allied with 'right-wing' Communists like Bukharin and Rykov, who supported gradual modernisation under the NEP. Zinoviev and Kamenev were expelled from the Politburo (1927) because they wanted the State to modernise Russia quickly by taking over the farms and the factories.

Having got rid of the 'leftists', Stalin then eliminated the right wingers like Bukharin and Rykov (1928–29), because Stalin decided to adopt fast modernisation policies for which Trotsky, Kamenev and Zinoviev had argued (see 6.10).

The Politburo was filled with Stalin's 'cronies' like 'Stone bottom' Molotov. Stalin now dominated the Communist Party.

6.9 Stalin eliminates his enemies

Before 1934 Stalin's treatment of his opponents was limited to dismissal from the Politburo and Party, but when Kirov, the popular head of the Leningrad Communist party was murdered (1934) Stalin ordered the **purge** of all possible anti-Stalinists. Great public show trials were staged in which old Bolsheviks like Zinoviev and Kamenev confessed to incredible crimes such as plotting to overthrow Stalin or spying for the Nazis. 35,000 army officers were arrested. By 1938 about 20 million had died through execution or exile.

Many Russians seemed to believe the confessions which were brought about by torture, because of Communist Party **propaganda**. People were encouraged to betray their friends and family to Stalin's police.

The **NKVD**, successor to CHEKA, carried out the executions. Yagoda, the NKVD chief, was arrested and replaced by the more ruthless Beria.

Stalin started the purges partly because he knew his economic policies (see 6.10) had made many enemies. He was also afraid of possible plots against his rule and he wanted to have total power in the USSR.

Stalin's new Soviet Constitution (1936) pretended to be democratic with everyone having the vote for candidates to the Supreme Soviet, but really everything was controlled by Stalin.

By 1938 the purges were weakening the USSR's industries and defence forces because many leaders were dead or in prison. Stalin called a halt to the purges. Hitler's early successes in the war (1941–42) were caused partly by the purges, and Stalin had to take generals and admirals out of prison to fight Hitler.

Stalin was on the verge of more purges when he died (1953). In 1956 Khrushchev condemned Stalin's cruelty at the 20th Party Congress (see 18.2)

6.10 Stalin's modernisation of industry

In 1928 Stalin decided to adopt Trotsky's ideas about fast modernisation, because Russia was not producing enough industrial goods. Stalin wanted the **USSR** to catch up with the industrialised West. Therefore Lenin's NEP was abandoned. A state planning commission, **Gosplan**, set five-year targets for industry and agriculture.

The first **five-year plans** (1928–32) stressed production in heavy industries (steel, coal, electricity, railways and machinery). These basic industries were vital for other industries and for the USSR's defence forces. By 1932 industrial output had doubled and the targets were beaten. Huge projects like the Stalingrad tractor works were completed.

The second five-year plan (1933–37) also concentrated on industrial goods, but the third plan (1937–43) concentrated on military goods to counter the threat from Hitler (see Chapter 9). Factories were built beyond the Urals so that western invaders could not reach them. By 1939 industrial production was third in the world behind the USA and Germany.

The Soviet people's wages were very low, as surplus profits were ploughed back into industry. The new industrial towns were overcrowded and food was short, so rationing had to be introduced. Workers were encouraged to produce more by propaganda about 'hero workers' like Stakhanov. Threats and punishments by industrial managers frightened workers into increasing output. 'Slackers' were accused of being criminals. Kulaks expelled from the land (see 6.11) provided cheap industrial labour in the Labour Camps.

The war with Hitler (1941–45) damaged Russia's industries. Machinery was worn out and mines were flooded, so the five-year plans (1946–50 and 1951–55) also concentrated on heavy industry. Trade agreements with Eastern Europe (see Chapter 19) helped Russia's exports and wages remained low.

6.11 Stalin's modernisation of agriculture

Under the NEP the peasants were not selling enough food, so Stalin decided (1928) to force the peasants to join state **collective farms**. These large farms would produce more food for town workers and for export to pay for industrial machinery. Tractors made in the factories could then be used on the large farms, and peasants not needed in the farms could be sent to work in industry.

At first Stalin tried to 'persuade' the peasants to volunteer for the collectives, but the richer peasants (kulaks) refused because they wanted to hold on to their own land. Therefore Stalin declared war on the kulaks. The army was sent to round them up, and 10 million of them were executed or removed to the Industrial Labour Camps (see 6.10). In protest the kulaks burned their crops and slaughtered their animals, which led to famine in the Ukraine in which another 5 million died. Stalin allowed a pause in the collectivisation process (1930) to allow the harvest to be collected.

By 1937, 99% of land was collectivised. Motor Tractor Stations helped grain output in 1940 to be 40% higher than in 1913. Exports of grain rose, bringing in foreign gold, but it was not until 1953 that livestock levels reached the levels of 1913.

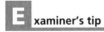

E xaminer's tip

i. Make two lists showing the benefits to the USSR of Stalin's rule and the costs of his rule.
ii. Be ready to explain whether you think the benefits outweigh the costs or vice versa.

6.12 How World War Two affected the USSR

The Russian army lost about 10 million soldiers fighting Hitler's German army. The Russian soldiers fought bravely, frightened of German cruelty if they were caught, and inspired by patriotic love of their country. Stalin's propaganda encouraged the people to defend their homeland. The purges of the officer class (see 6.9) had weakened the army, and this led to early defeats (1941–42) (see 12.6). Stalin had to recall many officers from the concentration camps to lead the defence of Russia.

The war caused the slaughter of cattle and loss of grain stocks and machines. The 1953 grain harvest was still below the 1913 level. Prices rose and food riots had to be put down by the Russian army. In 1950 Stalin put Khrushchev in charge of agriculture, and he planned to amalgamate the collectives so that bigger machines could be used to increase the supply of food.

About 15 million civilians died during the war due to starvation and murders by the German invaders. Most of Russia's factories had been destroyed, mines were flooded and the workers were worn out by war.

Stalin's five-year plans (1946–50 and 1950–54) concentrated on industrial goods and heavy industry, as had his earlier plans (see 6.10), so that Russia could defend itself and the eastern European states (see Chapter 9) against the West. The targets set out in the plans were achieved, and many new industrial centres were built behind the Urals. When Stalin died (1953) Russia was a modern industrial power.

Despite these achievements, Russia under Stalin failed to develop new industries like plastics and new lighter tractors instead of the heavy ones which ruined the soil. Heavy defence spending meant that consumer goods were in short supply.

6.13 Stalin and society in the USSR

Though there was a fair amount of artistic freedom under Lenin, Stalin crushed all non-Communist artists and writers. They were expected to produce works of social realism praising Stalin.

Education was controlled by the secret police. Books were used for indoctrination and pupils were encouraged to betray their teachers. Literacy, though, did improve and university education expanded.

Stalin attempted to crush the Orthodox Church by closing churches and persecuting priests and worshippers. Many priests were Party spies. In 1940 half the population were still believers, and when the war started Stalin relaxed the persecution to encourage patriotism.

Propaganda was used to bolster Stalin's rule. The 'cult of Stalin' began in 1929. His fiftieth birthday was celebrated by posters and statues. People were taught that 'Stalin is

Fig. 6.1 A French cartoon published in the 1930s
The banner held by the Russian citizen reads 'We are really happy'.

always right' and that he was the true heir of Lenin. Books and newspapers were censored by Communist Party officials so that only information and ideas favourable to Stalin were published.

Party 'apparatachiks' (officials), managers of collective farms and state factories, and members of the **CHEKA** all benefited from Stalin's rule. They had good jobs and privileges such as holidays, flats and good food.

In 1922 Lenin had incorporated the nationalities of Russia, Ukraine, Belorussia and Transcaucasia into the USSR. They were all controlled by the Communist Party. Later the Asian republics joined the USSR under Stalin. The 1936 Constitution did allow the peoples of the different republics some self-government, but any attempts by the nationalities to break away from control by Moscow were crushed. Towards the end of Stalin's rule Jews suffered persecution and many of them fled to Palestine (see Chapter 24).

Women were expected to bring up their children as loyal Soviet citizens. Many women were active members of the Communist Party and they worked in the factories and collective farms. They were also affected by Stalin's strict laws against abortion and divorce.

Summary

1 Between 1914 and 1917 Russia fought and lost the war with Germany. The Tsar, Nicholas II was blamed for the defeat.

2 The Tsar's German wife, Alexandra fell under the influence of Rasputin, who cured her son of haemophilia.

3 The war caused food shortages and there were many food riots and strikes in Petrograd. Soldiers refused to fire on the strikers.

4 In March 1917 the Tsar abdicated and was replaced by the Provisional Government, led firstly by Prince Lvov, and from July by Kerensky.

5 Workers and soldiers set up councils called soviets, which set up a rival government to the Provisional Government. The chief soviet was the Petrograd Soviet.

6 Lenin's Bolsheviks took control of the soviets, and planned a communist revolution. Lenin promised 'Peace, Bread, Land, Freedom'.

7 In November 1917 the Bolshevik Red Guards took control of Petrograd and a few other major cities. A Communist state was created, and opposition was crushed by the CHEKA.

8 There civil war (1918–22) between the Communists (Reds) and their opponents (the Whites). The Reds won due to Trotsky's genius and White divisions.

9 Lenin's War Communism policy helped to win the war. The Krondstadt mutiny forced Lenin to introduce the NEP, which helped Russia to recover from the war.

10 Stalin built up his power base before Lenin died, and he succeeded Lenin in 1924. By 1929 he had eliminated all his rivals, beginning with his main rival Trotsky.

11 Stalin's five-year plans set targets for industrial production. By 1941 the USSR was the third largest industrial nation.

12 Farming was collectivised by Stalin. The richer peasants resisted and Stalin crushed the peasants. This led to famine, but grain output rose by 1940.

13 Stalin 'purged' the USSR of all possible enemies. Millions of people were sent to labour camps, and millions more were executed.

14 The cult of Stalin was spread by propaganda and censorship. The secret police watched over everyone.

15 In 1953 Stalin died and was succeeded by Khrushchev, who condemned Stalin in the 1956 Part Congress.

Quick questions

1 Who were the following:
   i)   Nicholas II;
   ii) Alexandra;
   iii) Rasputin?
2 Which government replaced the Tsar's in March 1917?
3 What did Lenin promise the Russian people?
4 How did the Bolsheviks take power in November 1917?
5 Who, or what was the CHEKA?
6 What do the initials NEP stand for?
7 Who was Stalin's main rival after Lenin's death?
8 Name *three* industries listed in the five-year plans.
9 Which industry was affected by collectivisation?
10 What was the NKVD?

Chapter 7
China 1911–1949

7.1 The land, people, and government, 1900–1908

There were about 430 million Chinese people in 1900. Most of them were peasant farmers and workers. They lived in great poverty because their farming system was inefficient, their landlords took large parts of their crops as rent, and government officials took most of the rest as taxes. They also suffered from either disastrous floods when rains were heavy or from famine when rains did not come.

Most of the people lived in the eastern part of the country, because farming was almost impossible in the northern deserts and the western mountains.

Like farming, industry was backward and inefficient, and unable to provide enough goods for the huge population.

From 1861 to 1908 China was ruled by the Empress Tzu Hsi who belonged to the Manchu dynasty. She was an **autocrat** who did nothing to solve the country's problems. The officials in the capital, Peking, were corrupt and unable to control the remoter regions where 'war lords' 'ruled'. They had their own armies, imposed taxes over regions under their control, and defied government efforts to bring them under control.

7.2 China and the western world

By 1900 Japan had become a major industrial power, trading with the USA and modernising the country's industries and agriculture. China's rulers, however, thought that westerners were 'barbarians' from whom nothing could be learnt. They tried to prevent trade with the West, but a series of wars in the nineteenth century had led to China being opened up the western powers. The map (Fig. 7.1) gives some idea of the extent of western influence in China at the start of the century.

In the so-called 'Treaty Ports', Britain, France, Germany and other western countries built businesses and walled their estates to keep out the Chinese. They kept troops in their estates to guard against the danger of Chinese invasion.

Western influence was increased by the work of Christian missionaries. They also opened hospitals and schools, and many Chinese thought they were trying to destroy China's way of life. In 1900 a semi-religious organisation which taught the ancient form of self defence ('boxing') became the centre of anti-western feeling in China. In May 1900 the 'Boxers' attacked many European businesses and properties.

A huge international army invaded China, and captured and occupied the capital, Peking. The army forced the Chinese Government to sign a humiliating protocol (treaty): China had to pay huge sums in compensation to foreign firms and also had to agree to western troops being stationed in the capital to guard against further attacks. The treaty increased China's hatred of the West, and also increased opposition to the government which had been unable to stand up for China.

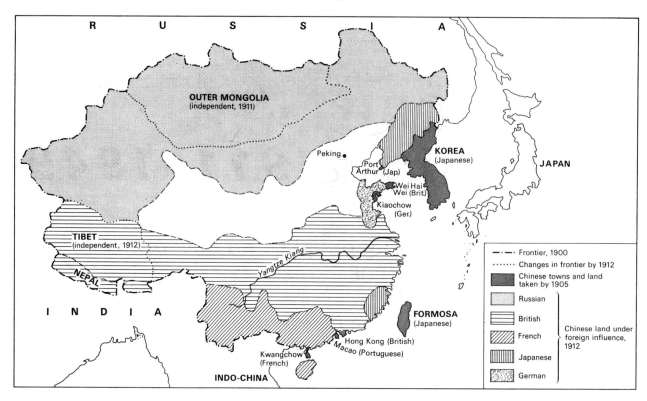

Fig. 7.1 China at the beginning of the Twentieth Century

7.3 The 1911 Revolution

The Empress died in 1908. The new Emperor was a two-year-old boy, Pu-yi. An anti-western war lord ruled as Regent on his behalf. Many Chinese realised that the traditional-thinking Government would not be able to get the foreigners out of China. They saw the need for China to become modernised in industry and agriculture. This called for the overthrow of the Manchu dynasty.

By 1911 the leader of this anti-Manchu and pro-westernisation policy was **Sun Yat-sen**. He was born into a Christian family and had become a doctor after his education in the British medical college in Hong Kong. He had the support of other western-educated Chinese, and the many Chinese who had emigrated to Japan and the USA, who supplied him with funds. In 1891 he founded a political party, the **Kuo Min Tang** (KMT).

Sun Yat-sen laid down the **Three Principles** of the KMT:

❶ Nationalism, or the end of foreign control of China;

❷ Democracy, so that ordinary people had a say in their government;

❸ People's livelihood, or a fairer sharing out of China's wealth, particularly its land.

In September 1911, after a bad harvest, the peasants in the Yangtse Province rose in rebellion, but were crushed by the army. On 10 October ('Double Tenth') there were a series of risings led by Sun's supporters in southern China, where sections of the army backed the rebels. By the end of November they controlled much of southern China, including cities such as Canton and Shanghai where anti-foreign feeling was high. In November 1911 the rebels captured Nanking, the old 'southern' capital of China, where they set up a Provisional Government.

Their armies then marched north to attack the Manchu capital of Peking. Here the army was commanded by General Yuan Shih k'ai. He defeated the rebels, drove them south of the Yangtse and then negotiated with them. On 24 December 1911 Sun arrived in China from the USA and was named the first President of the United Provinces of China. Yuan's army was much stronger than the KMT. He forced the boy-Emperor to **abdicate** , and Sun resigned as President of the Chinese Republic. Yuan did not see the need for reforms so Sun led a second revolution (July 1913) which Yuan put down. Yuan then captured Nanking, dismissed the elected Assembly, and in 1914 named himself the ruler of China.

7.4 Chinese war lords

Most Chinese accepted Yuan as leader, but he depended on the support of the army leaders. Many army generals were more powerful than the provincial governors appointed by Yuan. The badly paid and poorly disciplined soldiers often attacked the peasants and townspeople to get the food and money, which Yuan's government did not provide.

Yuan died in August 1916. His successor, Li Yuan Hun, restored the Constitution of 1912 and recalled the Parliament dismissed by Yuan in 1914. Li could not control the war lords who fought among themselves and against government troops to ensure control of their particular regions.

In the fighting the ordinary people suffered. Farms were ruined and millions died from famine. Town life became difficult as roads and drains were destroyed. Trade was disrupted by war and food became scarce.

7.5 Sun in power, 1917–25

E xaminer's tip

i. A useful way of studying this complicated topic is to make a timeline on which you put the key events in China's history from 1900.
ii. Make a list of problems which affected China from 1900–1925 and rank them in order of importance.

In August 1914, Japan (Britain's ally since 1902, see 2.7) declared war on Germany. President Yuan declared China was neutral in the war. Japan took control of the German colony of Kiaochow on the Chinese mainland, and then forced Yuan to make a series of humiliating concessions which increased Japanese control of China's mines and railways. Japan also won new trading rights in China, and Japanese financiers and military experts won powerful positions in the Chinese Government.

After Yuan had died, Sun called a meeting of the National Assembly in Nanking (1917) and named himself President of China. His government only controlled Canton and part of Kwantung province, and he depended on the support of a war lord. In the rest of China the war lords were in control, and no foreign government recognised Sun as President. The activities of the war lords enabled the western powers to increase their control over Chinese trade and industry.

The Japanese had a delegation at the Versailles peace talks (see 4.1). The peacemakers accepted Japan's claims to the former German colonies in China. This led to a rebellion by students (May 1919) who called for an elected government, western-style education, suppression of the war lords, an end to corruption in public life, and the expulsion of foreigners from Chinese trade and industry.

Sun tried to win the support of the students by proposing to fight the war lords. Lenin (see Chapter 6) had offered military help (1922), but Sun refused. One of his young supporters, Chiang Kai-shek, persuaded Sun to accept this aid, and the Russian Communists set up a military academy to train Chinese officers. Chiang and other KMT men went to Russia for more training and they brought equipment back to China for Sun's army. In 1924 Sun allowed members of the small Chinese Communist Party to join the KMT. When Sun died in 1925 Chiang became the leader of the KMT.

7.6 Chiang Kai-shek and Mao Tse-tung

In 1921 Mao Tse-tung (Mao Ze Dong in modern Chinese) was assistant librarian in Peking University, having taken part in the May 1919 rebellion. He was a founder member of the Chinese Communist Party (1921) and in 1924, along with Chou En-lai, he joined Sun's KMT. Chou was in charge of political education at Sun's Chinese Military Academy. Mao was in charge of political propaganda in Canton.

Chiang was backed by rich Chinese merchants and businessmen who wanted to end western power in China. He was also backed by left-wing members of the KMT who feared a Communist take over of their Party. Right-wing KMT members also feared the Communists, but opposed the moderate social reforms proposed by the KMT left wing, led by Madam Sun, the widow of Sun Yat-sen.

China's 'capital' was Canton, but western governments treated the war lords' government in Peking as the real Chinese Government. In 1929 Chiang set out to drive the war lords from Peking. He wanted to unite China under his KMT government and drive the foreigners out of China.

With 100,000 men he attacked the Yangtse Valley, and took Hankow and Shanghai. At the same time, Mao's political agents educated the peasants against their landlords, and town workers against their foreign bosses.

Chiang and his right-wing supporters resented the Communists' influence. In 1927 his business and gangster allies arrested and shot many Communists in Shanghai, including Mao's wife. They expelled the Russian Communist advisors and smashed the Shanghai communist organisation. Madam Sun thought that Chiang had betrayed her husband's principles but her sisters, one married to Chiang and the other to a rich businessman, welcomed Chiang's right-wing dictatorship.

In 1927 Chiang marched through Shantung and the Japanese-controlled port of Kia chow (see Fig. 7.2). He defeated many war lords who fled to Peking and to Manchuria. In 1928 Chiang took control of Peking, but made Nanking the capital of the new China. His government was right wing and controlled by businessmen and landowners. The KMT's Three Principles were ignored, and foreigners were not driven out. In return western governments recognised Chiang as China's new ruler.

7.7 Mao Tse-tung and the Kiangsi Soviet

While Chiang marched northwards, Mao and his small band of Communist followers gained control of an area north of Canton (see Fig. 7.2). Here, in what he called the Kiangsi Soviet, Mao and his followers educated the peasants, gave them more land in the land reforms, and organised a small Red Army. **Soviets** (or committees) were elected by villagers who saw Mao and the Communists share their hard life and treat them fairly, unlike Chiang's armies and the war lords.

Fig. 7.2 China in the 1930s

In 1931 the Japanese invaded Manchuria (see Fig. 7.2). We shall see in Chapter 10 how the League of Nations failed to deal with this aggression. Chiang did not resist this aggression either. He saw Mao's Communists as more of a problem. In 1930–31 Chiang fought three campaigns against Mao's Kiangsi Soviet. Mao's army followed four principles:

1. the enemy attacks, we retreat;
2. the enemy camps, we harass;
3. the enemy tires, we attack;
4. the enemy retreats, we pursue.

With the help of the peasants, Mao avoided defeat and capture. By 1931 Chiang had lost 21,000 men. In the 1932 campaign Chiang sent a million men and an airforce under two German generals to attack Kiangsi. By October 1934 Chiang's army had encircled the Communists. Mao decided that, rather than accept defeat he would lead his followers to a distant part of China.

7.8 The Long March, 1934–35

On 15 October 1934 120,000 men, women and children escaped from the Kiangsi area. Mao hoped to build a new soviet in the north-west, but Chiang's forces were too strong. 4000 communists were killed before his 'Reds' got to the Yangtse River. They then decided to make a march of 9600 km (6000 miles) to north China where Chiang's rule was weakest. The march lasted 368 days.

On the march they were attacked by Chiang's forces, by war lords, and by bandit gangs. Only 20,000 survived to reach Yenan where Mao set up a new soviet. Industry was developed, partly to provide arms. Peasant farmers were helped by the fixing of 'fair rents'. The landless got farms from unused land. New farming techniques helped improve output.

Mao and his leading supporters lived like every one else, in homes made in caves. Everyone worked on the land, in small industrial workshops, or as political agents in the area. **Propaganda** was used to win people's support. Plays, newspapers, cartoons and posters were all used to win support for Communism. Above all the army was trained, because, as Mao said, 'Political power grows out of the barrel of a gun'.

7.9 Chiang and the Japanese, 1931–37

Once the Japanese had conquered Manchuria (see 10.5), they took control of China's five northern provinces (see Fig. 7.2). Chiang did nothing to stop this gradual advance into China. He saw Mao's Communists as the main enemy. Mao said that 'Chinese ought not to fight Chinese', but that they should unite against the Japanese. In December 1936 Chiang was arrested after a revolt by some of his generals. To win his release Chiang, in negotiations with Mao's assistant Chou En-lai, agreed to a KMT-Communist 'United Front' against the Japanese. Mao hoped Chiang's KMT would exhaust themselves in this war.

On 7 July 1937 the Japanese attacked and took the Chinese capital Peking, and launched a full-scale war against China. They quickly took control of Nanking and the richest region, the Yangtse River valley.

Chiang retreated, hoping that the USA would one day come to his aid. Mao's Communists used guerrilla tactics against the Japanese, who failed to gain control of the countryside though they occupied most of the major cities. After the Japanese attack on Pearl Harbour in December 1941, the Chinese-Japanese war became part of the wider Second World War, with the USA providing much aid to both Chiang and Mao.

7.10 The Civil War, 1945–49

During the war against the Japanese, the US officials found that Chiang's forces were 'guilty of corruption, neglect, chaotic economy, hoarding, black market trading with the enemy'. They also approved of Mao's Party: 'It reduces rents and taxes, raises production and standards of living. People participate in government and the Communist leaders practice what they preach'.

After the defeat of Japan, Chiang had massive aid from the USA, but many Chinese opposed him. Businessmen suffered from massive inflation. Intellectuals hated the inefficiency and corruption of his government and armies. Patriots resented the small part Chiang had played in the war against Japan. Many of his soldiers refused to fight Mao and they deserted or sold their weapons to the Communists.

Mao, on the other hand, had the support of the peasants. He was admired by many intellectuals for his government's honesty, and by businessmen for the rule of law he established. Patriots admired Mao's fight with Japan after 1937.

In 1945 the KMT controlled the region south of the Yangtse and most of the northern cities, while Mao controlled the countryside. On 10 October 1945 Chiang and Mao signed an agreement to work together, but neither really meant to. Chiang could not accept Mao's ideas of social and land reform. Mao still saw the coalition as a step towards a Communist revolution.

In June 1946 Chiang attacked Mao's forces in Yenan, Shantung and Manchuria (see Fig. 7.2). Mao was forced to retreat, but in Spring 1947 his forces still controlled much of the countryside and threatened the rich Yangtse valley. In 1948 Mao, with a trained peasant army armed with Russian weapons, and with US arms sold by Chiang's soldiers, drove Chiang's dwindling army into its town bases. By January 1949 Mao had taken every city north of the Yangtse and many had surrendered without fighting.

In the winter of 1948–49 Mao took control of Manchuria. He ordered his armies to cross the Yangtse and to make their way south. He took Peking in the north. Mao's armies drove Chiang's forces into Nanking and Shanghai, where inflation ruined the middle classes who also became more pro-Mao.

The executions of hundreds of Chiang's opponents drove many **nationalists** to support Mao. Elsewhere rule by cruel war lords had started again, so that advances by Mao's armies were welcomed by peasants and workers alike.

In April–May 1949 the Communists took Shanghai and Nanking, and on 1 October 1949 Mao appeared at the Gate of Heavenly Peace in the Imperial Palace in Peking to read a speech in which he proclaimed the setting up of the 'People's Republic of China'. Chiang's forces held out for a time in Canton, but in December 1949 he and the last of his followers left mainland China for 'Nationalist China' or Formosa (Taiwan – see Fig. 7.1).

E xaminer's tip

i. Study carefully the weaknesses of the governments before Mao: Empress Tzu's failures, the fighting between Sun Yat-sen's KMT and General Yuan, the role of the war lords, the impact of Japan on China.
ii. Use key words to help you to learn the main actions made by Chiang Kai-shek and Mao Tse-tung.
iii. Analyse the reasons why Mao was able to defeat Chiang by 1949.

Summary

1 In 1900 China's industry and agriculture were backward and the war lords controlled many regions.
2 Unlike Japan, China despised the West which forced her to make many concessions to western traders and merchants. This led to several anti-western and anti-government risings.
3 Sun Yat-sen made the KMT the major political party and led the 1911 Revolution which was betrayed by General Yuan.
4 Sun was in power from 1917 to 1925 when he reluctantly accepted Russian aid.
5 Chiang Kai-shek, Sun's successor, defeated the war lords but betrayed Sun's Three Principles.
6 Mao Tse-tung, in the Kiangsi Soviet, won the hearts and minds of peasants, nationalists and intellectuals.

7 Chiang's attack on Mao led to the Long March, which caused the deaths of many of Mao's forces. At the Yenan Soviet Mao rebuilt the Communist power base.

8 Japan attacked China (1931), Manchuria (1932–37) and the northern provinces (1937–41). Chiang refused to oppose the invaders.

9 The 1945–49 Civil War was won by Mao's Communist Party. Mao won the support of many groups of people, while Chiang's corruption lost him support.

10 Mao established the communist 'People's Republic of China' in 1949.

Quick questions

1 Name the last dynasty to rule China.
2 Name:
   i)   the old 'Southern' Capital of China, and
   ii) the northern capital used by the last dynasty.
3 Name the religious nationalist movement whose anti-western attitudes led to the 1900 rising.
4 Name Sun Yat-sen's political party and list the Three Principles.
5 When was the Chinese Communist Party founded?
6 Who ruled China between 1927 and 1949?
7 In which regions did Mao have:
   i)   his first soviet;
   ii) a soviet founded after the Long March?
8 When did the Japanese:
   i)   conquer Manchuria;
   ii) occupy Peking?
9 Where and when did Mao proclaim the establishment of the People's Republic?
10 To which island did Chiang flee after Mao's victory?

Chapter 8
Germany 1918–39

8.1 Germany in 1918 after defeat in World War One

In November 1918 Germany was in chaos. The navy was in revolt and the Communists set up **soviets** hoping to start a revolution. A minority of Germans wanted to fight on, but General Ludendorf and other army leaders wanted to avoid Germany being invaded by foreign armies (see 3.8). Germany's politicians wanted to prevent a Bolshevik revolution, so Kaiser Wilhem II **abdicated** and was replaced by the moderate Socialist, Ebert. The German army and navy surrendered on 11 November 1918. In January 1919 Ebert's Social Democratic Party won the election for the General Assembly which moved to the small town of Weimar because of violence in Berlin (see 4.3).

8.2 German attitudes to the Treaty of Versailles

Examiner's tip

The Free Corps was a paramilitary organisation formed in 1918–19 by officers who recruited ex-soldiers and sailors, students and the unemployed. It was approved by the Army Minister in the Weimar government who used it to smash extreme left-wing risings. But the Corps was anti-republican and, in a campaign of terror, it assassinated government ministers. Many Corps' officers later led Hitler's SA.

The terms of the Treaty (see 4.2 and 4.3) were humiliating to Germany, so the **Weimar Republic** was born in defeat and hated by many groups in Germany. **Nationalists**, who mainly represented Army Officers and Industrialists, said the Government had 'stabbed Germany in the back.' They were loyal to the army which they felt had been betrayed. As Germany had not been invaded in 1918, many people did not realise that Germany had lost the war and that Ludendorf had asked for the **armistice**.

Many soldiers also felt betrayed since their sacrifices for Germany were in vain and they formed themselves into gangs of Free Corps. They wanted to restore the Kaiser and to smash the Communists and Socialists who they blamed for Germany's humiliation.

8.3 The Weimar Constitution

The Assembly produced a democratic constitution. The President was directly elected by all the people. He had powers to call elections for the **Reichstag**, to choose the Chancellor, to rule by decree and to use the army to put down revolution.

The Chancellor and his ministers needed the support of the Reichstag, but the system of proportional representation led to a large number of parties gaining seats, so no party obtained an overall majority. Weimar Republic governments were therefore often weak and unable to deal with the great problems facing post-war Germany.

8.4 Growing disorders in Germany, 19

Ebert's moderate socialist government was attacked by extreme right- and wing groups. In 1919 the right-wing Free Corps were asked by Ebert to put down the Communist ('Spartacist') uprising in Berlin. This showed that Ebert's government had lost control of Germany. The Free Corps murdered many politicians, and sympathetic judges often released the murderers. In 1920 the Nationalists, led by Wolfgang Kapp, tried to take power in Berlin. This **'putsch'** was put down by a general strike called by the Communist and Socialist trade unions. Many 'respectable' people already angry about Versailles were angry that the Government could not control Germany.

8.5 Reparations and hyper-inflation in 1923

Germany had to pay £6,600 million as **reparations** for war damages (see 4.2), but by 1923 the Government fell behind with the payments because it was short of money. The Government printed vast sums of money to solve the shortage, which led to increased inflation. The French army invaded the Ruhr, Germany's main coal and steel area, to force Germany to pay. German workers went on strike and production fell.

Inflation got even worse and money became worthless. Suitcases of money were needed to buy a loaf of bread. Communists again threatened revolution in many areas, and middle-class people blamed the Government for the loss of their savings and pensions, and turned against the whole idea of democratic government. Hitler's National Socialists tried to take advantage of this by attempting the **Munich Putsch** (see 8.8).

Table 8.1 Inflation under the Weimar republic

November 1918 £1	= 20 Marks
November 1921 £1	= 313 Marks
January 1922 £1	= 1000 Marks
June 1922 £1	= 1500 Marks
December 1922 £1	= 50 000 Marks
November 1923 £1	= 20 000 000 000 000 Marks

8.6 Recovery under Gustav Stresemann, 1924–29

In 1923 Stresemann became the new Chancellor and helped the Weimar Republic to recover. He issued a new currency (the Rentenmark) to replace the worthless Mark. He persuaded the French to leave the Ruhr in return for payment of reparations, so production rose and inflation fell.

In 1924 Stresemann negotiated the **Dawes Plan** which made reparations easier to pay, and in 1929 he negotiated the **Young Plan** which reduced reparations to £50 million a year (see 10.2). He persuaded American banks to provide loans to German industry, which helped Germany to produce more goods, so unemployment fell (see Fig. 8.1).

Stresemann signed the **Locarno Treaties** (see 10.2) which accepted Germany as an equal in Europe, and Germany also joined the **League of Nations** (see 5.3). It now seemed a stable country, and extremist parties became less popular there.

8.7 Weaknesses in the Weimar Republic's recovery

- The new prosperity depended on American loans, and if they stopped German industries would collapse.
- German nationalists were still unhappy with the democratic politicians, whom they blamed for defeat in the war and for the Versailles Treaty. They still resented the payment for reparations.
- Many middle-class people did not forgive the government for the loss of their savings in 1923, and still feared the threat of communism.
- Political violence by private armies was common in the Weimar republic.

8.8 The Nazi Party, 1920–28

Adolf Hitler, who had joined the German army in the war, was deeply shocked by Germany's defeat. He believed that Germany had been 'stabbed in the back' by the politicians who surrendered. After the war he joined, and then became leader of, the National Socialist Workers Party. Hitler was a fiery speaker and the Party grew quickly. Hitler's private army of Brownshirted Stormtroopers (the SA) attacked left-wing meetings and made Hitler appear a strong leader. In the 1923 elections the Nazis won 6% of the vote, and Hitler took advantage of Germany's economic problems (see 8,4) by trying to take power in the **Munich Beer Hall Putsch** with Ludendorf's support, but the putsch collapsed and Hitler was arrested.

In prison Hitler wrote *Mein Kampf*, outlining his hatred of all those who had betrayed Germany. He attacked the Weimar Republic, Jews and Communists, blaming them for the Versailles Peace Treaty (see 4.3). Hitler wrote of his plans for a Greater Germany by conquering eastern Europe where 'living space' would be created for the master 'Aryan Race' of pure bred Germans.

When Hitler left prison, he decided he would try to get power legally, but during the prosperous times under Stresemann (1923–28) the Nazis won only 2.6% of the vote in the 1928 Reichstag elections (see Fig. 8.1).

8.9 The collapse of the Weimar Republic and Hitler's coming to power, 1929–33

On 3 October 1929 Stresemann died, then on 28 October the American stock market crashed and the USA slid into depression (see 9.5). German banks and businesses that depended on loans from the USA had to close (see 9.9). Industrial production fell by 30% and unemployment rose to 5½ million in 1932 (see Fig. 8.1). The Government was short of money, but the new Chancellor, Bruning, failed to persuade the Reichstag to increase taxes or reduce unemployment benefit.

President Hindenburg called elections in 1930. Hitler, funded by industrialists who feared communism, recruited many people into his party. The 400,000 strong SA attacked communist and socialist meetings and offices. Goebbels organised Nazi **propaganda** through films, posters and rallies to persuade many voters that Hitler could make Germany great by attacking Jews, foreign bankers and Communists. The Nazi party became the second largest in the Reichstag, and violence between Nazis and Communists grew.

Hindenburg defeated Hitler in the 1932 presidential elections, but refused to use the army to suppress SA violence, possibly because Hitler had 13 million votes. In the 1932 Parliamentary elections the Nazis became the largest political party in the Reichstag, winning 37% of the vote.

Hitler refused to join a coalition government with other parties unless he was in control. The Nazis lost some seats in the November 1932 elections, but were still the largest party, so no stable government could be created. SA violence and Nazi demonstrations continued.

In January 1933 Hindenburg invited Hitler to become Chancellor and head of a government of Nationalists and Conservatives with only three Nazis in the Government. Hitler promised Hindenburg he would govern lawfully.

Nationalist and Conservative politicians such as Papen and Schleicher, representing landowners, industrialists and the army, hoped they could use Hitler to crush Communism and reverse the Treaty of Versailles. Socialists and Communists failed to unite to defeat Hitler in the Reichstag due to the rivalry between them, and because some thought that Nazi rule would soon collapse and that a Bolshevik revolution would follow.

8.10 Hitler's consolidation of power, 1933–34

Examiner's tip

i. Prepare for questions on why Hitler came to power by revising the weaknesses of the Weimar Republic and Hitler's skill in exploiting the Republic's weaknesses.

ii. Note that 8.9 shows you that Hitler was *handed power* by Nationalist and Conservative politicians.

iii. Some students get confused about the events of 1933. Note carefully that the Reichstag Fire occurred during the election campaign which Hitler called *after* he became Chancellor. Note also that the February 1933 emergency decree is *not* the same law as the March 1933 Enabling Act which was passed *after* the 1933 Election.

As soon as he came to power Hitler began a reign of terror against his enemies. The police, controlled by Goering, attacked the offices and meetings of the communist and socialist parties.

After the Reichstag fire of 27 February 1933 Hitler persuaded Hindenburg to pass an emergency decree banning socialist and communist meetings and allowing the arrest of left wingers.

In March 1933 Hitler called elections which the Nazis won with 44% of the vote. The Nazis joined with the Nationalists to ban the Communists from the Reichstag. Nazi gangs and the SA surrounded Parliament to force the politicians to pass the Enabling Act, which gave Hitler power to pass any law he liked. In July 1933 all non-Nazi parties were banned.

In May 1933 Hitler abolished all trade unions. Workers were also forbidden to strike. They all had to join the Nazi-controlled National Labour Front.

On 30 June 1934 Hitler ordered the murder of many SA officers in the 'Night of the Long Knives', because Roehm the SA leader was a threat to his power and unpopular with army chiefs jealous of the SA's powers.

When Hindenburg died in July 1934 Hitler became **Fuhrer**, as both Chancellor and President. Everyone in the army swore an oath of personal loyalty to Hitler.

8.11 The Totalitarian State

The Gestapo (SS), the secret police force led by Himmler, terrorised opponents of the Nazis by murdering and imprisoning them. It had secret files on all important Germans. Nazi **propaganda** was organised by Joseph Goebbels to persuade Germans to believe in Nazism.

All newspapers were controlled by the Nazis. German-made films put forward Nazi ideas, and radio was used to broadcast Hitler's speeches and Nazi Party rallies. Writers and artists were forced to fit in with Nazi ideas, and it was impossible to perform the plays or music written by Jews. German sporting victories were used to bring honour to Nazism, and the 1936 Berlin Olympics was a propaganda triumph.

By 1936 most young people had joined the Hitler Youth movement which became compulsory in 1939. Girls were taught how to be good German mothers, and boys were taught how to be soldiers. They were taught that 'Hitler is always right', and told they should betray their parents to the Gestapo if they were disloyal to Hitler.

Education was totally controlled by the Nazis. All teachers had to be pro-Nazi. Pupils were encouraged to betray non-Nazi teachers. Text books were written to put forward Nazi ideas, especially in history and biology. Women were encouraged to be good Nazi mothers and expected to have as many babies as possible so that the Nazi Aryan race could expand.

Racial minorities were persecuted. Hitler and many Germans thought the Jews were subhuman, and blamed them for the problems of the Weimar republic and corrupting the pure German race. The Nazi newspaper, Die Sturmer, specialised in attacking Jews.

In April 1933 Jewish shops and businesses were **boycotted**. The 1935 Nuremburg Laws took German citizenship away from Jews, and banned marriages between Germans and Jews. All Jews had to wear the yellow Badge of David on their coats to mark them out as non-Germans.

On 9 November 1938 the Nazis organised 'Crystal Night' when Jewish homes, businesses and synagogues were attacked. 40,000 Jews were sent to concentration camps, which became Death Camps for the murder of 6 million Jews in the 'Final Solution' 1941–45.

Other minorities such as gypsies and homosexuals, and Christians who actively opposed the Nazis were also rounded up into concentration camps.

8.12 Why many Germans supported Hitler

Workers were pleased that unemployment almost disappeared (see Fig. 8.1). Work was provided in factories rearming Germany. Public works such as motorway building and slum clearance also provided work. The 'Strength with Joy' organisation gave workers welfare benefits such as cheap holidays and convalescent homes.

Army leaders were pleased because Hitler was promising to make the German army great again (see 10.5).

Industrialists were grateful to Hitler for destroying communism and trade unions. Many of them got contracts for public works and rearmament. They welcomed the

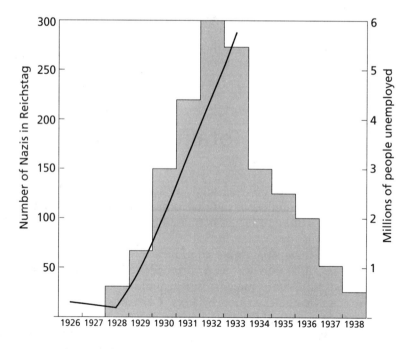

Fig. 8.1 The Nazi Party grew as unemployment grew

policy of **'autarchy'** which aimed to make Germany self-sufficient in many products such as oil and food.

Farmers were happy because prices were fixed to give them a profit, and they could not be forced by bankers to sell their land to clear their debts.

Summary

1 In November 1918 the Kaiser abdicated and a republic was declared. The first President of the Weimar Republic of Germany was the socialist Friedrich Ebert.
2 German Nationalists blamed the Republic for Germany's defeat and the Treaty of Versailles, saying that Germany had been 'stabbed in the back'.
3 The Weimar Republic's constitution was democratic, but the system of proportional representation led to political instability.
4 There were many clashes between right-wing groups and Communists.
5 Germany had to pay £6,600 million in reparations. The Government printed the money which led to massive inflation. The crisis was made worse by the French invasion of the Ruhr.
6 Gustav Stresemann led Germany's recovery by issuing a new currency and negotiating with European nations.
7 Adolf Hitler's National Socialist Party (Nazis) tried to take power in the 1923 Munich Beer Hall Putsch, but Hitler it failed and Hitler was imprisoned.
8 The 1929 Wall Street crash led to bankruptcies in Germany, and by 1932 there were 6 million unemployed in Germany.
8 The Nazi Party became more popular between 1929 and 1933. Hitler's book *Mein Kampf*, speeches and party organisation all attracted many voters in the 1930 and 1932 elections.
10 Hindenburg invited Hitler to become German Chancellor in January 1933.
11 Between 1933 and 1934 Hitler and the Nazis created a one-party state by abolishing all other parties and trade unions, and by murdering opponents.
12 Between 1934 and 1939 the Nazis took complete control of Germany by use of SA and Gestapo terror, Goebbels' propaganda machine and the Hitler Youth movement.
13 Jews were singled out for special persecution, starting with the boycott of shops, followed by the Nuremburg Laws, 'Crystal Night', and the rounding up of Jews in concentration camps.
14 Many Germans welcomed Nazi economic policies of public works, self-sufficiency and rearmament, which almost abolished unemployment.

Quick questions

1 What was the name of the German Republic in 1919?
2 Who were:
   i)   the Spartacists, and
   ii) the Free Corps?
3 How did the German Government's policy of printing money affect Germany in 1923?
4 Who led the recovery of the German economy from 1923 to 1929?
5 Where and when did Hitler try to get power by force?
6 Which book did Hitler write while in prison?
7 Which people did Hitler call 'the master Aryan race'?
8 Who invited Hitler to become Chancellor in 1933?
9 By which Act did Hitler gain the power of a dictator?
10 Which Nazi group suffered during 'the Night of the Long Knives'?
11 Which ministry was Goebbels the head of?

Chapter 9
The USA 1919–39

9.1 Causes of the 1920's economic boom, 1919–29

The First World War helped American industry, since countries that could not buy from Europe bought American goods during and after the war.

President Harding's Republican Government introduced the Fordney–McCumber tariff (1922), which raised import duties on foreign goods so people bought home-produced goods. Income taxes were also reduced so that people had more money to buy these goods.

Growing demand for cars led to the growth of many allied industries such as petrol, glass, tyres and road building. Greater use of electricity and mass-production techniques helped American industries to make cheap, high quality goods. Henry Ford's moving assembly line produced cars which workers could afford. Four million new jobs had been created in the car industry.

Advertisements on the radio, in cinemas and in newspapers also encouraged people to buy more goods.

Hire Purchase (HP) credit helped workers to buy what they needed; the loan was repaid, with interest, in instalments.

9.2 The effects of the boom: prosperity of the 'Roaring Twenties'

The growth of incomes meant people could buy more consumer goods such as cars, radios, watches, vacuum cleaners and washing machines. In 1930 there were two cars for every three American families.

People had more money to spend on entertainment. The film industry grew, first with the silent movies and, after 1927, with the 'talking pictures'. Hollywood was the capital of the film industry, creating film stars like Charlie Chaplin and Rudolph Valentino. Walt Disney's cartoon characters, Mickey Mouse and Donald Duck delighted adults and children. Cecil B. de Mille was a leading producer of epic films. By 1937 75 million people went to the cinema every week.

Jazz clubs and dance halls also became very popular. Louis Armstrong and Duke Ellington won a loyal following from black and white people alike. Dances like 'the Charleston' and 'the Black Bottom' were very popular with young people who had the money to spend in their leisure time.

Spectator sports grew in popularity especially baseball, football and boxing, creating heroes like Jack Dempsey (world champion in boxing), and George 'Babe' Ruth (baseball player for the New York Yankees).

Women's opportunities grew. Many women carried on working as they had done during the war when men were at the front. The consumer industries also provided work and increased opportunities for leisure. In 1920 women voted for the first time. Labour-saving devices in the home, and knowledge about birth control helped to liberate women from tedium and large families. The 'flappers', with their bobbed hair and fashionable short skirts, driving their cars were signs that a 'new woman' was emerging in the prosperous America.

Most Americans thought that the boom would go on for ever. In 1928 President Hoover said 'We in America are nearer to the financial triumph over poverty than ever before.' The Wall Street stock market boomed as millions of Americans bought shares in profitable companies hoping to 'make a quick buck'. Often they bought shares on credit, as they did when buying other goods.

9.3 The economic problems hidden behind the boom

Examiner's tip

Prepare for questions on the USA during the 1920's by making two lists showing the positive and negative aspects of life in the USA. Be ready to show whether life in the USA was good in these years. The answer should show both sides of the question and give a conclusion.

Farmers did not share in this prosperity. During the 1920s food prices fell because farmers produced too much food. Food exports fell because European farmers also produced more food. As a result farm workers' wages fell and many of them lost their jobs and homes.

The black population was also left out of the prosperity. In the south, white farmers sacked black labourers first, which forced them to look for work in the cities and take lowly paid jobs. Overcrowded slums sprang up. Black people suffered segregation in schools and public places, and often lost their voting rights.

The shipbuilding, coal and textile industries did not share the boom either. Shipbuilding was hit by the fall in exports and the end of the war. Japan and India developed their own textile industries, and introduced **tariff barriers** against American exports. Oil and electricity were more efficient than coal as fuel.

Workers and their families affected by these problems reduced their spending, so by 1929 the new industries had to reduce production. Profits made by businesses fell and unemployment began to rise (1928–29).

9.4 A violent society

The '**Red Scare**' describes the fears of Republicans and businessmen that Communism was being spread by immigrants and trade unionists. Mitchell Palmer, the Attorney General, sent troops and police to raid trade union offices and arrest the leaders. Trade unionists retaliated with bombs and violent attacks on factories.

In 1920 two Italian immigrants, Sacco and Vanzetti, were convicted and executed for murder, despite protests against a lack of evidence. The jury believed that the foreigners were dangerous communists.

Prohibition of the alcohol trade (1920) led to increased violent crime. Temperance movements had argued that the law would make America more hardworking and 'moral', but the law was impossible to enforce. Gangsters like Al Capone made millions by illegally 'bootlegging' alcohol and selling it in 'speak-easies'. There were gun fights among rival gangs. Capone was one of the most powerful men in Chicago, and was only arrested for non-payment of tax. When prohibition was stopped (1933) the violence declined.

The **Ku Klux Klan**, with five million members, attacked blacks, Jews, Catholics and Communists with lynchings, assaults and whippings. The Klan, based in the south, believed that true Americans were white, Anglo-Saxon Protestants (WASPS).

The Quota Immigration Law (1921) almost stopped immigration of peoples from Europe. Republicans believed the law would help to save American jobs. The dream of America being the 'melting pot society' was ended.

The growth of religious fundamentalism may have been a reaction to the growing violence and divisions in society. Many states banned the teaching of Darwin's theory of evolution following the 'Monkey Trial' (1925), when the Tennessee school teacher, John Scopes, was found guilty of breaking state law by suggesting that Darwin's theories were correct.

9.5 The end of prosperity – the October 1929 Wall Street crash

In September 1929 share prices on Wall Street began to fall, because some investors sold shares when they realised profits of American businesses were falling. The wave of selling continued in October as people tried to get some money from their shares, and on 29 October 16 million shares were sold.

Banks which had lent money to people to buy shares tried to get their money back, and when the loans could not be repaid the banks went bankrupt. Savers lost their money and mortgage payers lost their homes and farms.

Many businesses also went bankrupt, since the banks stopped lending money to them. Unemployment rose from 3 million to 14 million (1929–32).

9.6 The Great Depression

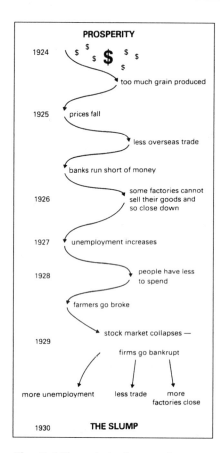

Fig. 9.1 The spiral of unemployment

Rising unemployment created a vicious spiral (see Fig. 9.1) by which people had to reduce their spending, forcing industry to reduce production, so even more people lost their jobs and homes.

Thousands of unemployed people marched to Washington to demand action from President Hoover. Their shanty towns were called 'Hoovervilles', which police and troops tried to smash up. Some farmers tried to stop the banks taking over their farms with the slogan 'In Hoover we trusted, now we are busted'. Bing Crosby's song 'Brother, can you spare a dime' summed up the desperation of poor Americans.

President Hoover believed in 'rugged individualism' and 'laissez faire' economics, which meant businesses and individuals should help themselves. He was reluctant to spend government money on programmes to put the unemployed to work, though some money was lent to some businesses to save them from bankruptcy.

9.7 Franklin Delano Roosevelt's New Deal, 1933–39

In November 1932 Roosevelt defeated Hoover in the presidential election. He promised a 'New Deal for the forgotten man.' In his inaugural speech (March 1933) Roosevelt told the American people that 'the only thing we have to fear is fear itself'. He promised 'Relief', 'Recovery' and 'Reform' in the 'first Hundred Days' of his Presidency.

During his Presidency Roosevelt spoke to the nation on the radio in his 'fireside chats', to help the people to be more hopeful about the future. He believed, unlike Hoover, that the Government did have a duty to help people find work. He tried to make his presidency 'accessible', and when ordinary people wrote to him, Roosevelt replied to his people. He introduced a series of measures known as the '**Alphabet Laws**'.

- Under the **Emergency Banking Act** (March 1933) the Government lent money to some banks to help them trade, and closed the weak ones. Roosevelt talked to the nation on the radio about putting money back into the banks. He told them their money was safe. At the same time the **Federal Emergency Relief Administration** (FERA) gave 500 million dollars of food and aid to the poor.
- The **Civilian Conservation Corps** (CCC) provided young men with work in conservation projects.
- The **Agricultural Adjustment Act** (AAA) paid farmers to grow less food, which helped prices and farmers' incomes to rise.
- The **National Industrial Recovery Act** (NIRA) set up the CWA (**Civil Works Administration**) for the building of roads, bridges, hospitals and schools. The **Works Progress Administration** (WPA) replaced the CWA (1935), employing 8 million workers who could buy goods made by industry. Harry Hopkins organised these public works agencies.
- The **National Recovery Administration** (NRA) encouraged employers to treat workers properly, abolishing child labour and introducing trade union rights and the eight-hour day.
- The TVA (**Tennessee Valley Authority**) built dams which provided work, electricity and irrigation for infertile land.
- The **Social Security Act** (SSA) provided pensions for most workers, and funds for the unemployed and disabled, and the Wagner Act gave trade unions legal rights to bargain with employers.

Although he was opposed by many Americans, Roosevelt had shown that the Government did care about the people. He was re-elected President in 1936, so although the New Deal did not solve the problems of unemployment, America was a more united country under Roosevelt because the Government was prepared to help people solve their problems of poverty and unemployment. Roosevelt's policies helped to avoid the threat of revolution which had been experienced in Russia (see Chapter 6), and Germany (see Chapter 8).

9.8 Opposition to, and failures of, the New Deal

The New Deal was opposed by businessmen who objected to the growth of trade unions, the regulation of hours and wages, and increased taxes.

The Supreme Court ruled the NRA and AAA to be unconstitutional, and after Roosevelt won the presidential election (1936) he tried, but failed, to persuade Congress to appoint younger judges who would support the new Deal.

Huey 'Kingfish' Long thought Roosevelt had failed to do enough for the poor.

Long's policy of 'Share our Wealth' demanded taxes on the rich to give more to the poor. He became very popular and many people thought he might win the 1936 presidential election, but he was assassinated in September 1935.

8 million people were still out of work in 1937, and in 1938 Roosevelt cut government spending which caused a new recession, and unemployment rose to 10½ million. Unemployment only fell to below 1 million in 1943 due to the rearmament caused by World War Two.

The AAA drove many tenants off the land, and these 'Okies' (from Oklahoma) were forced to search for work across America. The NRA regulations were not compulsory, so conditions for many workers did not improve. The Social Security Act (1935) laid down no national rates of benefits and there was no state medical care system.

9.9 Foreign policy

In 1919 most Americans supported **isolationism**. The Congress rejected Woodrow Wilson's wish for the USA to join the League of Nations. The Republican, Harding, won the presidential election (1920) promising to stop America from being 'entangled' with the world's problems. Most voters did not want their young to die in foreign wars. German and Irish Americans especially resented American support for Britain in World War One.

The **Neutrality Laws** (1935 and 1937) were passed to keep America out of wars with the dictators that had come to power in Europe.

Harding's successor, Coolidge, refused to cancel the **war debts** owed by her war allies, Britain and France. American **tariffs** (see 9.1) had stopped Britain and France from selling their goods to America, so the debts were not repaid quickly. America did lend Germany money to pay the reparations to the allies (see 4.2 and 8.5–6). Britain and France sent this back to America. After the Wall Street crash (see 9.6) America demanded the money back from Germany (see 8.9), so that the allies were forced to canel their repayments of their US loans.

Harding did call the **Washington Naval Conferences** (1921–22), where Japan agreed to limit the size of her navy and to withdraw from Chinese territory. However, Japan was still dominant in the Far East, and under the policy of 'non-entanglement', America refused to act when Japan invaded Manchuria in 1931 (see 10.3).

The United States dominated Latin American, but in 1933 Roosevelt produced the 'Good Neighbour' policy which stated that the United States would not intervene in any Latin American state. America also gave economic aid to Latin American states.

America did not join the war against Germany and Japan in 1939, but Roosevelt did persuade Congress to sell war material to Britain. When Germany and Japan threatened to dominate Europe and Asia in 1940, America started to send massive aid to Britain (see Chapter 12).

Summary

1 There was an economic boom from 1919 to 1929. The American people bought a wide range of consumer goods.

2 Henry Ford's cars were mass produced on continuous assembly lines.

3 During the 1920s many people became rich buying shares, often on credit.

4 Farmers did badly in the 1920 since over-production of food drove down prices and profits.

5 Black people suffered from poverty, discrimination and segregation during the whole of the period 1919–29. The Ku Klux Klan persecuted black people and other minorities.

6 The 'basic industries' (coal, shipbuilding and textiles) did not share in the boom of the new consumer industries.

7 Violent crime increased as a result of the prohibition of the alcohol trade. Gangsters like Al Capone became powerful.

8 In 1929 the Wall Street crash started the Great Depression, when unemployment rose to 14 million and many businesses went bankrupt.

9 The Republican President, Hoover, did not think the Government could do much to solve the country's problems.

10 Franklin Delano Roosevelt (FDR) became the President of America in 1932, and his 'New Deal' helped to create jobs and greater security.

11 A series of 'Alphabet Laws' were passed under the New Deal, and unemployment fell, but it was the Second World War that really got America back to work. Rich people did not like paying taxes, and the socialists thought that the New Deal did not do enough for the people.

12 American foreign policy was 'isolationist', but America did help Germany with reparations, and Britain in the war against Hitler.

Quick questions

1 Which car maker was most responsible for 'assembly line' production?
2 What do the initials HP stand for?
3 Which of the following industries did not share in the boom of the 1920s:
   i) film;
   ii) steel;
   iii) agriculture;
   iv) electrical goods?
4 In what year did the boom of the 1920s come to an end?
5 In which city did Al Capone have most power?
6 Which President referred to 'rugged individualism?
7 What event started the Great Depression?
8 What did the following initials stand for: i) CCC; ii) NRA; iii) AAA; iv) TVA?
9 What word best describes American foreign policy during the years 1919 to 1939?

Chapter 10
International Relations 1919-39

10.1 Collective security

The League of Nations was supposed to maintain peace through collective security (see 5.6): if one state attacked another, member states would act collectively (together) to stop the aggressor, either by economic **sanctions** or military force (see 5.1). This aim was never achieved, and some of the reasons for this include:

- The League had no army of its own: Article 16 of the Covenant expected member states to supply troops if needed, but the 1923 League Resolution allowed each state to decide for itself whether or not to fight, so collective security was finished.
- The 'isolationist' USA refused to join the League (see 9.9).
- The League relied on Britain and France to act in the name of collective security, but in 1925 the British Conservative Government told the League it would not commit troops to defend the Treaty of Versailles.

10.2 Acting outside the League

When Germany found it difficult to pay the **reparations** instalments, two USA bankers, Dawes and Young drew up plans (1924 and 1929) which lowered the amount of money which Germany had to pay (see 8.6). The Treaty of Versailles had therefore been modified without the League's approval.

The 1925 **Locarno Treaties** were drawn up by Britain, France and Germany and were also signed by Belgium and Italy. The Treaties guaranteed Germany's western borders with France and Belgium, but did not guarantee Germany's eastern borders with Poland and Czechoslovakia.

At Locarno, therefore, the Great Powers were weakening collective security and the authority of the League of Nations by suggesting that Germany might be allowed to take over parts of eastern Europe where many Germans were living as a result of the Versailles Treaty (see 4.2 and 4.3).

10.3 Japan, the League and Manchuria: Case Study 1

Japan, an important industrial nation and a member of the League Council, suffered from the world depression which followed the Wall Street crash (see 9.5 and 9.6). Japan was unable to sell enough goods, and her people suffered massive unemployment, so she decided to invade Manchuria (see Fig. 7.2). Japan saw Manchuria as a source of raw materials, a market for her goods, and living space for her growing population. As we saw in Chapter 7, Japan had forced China to give up part of this area (see Figs 7.1 and 7.2).

In September 1931 there was an explosion on the South Manchurian Railway which Japanese soldiers controlled. Japan used this explosion as an excuse to seize Mukden, the capital of Manchuria, and within five months Japan had occupied all of Manchuria, in spite of the League's condemnation of this aggression.

Chiang Kai-shek, the Chinese President, appealed to the League to act, and the League sent a commission under Lord Lytton of Britain. Lytton's Commission condemned Japan as an aggressor. The League accepted the Report and refused to recognise Japan's renaming of the area as Manchukuo. Japan left the League, which took no further action against Japan. This showed that in spite of the Covenant (which Japan had signed), force could win in the end, and the aim of enforcing collective security' (see 10.1) had failed.

The British cartoonist Low showed how the League had been humiliated by Japan (1931–32), and how the British Foreign Secretary, Sir John Simon, was trying to repair the damaged League.

Fig. 10.1 *Evening Standard* cartoon. Japan trampling on the League of Nations; Britain repairs its face.

10.4 Italy, the League and Abyssinia: Case Study 2

In 1925 Mussolini, the dictator of Italy, proposed Abyssinia for membership of the League of Nations. In the nineteenth century Italy had already conquered lands bordering Abyssinia, and in 1934 there were border clashes between Italians and Abyssinians. Mussolini threatened to invade Abyssinia. The Abyssinian Emperor appealed to the League, but was told to negotiate with Mussolini who sent troops into neighbouring Somaliland and Eritrea.

In October 1935 Italian troops invaded Abyssinia, supported by a large airforce and using chemical weapons (poison gas) against the poorly armed tribesmen. The League condemned Italy as an aggressor and imposed economic **sanctions** against her. Countries were asked not to trade with Italy. However, this was merely a public relations stunt:

- Coal, steel and oil were excluded from the list of goods which came under the sanctions.
- Austria and Germany ignored the sanctions completely and then sold arms to Italy.
- Britain and France allowed free passage of Italian ships through the Suez Canal, which they controlled.
- Laval, French Foreign Secretary, publicly supported Italy's claims to an African Empire (see Fig. 10.2).

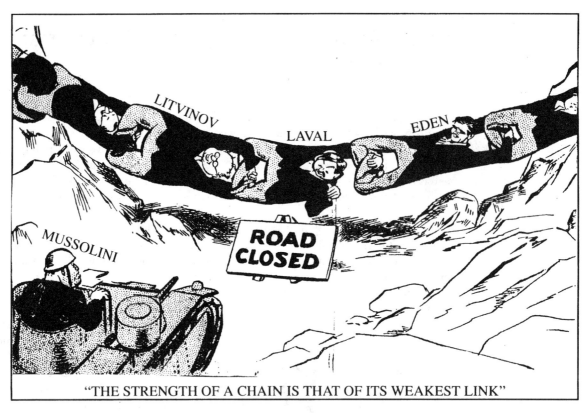

"THE STRENGTH OF A CHAIN IS THAT OF ITS WEAKEST LINK"

Fig. 10.2 A British cartoon drawn by David Low in 1935

Examiner's tip

i. Students sometimes get confused about the details of the Locarno Treaties, the Manchurian and Abyssinian crises. Study them carefully.

ii. A useful way of revising these issues would be to make a list of key words which help you to revise the main points.

iii. Note the similarities and differences between the Manchurian and Abyssinian crises and the reasons why the League was weak at these times.

In December 1935 the British Foreign Secretary (Hoare) signed a Pact with Laval. The Hoare-Laval Pact would have allowed Italy to take two-thirds of Abyssinia, including the coastal area, so that Abyssinia (renamed Ethiopia) would be 'landlocked'. When this Pact was published there was much anger that Hoare had to resign and the Pact had to be dropped.

The Italian conquest went ahead. By May 1939 the whole of Abyssinia was under Italian occupation and the Abyssinian ruler went into exile. Mussolini's success showed that the League of Nations was very weak, and that the political reality was 'might is right'.

10.5 Hitler's aggressive foreign policy, 1933–35

One of the reasons for Hitler's popularity among Germans in 1933 was his condemnation of the terms of the Treaty of Versailles (see 4.2 and 4.3). Most British politicians sympathised with the German people's anger over the Treaty, though most French people hoped the terms of the Treaty would last for ever.

In 1933 Hitler ended Germany's membership of the League of Nations (see 5.6) and set about undoing the terms of the Versailles Peace Treaty. The League of Nations failed to prevent Hitler's policies:

- He introduced conscription and enlarged Germany's armed forces.
- The building of a large navy, army and airforce was forbidden by the Versailles Treaty (see 4.2), but pleased German nationalists, businessmen and workers who found employment after the depression (see 8.12)
- In July 1934 Austrian Nazis murdered the Austrian Chancellor Dollfuss and asked Hitler to help them take control of Austria. The new Chancellor, Schuschnigg, appealed to Mussolini to stop Hitler invading Austria. Mussolini did not want German forces to be near the Italian frontier, so he sent Italian troops to the

Brenner Pass, forcing Hitler to call off his plans for taking over Austria. The German plans to break the Treaty by uniting Germany and Austria were stopped by force, but not by League action.

In April 1935 Mussolini signed the 'Stresa Front' with Britain and France to resist Hitler's attempts to revise the Versailles Treaty. In June 1935 Hoare, the British Foreign Secretary angered France and Italy when he signed the Anglo-German Naval Agreement which allowed the German navy to be 35% of the size of Britain's navy. This was against the Versailles treaty and encouraged Hitler to break more terms of the treaty because Britain would not oppose him. The agreement was part of the British policy of **appeasement** of Hitler. It alarmed Mussolini who decided to become closer to Hitler. The French realised Britain would not defend them against Germany.

10.6 Three steps towards war, 1935–38

1. In March 1936, while Britain and France were occupied with the Abyssinian crisis, Hitler ordered German troops to march into the Rhineland (see Fig. 10.3). This was forbidden by the Treaty of Versailles and the Locarno Treaties (see 10.2), but the British government was not willing to stop Hitler 'occupying his own backyard'. France did want to stop Hitler because the Rhineland was the barrier between France and Germany, but they were powerless without Britain. A small force could have stopped the invasion, but when no one stopped the invasion Hitler claimed he was 'always right'. British 'appeasement' encouraged Hitler to demand more.

2. In November 1936 Hitler signed the anti-Comintern Pact with Japan, which Italy joined in November 1937. All three aggressive nations were now linked together.

3. On 11 March 1938 Hitler ordered the German invasion of Austria. He had bullied the Austrian Chancellor Schuschnigg into allowing Austrian Nazis to join the Government. Schuschnigg had also called off a **plebiscite** about whether the Austrians wanted to join up with Germany. The Austrians did not resist the invasion and most of them welcomed the *Anschluss* (Union) between Germany and Austria, which was announced on 13 March 1938. This broke another part of the Versailles Treaty, but Britain and France did not take any action.

The map in Fig. 10.3 shows how Czechoslovakia was now caught between Germany and Austria; 'a prey inside two jaws'.

10.7 Czechoslovakia, 1938–39: Case Study 3

Czechoslovakia was formed by the Treaty of St Germain (see 4.4). There were many German speakers in the Sudetenland (see Fig. 10.3), many of whom were supporters of a Nazi-style party led by Henlein. Henlein complained of ill-treatment by the Czech government, and Hitler threatened to invade to 'protect' the Nazi supporters, as he had done in Austria (see 10.6)

The British Prime Minister, Neville Chamberlain, tried to settle things peacefully. His Foreign Secretary, Eden, resigned over this latest example of **appeasement**. Chamberlain's policy led to four important meetings:

1. In August 1938 Britain persuaded the President Benes of Czechoslovakia to allow the Sudeten Germans to have self-government, but this failed to satisfy Hitler who called Czechoslovakia 'an artificial state'.

2. On 15 September 1938, at the Berchtesgaden meeting, Chamberlain and Daladier of France agreed with Hitler to force Benes to give up to Germany any region where 50% of the people were German.

Fig. 10.3 Hitler's expansionist policy, 1933–38

③ On 27 September Chamberlain flew to meet Hitler at Godesburg after Benes had refused to accept the demands on the Czechs. Chamberlain asked Hitler not to invade Czechoslovakia until he had the chance to ask the Czechs to give in to Germany's demands.

④ On 29 September Chamberlain flew to Munich where he met with Hitler, Daladier and Mussolini. 'The Big Four' decided that Germany should occupy the Sudetenland. The Czechs and their **USSR** allies were not invited to the meeting. On 30 September Chamberlain flew home with a 'piece of paper' signed by Hitler promising 'Peace in our Time'. The loss of the Sudetenland meant the Czechs lost most of their resources and defences. In October and November 1938 Hungary and Poland took Slovakia and Moravia with its coal fields and steelworks.

10.8 And so to War

Hitler ignored the Munich agreement, and on March 15 1939 German troops invaded the rest of Czechoslovakia. Britain and France began discussions about ways of stopping Hitler.

In April 1939 Britain promised Poland help if Germany attacked, but Britain and France were unwilling to join with the USSR in an anti-Nazi Alliance.

Stalin feared Britain and France might join with Hitler in a war with the USSR. Stalin and Hitler signed the Nazi-Soviet Pact negotiated by Molotov and Ribbentrop in July 1939. The USSR and Germany agreed they would not fight each other, and they agreed to carve up Poland between themselves. Hitler was pleased as this meant that Germany would not have to fight on two fronts as it had done in 1914 (see Chapter 3).

On 1 September 1939 Hitler ordered the German invasion of Poland. He wanted control of Danzig and the Polish Corridor which, after the Treaty of Versailles (see 4.2) separated East Prussia from the rest of Germany (see Fig. 10.3).

On 3 September Britain and France declared war on Germany. On 15 September the USSR invaded Poland and the Baltic States which she had lost in the Treaty of Brest Litovsk (see 6.5). In a futile gesture the League expelled the USSR from membership.

Summary

1 Collective security was the policy of the League of Nations, but could not be enforced as no country was willing to send forces to war.
2 In the 1920s reparations were reduced and the Locarno Treaties were signed.
3 The League was exposed as weak by the Manchurian crisis.
4 The League failed over Abyssinia in 1935–36.
5 Hitler left the League and started to rearm Germany.
6 In 1934 Mussolini stopped Hitler's plans to invade Austria.
7 In 1935 the Stresa Front was formed to oppose Hitler.
8 The 1935 Anglo-German Naval Treaty broke the Treaty of Versailles.
9 Germany occupied the Rhineland (1936) and Austria (1938).
10 Czechoslovakia was divided up 1938–39.
11 The Nazi-Soviet Pact (1939) carved up Poland and helped Hitler fight on one front.
12 War broke out in Europe in September 1939 after Germany's invasion of Poland.

Quick questions

1 On which *two* countries did the League most depend to uphold collective security?
2 Name the *two* US bankers who arranged the reduction of German reparations.
3 In which year were the Locarno Treaties signed?
4 Name *five* Countries which signed the Locarno Treaties.
5 Why did France welcome one of the Locarno Treaties?
6 When did Japan invade Manchuria, and who led the League Commission to examine Japan's invasion?
7 In which year did Italy complete the conquest of Abyssinia?
8 Name:
   i)   the British Foreign Secretary, and
   ii) the French Foreign Minister
       who were in office when Italy invaded Abyssinia.
9 How did Hitler break the Treaty of Versailles over the Rhineland in 1936?
10 Name the *three* countries of the Stresa Front, 1935.

Chapter 11
India 1900–1949

11.1 Government and people, 1901

Queen Victoria, Empress of India, died in 1901. The 300 million Indians were governed by a few thousand British officials, led by the **Viceroy** who ruled on behalf of the King or Queen. He was helped by a **Central Council** consisting of British civil servants and army officers.

India was made up of many separate states. The majority of people were Hindu, and the largest minority were Muslims. While most states were governed by British officials (aided by state Councils), Indian Princes were allowed to rule in some States with the help of British officials.

11.2 Wealthy Indians and the demand for change

A small number of Indians, apart from the Princes, were very wealthy, namely landowners, merchants, bankers and owners of small factories.

Some Indians were educated in British schools in India, and others in schools and Universities in Britain. They were not allowed into the higher ranks of the Indian Civil Service and were not given a say in the running of their own country.

In 1885 some of these rich, well-educated Indians held the first **Indian National Congress**. Most of its members were Hindus who were normally more successful in trade and better educated than the Muslims. Some Congress members wanted social reform to help the poor. Others wanted political reform to help the better educated get on. Others, more extreme, called for an armed uprising to get the British out of India.

11.3 Political reforms, 1909–19

In 1909 John Morley, the British Secretary of State for India and Lord Minto, the Viceroy of India pushed through the **Morley-Minto reforms**.
- The Viceroy's Central Council was enlarged to include 27 members to be elected by Indians. The majority of members were British, appointed by the Viceroy.
- Indians could be elected to state Councils, but would be in a minority there too.
- The **franchise** was based on a property qualification, so the majority of voters were Hindu.
- There was separate representation for Muslims, which pleased the **Muslim League** formed in 1906.

During the First World War (1914–18) Indian troops fought for Britain. Congress and the Muslim League called for political reform, which the British promised would come 'after the war'. The Russian Revolution (see 6.2) showed how an unpopular government could fall, and the break up of the Austro-Hungarian Empire (see 4.4) showed how Empires could fall.

In 1917 Montagu, Secretary State for India, promised more self-government by Indians 'at some distant future'. Indians thought that this meant immediate independence, but most British politicians thought it meant 'say, in 500 years time.' In 1919 **Montagu** passed a series of important reforms.

- The Central Council was enlarged again, with a majority of Indians.
- A Council (Upper House) was created for the Princes and large landowners in British-governed States.
- A **Chamber of Princes** was created in Indian-governed States to discuss matters of common concern with the British-governed States (e.g. trade, postal services and defence).
- Provincial Councils were to have a majority of Indians from which the British Ministers had to get agreement for decisions.
- The franchise was extended so that 5 million people voted for the Provincial Councils. One million voted for the Central Council. You should note that only a very small minority of Indians voted.

Many Indians thought these reforms had not gone far enough, while the British thought that they had been generous but sensible to give Indians only a little power. They did not believe the Indians could be trusted to govern themselves.

11.4 Gandhi and politics, 1914–19

Gandhi, born to a rich family, had gone to London University and became a British-trained barrister. He spent some years (1893–1914) in South Africa leading campaigns against its cruel racial laws, and was often imprisoned. Many Indians in South Africa opposed his non-violent policies. He went to London to organise an Indian ambulance corps, hoping that this would lead to more concessions from the British.

Back in India in 1919, he became the religious leader of the nationalist movement: his supporters called him Mahatma (or 'Great Soul'), and in 1920 he became their accepted political leader. He asked his supporters to adopt a policy of non-violence: to refuse to obey 'unfair' laws, and to pay 'unfair' taxes, and to **boycott** British-made goods. This non-violent policy was known as the 'satyagraha' or 'soul force'.

One unfair law allowed British judges to try cases of terrorism without a jury. Another law allowed people to be sent to prison without a trial.

On 6 April 1919 Gandhi called a 'hartal', a day on which Indians would fast and pray and not go to work. Gandhi hoped this would encourage the British to give in to demands for more reforms and grant independence.

In some places the hartal led to rioting. General Dyer's armed force put down the rioters in the Sikhs' holy city of Amritsar in the Punjab. The Punjab state council banned meetings in the hope that the unrest would die down.

On 18 April 1919 a peaceful but illegal gathering took place in Amritsar, in a square which had only one narrow exit. Dyer commanded the troops sent to disperse this gathering. The crowd could not or would not disperse. Troops opened fire and 379 Indians were killed with 1200 left wounded.

This **Amritsar Massacre** was an important turning point. Congress changed from being a moderate middle-class party to being a mass movement supported by millions of angry Indians. Relations between the Indians and the British were never the same again.

11.5 Gandhi and politics, 1920–35

Strikes and violence grew despite Gandhi's call for non-violence. In 1921 Gandhi supervised the burning of British goods in Bombay, and this led to looting and murder. As a result Gandhi called off his policy of civil disobedience and non-cooperation with the government, but he was arrested in 1922 and sentenced to six years in prison. He was released in 1924, and in 1927 he was elected President of Congress, but refused to take the post, leaving it to Motilal Nehru, the Hindu leader.

In 1928 the British sent a Commission, led by Sir John Simon, to see how the reforms of 1919 were working. Gandhi boycotted the Commission which had no Indian members. Congress supported Nehru's demand for complete **Dominion** independence such as Canada, Australia, New Zealand and South Africa enjoyed.

In 1930 the Simon Commission recommended an increase in the powers of Provincial Governments and indirect elections for the Central Council.

Gandhi made his 250-mile-long march from Ahmedabad to the sea, where he produced salt from sea water. This deliberately broke the law which said that only the Government could make salt. The march drew millions of ordinary Indians into the anti-British campaign. Violence grew and Gandhi was imprisoned.

The Viceroy freed Gandhi and persuaded him to attend the second Round Table Conference in London (1931). The first Conference (1930) had failed because Congress was not represented and Gandhi was in prison. The second Conference failed because Muslim and Congress representatives would not agree about the nature of the Indian Parliament.

When he returned to India Gandhi called another campaign of non-cooperation. He was imprisoned again, and after his release he retired to his 'ashram' (prayer centre), stating he was discouraged by Muslim-Hindu divisions and Nehru's support for extremist, violent 'direct action' against the British.

Examiner's tip

i. Revise carefully the *different views* held by people in India and the reasons for the gradual changes in British policy up to 1939.
ii. You should revise Gandhi's career by revising the reasons behind his actions, the various acts of defiance of the British, his successes and his failures.

11.6 The Government of India Act, 1935

This was a major step towards Indian independence.
- A central, elected Indian assembly was to have a say in all matters except defence and foreign affairs.
- The eleven Provincial Assemblies were to have almost total control of local affairs.
- The franchise was extended so that 35 million people had the vote, but still on a small property qualification, so the poor did not vote.
- Some seats in all Assemblies were reserved for religious minorities.
- However, many Indians said these reforms did not go far enough.
- India was denied the right to control its foreign and defence polices.
- The conservative, pro-British Princes were given one-third of the seats in the Lower House of the Central Assembly, and two-thirds of the seats in the Upper House.
- The Viceroy's Ministers were not answerable to the Central Assembly.
- The Act ignored the fears of the Muslims that the Hindu majority would treat them unfairly. In the 1937 elections Congress won control of eight of the eleven Provinces. The Muslim leader Jinnah demanded a separate state for Muslims, called Pakistan, but Congress and Gandhi were determined to keep a united India.

11.7 India and the War, 1939–45

In September 1939 the Viceroy, without consulting Congress, 'speaking for India', declared war on Germany. Nehru demanded immediate independence for India if India was to fight. Britain refused this demand so Congress opposed Indian participation in the war. Many Congress leaders were imprisoned without trial. Gandhi, a **pacifist**, was arrested for opposing the war, and Congress Ministers in the provinces resigned. The more warlike Muslims supported the Viceroy and the war, and stayed in the provincial governments. In 1940 Jinnah demanded a separate Pakistan.

With the Japanese successes in Burma and elsewhere (see 12.7), Gandhi and other leaders claimed that India would be safe if Britain left.

'Quit India' was their slogan against the British. In 1942 the British Mission, led by Stafford Cripps, went to consult Congress. He promised:
- Dominion status (like Canada and Australia) after the war;
- India's right to leave the Commonwealth if she decided;
- India's right to work out its own **constitution**.

Nehru wanted to accept this, but Gandhi opposed it and called for a campaign of civil disobedience. This led the British to put the Congress leaders back into prison. In 1945 Wavell, the Viceroy, freed the Congress leaders and held a Conference where he tried to get the Muslims and Hindus to agree to future government of India. Muslims refused to accept Nehru's policy that Congress (which had some Muslim members) had the right to name which Muslims should be included in a future Indian government.

11.8 The last days of the Raj, 1946–47

xaminer's tip

In 1947 Britain's poor economic position forced her to end her part in the civil war in Greece (see 15.3) and to give up her mandate in Palestine (see 23.5). Other imperialist powers were similarly impoverished because of the recent war. Holland was unable to regain control of the Dutch East Indies (now Indonesia), while France was unable to keep control of French Indo-China (now Laos, Kampuchea and Vietnam).

In August 1946 Wavell invited Nehru to form a government. Jinnah, head of the Muslim League, was a minister in that government, but he said that Muslims would use violence to get a separate Pakistan. Local Muslim leaders started to use violence and there were massacres of Hindus, Sikhs and Muslims. Provincial governments were unable to stop the killings and India was on the edge of civil war. Jinnah's Muslim League made it impossible for Nehru's government to work properly.

11.9 A partitioned India

Talks with Nehru, Gandhi, Jinnah and other leaders showed Mountbatten that India would have to be partitioned. He announced that independence would take place on 15 August 1947. The Indian Independence Act was rushed through the British Parliament. It created **Pakistan** for the Muslim majority areas in north-west and north-east India, which were a thousand miles apart. The rest of India was called India. Nehru became the Prime Minister of Independent India, while Jinnah became the first Governor General of Pakistan. Jinnah died soon after independence and the Pakistan Prime Minister, Ali Khan, was assassinated in 1951. These events increased Pakistan's difficulties after partition.

The **Partition of India** led to many problems.
- The Punjab Province was split between India and Pakistan. The Sikh community's holy city, Amritsar, was in India, leaving the Sikhs in Pakistan cut off.
- While a boundary commission was meeting (March 1947) Muslims attacked Sikhs in Amritsar and also murdered thousands of Hindus there. The warlike Sikhs fought back. The police, who were also divided on racial grounds, took little or no action.
- Five million Hindus left West Pakistan for India, and one million Hindus left East Pakistan for India. Five million Muslims left India for West Pakistan, and at least $1\frac{1}{2}$ million were killed as they made their way to their new homes. Gandhi himself was assassinated in 1948 by a Hindu fanatic who thought that Gandhi had been 'soft on the Muslims'.
- It was not only territory that had to be shared between the new states. Irrigation schemes had to be partitioned, with the worry that Muslims and Hindus would not

E **xaminer's tip**

i. Some students become confused between Nehru, Jinnah and Gandhi. Take care to study how they were both similar and different from one another.
ii. Make lists of reasons
a) why India was partitioned and
b) the effects of Indian independence and partition.

share 'their' water. The army and navy, civil service and the railways also had to be shared.

On top of these problems, India and Pakistan had major social and political problems:

- The majority of voters could not read or write.
- Thousands died each year of hunger, and famines were a regular feature of life.
- Poverty and inequality (often caused by the Hindu **caste** system) would have to be attacked.
- The populations of both states were increasing and the Governments of India and Pakistan had problems with housing, feeding, clothing and educating the people.

Summary

1 The Congress Party was founded (1885) by well-off Indians who wanted social and political reforms.
2 The Morley-Minto reforms (1909) gave some Indians a small share in central and provincial governments.
3 Montagu promised self-government at 'some distant future' (1917).
4 In 1919 the role of Indians in government was increased, although only a few Indians had the franchise.
5 Gandhi, the Congress leader, called for non-violent methods to be used against British rule.
6 The 1919 Amritsar massacre was a major turning point.
7 The 1931 Round Table Conference was ignored by Gandhi whose 'march for salt' drew millions of Indians to support him.
8 In 1935 the Government of India Act was a big step towards independence.
9 Muslims, led by Jinnah, demanded a Muslim state of Pakistan.
10 Congress opposed Indian participation in the war (1939–45). Gandhi's 'Quit India' campaign led to his arrest.
11 In 1946 when Nehru formed the government of India there were many religious and racial massacres.
12 In 1947 Mountbatten partitioned India, which caused many short-term and long-term problems for the governments of India and Pakistan.

Quick questions

1 In what year was the Indian Congress founded?
2 What was the religion of the majority of Indian people?
3 Name:
   i) the Secretary of State, and
   ii) the Viceroy.
      responsible for the 1909 government reforms.
4 What did Montagu promise India in 1917?
5 What was a 'hartal'?
6 To which religious group is Amritsar a holy city?
7 Against what was Gandhi protesting in his 'march to the sea'?
8 Why was 1935 an important year in Indian history?
9 Which religious group was led by Jinnah?
10 Why was Gandhi imprisoned in 1940?
11 Who was the last Viceroy of India?

Chapter 12
The Second World War, 1939–45

12.1 Poland partitioned, and the 'Phoney War'

The Germans invaded Poland on 1 September 1939. They used a combination of tanks, bombers, parachute troops and soldiers carried in lorries, in what was called **'blitzkrieg'** (lightning war). They overwhelmed the small, slow and old-fashioned Polish forces, who also had to fight Russian troops who had invaded from the east on 15 September. On 3 October Poland surrendered and was partitioned between Germany and Russia.

Britain and France could not save Poland. The French had built their **Maginot Line** ('a battleship on land') which the Germans were unwilling to attack. The Germans had the **Siegfried Line**, which the British and French were unwilling to attack. So, for six months there was almost no action on this western front. Many people described this a period of 'Phoney War'.

12.2 Blitzkrieg in the west

On 9 April the Germans invaded Denmark and Norway to prevent Britain from taking control of the Norwegian coastline and the routes by which Swedish steel got to Germany. The 'blitzkrieg' tactics forced Denmark to surrender on 9 April. Norway held out a little longer, helped by British troops in the north, but south and central Norway fell to the Germans, partly because of a Norwegian 'fifth column' under Quisling. When the British forces were forced to withdraw from the north (May 2) Quisling, a German puppet, became the administrator of Norway.

The loss of Norway led to the resignation of Prime Minister Chamberlain, and Churchill becoming Prime Minister (10 May) on the very day on which German troops invaded Belgium, Luxembourg and Holland.

Once again, it was 'blitzkreig': Rotterdam was devastated by bombing, and German parachutists landed behind Dutch and Belgian lines, cutting off thousands of troops who had to surrender. The French Maginot Line had not been built along the Belgian border so, as in the First World War (see Fig. 3.1), German troops invaded France from the north, by-passing the Maginot Line. Holland and Belgium surrendered, and British troops defending Belgium were pushed back to the coast at **Dunkirk**. Here about

340,000 British and Allied troops were attacked by German land and air forces, but Hitler called off an attack by the army: maybe he wanted to give the German airforce (Luftwaffe) a chance to finish off the allied troops; maybe he hoped to force Britain to make a negotiated peace. In any event, about 300,000 allied forces were ferried off the beaches in small ships, either to larger ships which took them off to England or, in many cases, directly across the Channel.

The Germans continued to invade the rest of France itself, dive bombing refugees on the crowded roads. On 14 June 1940 they took Paris. Prime Minister Reynaud resigned, and Marshall Pétain, hero of Verdun in the First World War (see 3.2), became head of the French government. On 22 June he signed an **armistice** with Germany: the Germans occupied the north and the west of France, while the rest of France was governed by Pétain from the town of Vichy. Britain now stood alone against a German-controlled Europe.

12.3 The Battle of Britain

Hitler's plan for the invasion of Britain (**Operation Sea Lion**) depended on German control of the air over the Channel and the south of England.

This led to a period of aerial war over southern England which was called 'the Battle of Britain'. Germany had Heinkel bombers, Junker 'stuka' dive bombers and Messerschmitt fighter planes. The British depended on the Hurricane and the Spitfire and, most importantly, the chain of radar stations along the coast which had been developed by Robert Watson-Watt. These provided the RAF with warning of the approach of German planes, and allowed British planes to be accurately and quickly sent to meet the incoming planes.

The Battle of Britain was fought in four stages:

1. 10 July–7 August: German attacks on coastal shipping and vital inland targets were meant to force British fighters into the sky. The Germans lost many more planes than they had expected.
2. 8–23 August: large-scale attacks on airfields destroyed many RAF planes and buildings. Foolishly, the Germans did not attack the vital radar stations.
3. 24 August–6 September: the Germans switched targets and turned to the bombing of factories and military targets, hoping to lessen Britain's ability to fight.
4. 7–30 September: all RAF fighters were sent to the south to protect Britain against the planned invasion. Huge raids by day led to desperate air fighting over southern England during the warm summer. The Germans lost 1,733 planes, the RAF lost 900. The loss of 700 RAF pilots was more serious and left the RAF undermanned, but the Germans thought their losses were too heavy. They called off the attack and switched to night bombing of British cities (see Chapter 13). Hitler gave up his invasion plans, and Britain had been saved by the RAF. Churchill said 'Never in the field of human conflict was so much owed by so many to so few'.

Examiner's tip

i. You should revise the reasons for Germany's success in the first year of the war, and the reasons for the outcome of the *Battle of Britain*.

ii. Note the link between the Battle of Britain and the Battle of the Atlantic, and study the reasons why Britain won the *Battle of the Atlantic* and the effects of the victory.

12.4 The Battle of the Atlantic

Hitler then decided to attack the **convoys** of shipping which brought food and raw materials to Britain, taking about 15 days to cross the Atlantic. 'U-Boats' in 'wolfpacks' waited until the convoys had little cover from air or surface vessels, then attacked. German heavy bombers (Condors) attacked shipping in British waters which were also heavily mined. Battleships, such as the *Bismarck* and *Prince Eugen*, were meant to attack merchant shipping, but did less damage than the submarines. After 1942 Britain lost fewer ships and won the Battle of the Atlantic. The reasons for this victory were:

- British escort ships were better equipped with radar to locate U–Boats. bomb throwers and more effective depth charges to destroy submarines.
- Better quality escort ships, faster frigates and corvettes could attack the German submarines when they surfaced.
- Bomber planes also played a part against the U–Boats in 1942 and 1943.

12.5 The Balkans and the Middle East

In June 1940, with France collapsing, Mussolini declared war and invaded France. In October he invaded Greece, but the Greeks defeated the Italians and invaded Albania, which Italy had conquered in April 1939.

The Germans had to come to the aid of their ally, hoping also to gain influence in the Balkans, the pathway to Britain's Middle East oil interests and to the vital Suez Canal. By the early summer of 1941 the Germans had control of almost the whole of the Balkans (see Fig. 12.2). Rumania and Hungary signed alliances with Germany (November 1940), as did Bulgaria (March 1941). In April 1941 Germany invaded and conquered Yugoslavia and invaded Greece, from where British troops were forced to retreat to Crete (see Fig. 12.1).

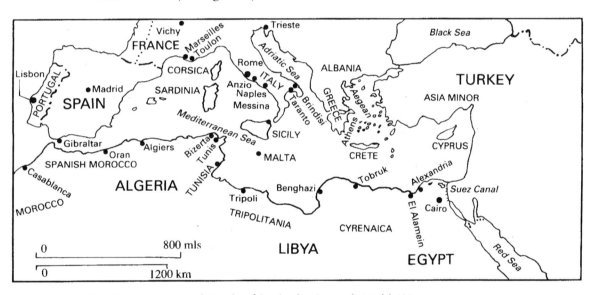

Fig. 12.1 Europe and North Africa in the Second World War

In September 1940 Italian troops advanced from Libya to Egypt. British and **Dominion** troops were rushed out, along with tanks from Britain. The Royal Navy defeated one Italian naval force at Taranto (November 1940), and another at Matapan off the coast of Greece (1941). In February 1941 British forces drove the Italians back to Benghazi, which forced Hitler to send troops to help.

Led by **Rommel** ('the Desert Fox') the Germans drove the British from Libya, but they did not receive the supplies they needed due to Hitler's war with Russia (see 12.6), so the British re-took Libya. British supplies were reduced by the bombing of Mediterranean convoys by planes based in Italy. The British base of Malta was under constant air attack. In May 1942 Rommel received extra supplies and drove the weakened British forces from Libya and deep into Egypt, threatening the Suez Canal and the Gulf oil fields. The German African army threatened to link up with the German forces which had conquered much of southern Russia.

The new British General, **Montgomery**, received extra supplies and halted Rommel's advance at the first battle of **El Alamein** (July 1942). He then defeated Rommel at Alam Halfa (August 1942) before defeating him decisively at the second

E **xaminer's tip**

El Alamein, October 1942, was one of the war's 'turning points'. Others were **Stalingrad**, January 1943 (see 12.6) and the US naval victories in the **Coral Sea**, May 1942 and at the **Midway**, June 1942 (see 12.7)

battle of El Alamein (October 1942). After this the British Eighth Army ('the Desert Rats') chased the Germans and Italians as far as Tunis (May 1943).

In November 1942 American, British and French troops, commanded by General Eisenhower, landed in Morocco and in Algiers (**Operation Torch**). They advanced towards Tunis, and in May 1943 the fighting in North Africa was over.

12.6 Russia, 1941–44

Examiner's tip

i. Study the reasons for Germany's success in the Balkans, Libya and Russia (1940–42), and the reasons why Germany's armies were defeated in Africa (1942–43) and in Russia (1942–44).

ii. Examiners expect you to explain the importance for the war of these turning points.

Hitler issued a secret document known as 'Operation Barbarossa' (18 December 1940).

This was the plan for the invasion of Russia. He hoped to crush communism, to get the wheat fields of the Ukraine, and the oil of the Caucusus. He also wanted to provide German people with extra living space ('**Lebensraum**'). Then, with most of Europe and Russia under his control, he would be able to attack Africa, the Middle East oil fields and the route to India.

The invasion was delayed because troops were sent to help Italy in Greece (see 12.5). On 22 June 1941 a five-pronged invasion was launched to drive towards Leningrad, Moscow, the Ukraine, Stalingrad and the Crimea. The blitzkrieg methods worked, and the Germans drove deep into Russia. By the end of 1941 they had taken the Baltic

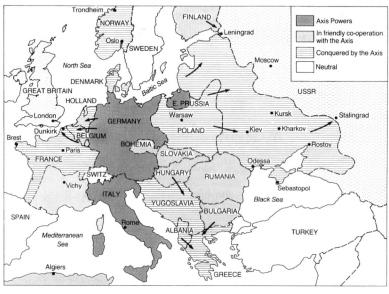

Fig. 12.2 The Axis powers in victory, 1939–42

States and were besieging Leningrad, had taken the Ukraine and reached the Black Sea, and had reached the outskirts of Moscow.

The advance ground to a halt in the bitter Russian winter. In June 1942 the Germans began to advance again towards the southern oil fields and the capture of Moscow. They were halted by Russian resistance at **Stalingrad** (September 1942) where, after five months of bitter fighting, the Russian Commander Zhukov surrounded the Germans. In January 1943 the German commander, von Paulus surrendered along with his 100,000 soldiers, including 24 generals.

The Russians then began to push the Germans back. In July 1943 3,000 tanks fought the battle of Kursk, which ended in a Russian victory. In June 1944 the last German forces were driven from Russia by armies which liberated Rumania and Bulgaria (September 1944), Hungary (January 1945), and Poland (February 1945).

12.7 Italy, 1943–44

Stalin asked the western allies to open a **'Second Front'** against the Germans. In July 1943 British and American troops crossed from North Africa to Sicily (see Fig. 12.1) which was captured in August. In September 1943 the Allies invaded the Italian mainland and took the port of Salerno in a vital battle. Many Italians now changed sides: the King imprisoned Mussolini and a government under Marshall Badoglio sought an **armistice**.

Hitler rushed troops to stop the Allied advance, and they took control of Rome. Mussolini was rescued by German paratroops and the Germans set him up as head of a new government in the north. The Allied advance up the 'leg' of Italy was slow due to the many rivers and mountains and the fierce German resistance. The destruction of the monastery of Monte Cassino was seen as vital by the Allies because it was a German strong point. Many Italians regarded the Allied bombing of the monastery as barbaric.

In June 1944 the Allies took Rome, but the north was not conquered until April 1945 when Mussolini was captured and killed by Italian **partisans**. His body was hanged upside down with his mistress in Milan, where he had first set up his Fascist Party.

12.8 The Japanese War

Japan was already at war with China (see 10.3 and 7.9). In July 1941 the Vichy government of France allowed Japan to take control of Indo-China (now Laos, Cambodia and Vietnam). When Japanese troops moved into Indo-China, the USA stopped the sale of oil to Japan, as did Britain and Holland. The USA said that, to restore trade, Japan would have to withdraw from both China and Indo-China.

The military government in Japan decided to go to war to gain control of the oil and other raw materials in the Dutch and British colonies in the region. On 7 December 1941 Japanese planes destroyed the US fleet anchored in the Hawaiian base at **Pearl Harbour**. At the same time Japanese forces attacked the Philippines and British bases in Malaya, Singapore and Hong Kong and Burma. By May 1942 they had taken these bases and now threatened India. May 1942 was a 'turning point' in the war as seen by:

- the US naval victory at the **Coral Sea** (May 1942);
- the naval victory at **Midway Island** (June 1942);
- the success of the British 'Forgotten Army' which held the Frontier between India and Burma.

In June 1943 US forces began the process of 'island hopping' in which, in costly battles, they gained control of many islands and their airfields.

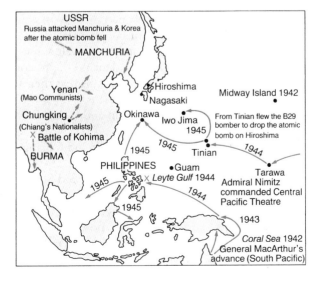

Fig. 12.3 The defeat of Japan

In June 1944 British and Indian troops in Burma defeated the Japanese at Kohima on the Indian border, while Australian troops began to drive the Japanese from New Guinea.

After the naval victory at Leyte Gulf (October 1944) the US forces took most of the Philippines back, and took the capital Manila in February 1945. From island air bases US planes bombed the Japanese mainland, but their armies faced stiff resistance from Japanese troops and from 5000 Japanese kamikaze pilots.

The USA planned two invasions of Japan. Southern Japan was to be taken in 1945 and Honshu in 1946. Casualties were expected to be high. In January 1945 Japan rejected peace proposals made by Allied leaders meeting in Potsdam (see 12.9). On 6 August 1945 an atomic bomb was dropped on **Hiroshima**. A second bomb was dropped on **Nagasaki** (9 August). On 15 August Japan surrendered.

12.9 The defeat of Germany

Examiner's tip

i. Be ready to explain why the Italian and Japanese campaigns were important for the outcome of the war.
ii. Study carefully the reasons for the Allied victory over Nazi Germany (Battles of Britain and the Atlantic, the Middle East battles, the Russian campaign and Allied invasions).
iii. You may be asked to discuss which factors were the most important.

On 6 June 1944 ('D-Day') US, British and Canadian forces landed on the Normandy beaches in **Operation Overlord**. Five thousand ships, protected by airforces in complete control of the skies, carried millions of men and tons of supplies across the Channel.

British engineers produced an artificial harbour ('Mulberry') which was towed across the Channel to make the landing of more troops and supplies easier. A Pipeline under the ocean (PLUTO) was created to ensure supplies of fuel for tanks, lorries and aircraft.

The Allies suffered heavy casualties before they could break out of the beaches and advance inland. Here, too, they suffered at the hands of superior German tanks and stiff resistance. However, the Germans were overwhelmed by the constant stream of supplies from US and British factories, and were hampered by the work of French **partisans**. By September 1944 the Allies had freed France and Belgium in spite of the disaster at Arnhem, where British paratroopers tried to take the Rhine bridge at Arnhem in Holland.

In December–January 1945, the Germans made a counter-attack in the Ardennes area, but by the spring of 1945 the Allies had crossed the Rhine and advanced into the heart of Germany. Meanwhile, as we have seen, the Russian forces advanced from the east, reaching east Berlin in April 1945. On 1 May Hitler shot himself and on 7 May the German surrender was signed at Rheims. The war was over in Europe at least.

12.10 Wartime conferences between Allied leaders

1. August 1941. Churchill met Roosevelt before the US entered the war. They drew up the Atlantic Charter which promised that every country would have the right to choose its own government after the war (see 14.1).
2. December 1941. In Washington, Roosevelt and Churchill agreed that Germany, not Japan was the main enemy.
3. August 1942. In Moscow Churchill explained the US-British plans to Stalin and got him to agree to the Allied invasion of North Africa.
4. January 1943. At Casablanca, Churchill and Roosevelt agreed on the invasion of Italy rather than of France. They agreed to demand the unconditional surrender of the Axis Powers to stop any future German claims that their forces had been 'stabbed in the back' by peace-making politicians.
5. 5 August 1943. At Quebec, the USA, Britain and Canada agreed plans for the invasion of Japan.
6. November 1943. In Cairo, Churchill, Roosevelt and Chiang Kai-shek agreed on the plans for the defeat of Japan.
7. November 1943. At Tehran, Churchill, Roosevelt and Stalin agreed that the western allies would open a second front in France, that there should be an international organisation to succeed the League of Nations, and that the USSR would declare war on Japan 'at some suitable moment'.
8. February 1945. At Yalta, Roosevelt, Stalin and Churchill agreed on the division of post-war Germany into zones of occupation. Russia was to take part of eastern

Poland which was to get land from east Germany. They also agreed to hold a conference in San Francisco to launch the United Nations Organisation (see Fig. 15.1 and Chapter 21).

9 July–August 1945. At Potsdam, Stalin, Truman (Roosevelt had died in April) and Churchill (replaced by Attlee after Churchill lost the British General Election on 26 July) failed to agree on many things as it became clear that Stalin was determined to control eastern Europe (see 15.1 and 19.1), while the US and Britain wanted control of the west.

Summary

1 1939–40: The German 'blitzkrieg' conquered Poland, and was followed by the 'phoney war'.
2 In 1940 the Germans defeated the Baltic states, Belgium, Holland and France.
3 July–September 1940: Britain eventually won the 'Battle of Britain'.
4 British victory in the Battle of the Atlantic ensured that her lifelines would be kept open.
5 Germany conquered the Balkans and North Africa 1940–42.
6 German invasion of the USSR was at first successful, but after the 'turning point' of Stalingrad (1942–43) the Germans were defeated.
7 The Allies invaded Italy (1943–44) as the 'Second Front'.
8 Japan had many initial successes, but the defeats at the battles of the Coral Sea and Midway were 'turning points' in the war against Japan.
9 Germany was defeated in May 1945 after fierce fighting following the June 1944 'D-Day' Normandy Landings.
10 Several Allied Wartime Conferences shaped plans for the war and world order after the war's end.

Quick questions

1 Which country first suffered from 'blitzkreig'?
2 What name was given to the French fortifications on the Franco-German border?
3 When did the 'phoney war' come to an end?
4 In which French town was a pro-German government set up in 1940?
5 What invasions were planned by:
   i) Operation Sea Lion;
   i) Operation Barbarossa;
   iii) Operation Overlord?
6 Name the battles which marked 'turning points' in:
   i) North Africa;
   ii) Russia;
   iii) the Far East?
7 What were i) Mulberry, and ii) PLUTO?
8 Who commanded i) the German, and ii) the Russian forces at Stalingrad 1942–43?
9 When and where did the USA drop the first atomic bomb?
10 When did Hitler shoot himself?

Chapter 13

The British Home Front, 1914–18 and 1939–45

1914–18

13.1 'Over by Christmas'

Cheering crowds in London and elsewhere greeted the British declaration of war on 4th August 1914. Crowds of men, young and middle-aged, rushed to volunteer to serve in the forces. Mothers, wives and girlfriends urged them on; in the words of the popular song, they said 'We don't want to lose you, But we think you ought to go, For your King and your country, Both need you so.' **Propaganda** in the form of the famous Kitchener poster, military bands leading processions through towns and villages, and speeches by politicians attacking the 'vile Hun', all contributed to the fervour. So, too, did early war poetry, notably that of Rupert Brooke: 'Now, God be thanked Who has matched us with His hour, And caught our youth, and wakened us from sleeping'.

13.2 The Liberal Government's attitude to war, 1914

Traditionally the Liberals had opposed war: they were the party of free trade and universal peace. One Minister resigned as soon as war was declared, and others did so afterwards. Prime Minister Asquith and the rest of the Government, thought that the war should be left to the generals, officials and munitions makers, with the Government playing little part. The Government did push through a **Defence of the Realm Act** (DORA) which was to be amended and strengthened by later legislation. This allowed trials by military courts (courts-martial) of anyone who broke such laws as the Government might make for the safety of the nation in wartime. It also allowed the Government to censor reports and stories which newspapers might have wanted to print. Later on, DORA allowed the Government to take control of industry, of raw materials and of food supplies (see 13.3 and 13.7).

13.3 The new reality, 1914–16

The heavy losses on the Western Front (see 3.2), and reports that there was a shortage of shells and other munitions, led to demands for sweeping changes in government policy. In 1915 Lloyd George became Minister for Munitions, and the **Munitions of War Act** (1915) allowed the Government to limit the profits made by munitions' makers, to take over some industrial firms, and to open new Government-owned munitions factories. The Government forced firms to adopt US machines and methods which produced arms and weapons at great speed, even though most of the workers were previously unskilled.

The heavy losses in the trenches (see 3.2) obliged the Government to bring in the **Conscription Act** (1916), which forced every man aged between 18 and 40 to register for service in the forces. Millions were made to join one or other of the services. Twenty-seven Liberal MP's voted against their government over this Act. Many young men became 'conscientious objectors', either refusing to register, or refusing to enlist in the forces once they had registered. They were harshly treated by the courts, being sent to prison or made to serve in ambulance units. They were also mocked by their neighbours, many of whom lost sons, husbands and brothers in the war.

13.4 Soldiers versus civilians

Fig. 13.1 A totally misleading representation of life at the front

In 1917 a US Senator said: 'The first casualty, when war comes, is truth'. By this time most soldiers had come to resent the ways in which civilians at home saw the war. They were angered by the high-living of those who made money out of the war, who were described by the steel maker, Baldwin, as 'hard-faced men who did well out of the war'. They hated the popular, pro-war songs sung in the Music Halls, the posters and cigarette cards (see Fig. 13.1), and postcards which showed the trenches as some jolly hunting scene. A new breed of poets – soldier-poets or war poets – spoke for the mass of the serving men, and included Wilfred Owen, Siegfried Sassoon, Robert Graves, R.L Thomas and others.

13.5 Women and war

The expansion of the munitions industries and the 1916 Conscription Act led to a great shortage of manpower. Women had to fill these vacancies. Women also joined the armed services, nursing organisations, became bus and tram drivers, delivered milk and worked on the farms and the railways. They won a great deal of respect for helping Britain to win the war, and they earned decent wages. It became almost inevitable that, after the war, they got the **franchise** .

13.6 Air raids

Between January 1915 and June 1918, London, Dover and towns on the east coast suffered from air raids by German Zeppelin and Gotha bombers. The heaviest casualties were during a raid on London on 13 June 1917, when 594 people were killed or injured. By the end of 1917 anti-aircraft weapons were in place and brought down a number of planes.

13.7 The effects of the submarine campaign

Once the German U-Boats started torpedoing food-carrying ships, there was a shortage of food at home. British farmers had almost given up wheat production by 1914 to concentrate on dairy farming. In 1917 the Government pushed through the **Corn Production Act** to reverse this process; the Act guaranteed farmers a minimum price for their output. They ploughed up land which had been left idle for years, as well as their rich pastures.

By 1918 there was a 50% increase in British food production, but there was still a food shortage. A new **Food Ministry** encouraged a system of voluntary **rationing**, but this failed so that everyone got a weekly ration of sugar, butter, margarine, jam, tea and bacon. Many Liberal MPs opposed this fresh attack on 'the free market'. Compulsory rationing was introduced.

13.8 Working people and the war

Many wartime homes had higher incomes than they had in 1913. There was more employment at higher wages, many married women had work, and soldiers had to send regular 'allotments' to their families. More people had a better diet (meat, fruit and vegetables) than they had in 1913, and were healthier – the improvement in children's health is seen in the reports from school medical officers.

Trade union leaders were involved in national and local committees set up to help increase production. Unions gave up their rights to strike (although Glasgow engineers had to be forced by the courts to accept this) and allowed unskilled workers (including women) to do work once done only by skilled men. The TUC hoped that after the war the Government would 'use its powers and increased taxes to make life better for our people'.

Labour politicians joined Lloyd George's Coalition Government in 1916, giving the party some added responsibility, as well as experience in government. With the Liberal Party badly split during the war, the Labour Party became the second largest party after General Elections in 1918 and 1922.

1939–45

13.9 Early preparations

There was none of the public welcome for war in 1939 that there had been in 1914. However, preparations for war had been made well before it began. **Conscription** of men aged 20–21 had been brought in in April 1939, and was extended to those aged 19–41 once war started in September. Essential workers were not conscripted. Instead they had to submit to 'direction of labour', being forced to leave non-essential work to go to munitions factories.

Air raid shelters had been dug in parks and other public places in September 1938, during the Munich Crisis (see 10.7). An **Air Raid Precaution Act** (ARP) had been passed in September–October 1937. This had led to the formation of ARP teams in towns and cities, with air raid wardens empowered to direct people to shelters in event of bombing, and taught to deal with the effects of such bombing.

Long before war started, everyone had been issued with a **gas mask**, and they were legally obliged to carry the mask wherever they went – school, work or play.

13.10 Government powers increased

DORA (see 13.2) was renewed and strengthened. **Emergency Powers Acts** of 1939 and 1940 allowed the Government to imprison German nationals and British Fascists such as Oswald Mosley without trial, to control and censor newspapers, some of which (the Communist *Daily Worker*) were shut down for a time, while the *Daily Mirror* was threatened with closure when it became too critical of the Government.

Industry was brought under government control, and government officials were appointed to run the railways, road transport and the docks. The **Ministry of Fuel and Power** was set up in 1942 to run the coal industry.

The Government controlled power supplies and supplies of raw materials which went to firms doing essential work. Ernest Bevin, once leader of the Transport and General Workers Union, joined Churchill's Coalition Government (May 1940) as Minister of Labour. He was responsible for the 'direction of labour' (see 13.1), and for the **Conscription Act** (1941) which forced unmarried women to join one of the services or to go to work in an essential industry. He also got unions to allow unskilled workers to do work once done only by skilled workers and to work longer hours, so that more munitions could be produced.

Lord Beaverbrook, owner of the *Daily Express*, became Minister of Aircraft Production in 1940 to help ensure a plentiful supply of planes. He persuaded motorcar firms to produce planes, co-operated with Bevin to get the unions on his side, and ensured that firms got the supplies of raw materials they needed.

13.11 Evacuees

Everyone expected that, once war started, enemy planes would bomb cities and towns. So, in September 1939, millions of children were taken from their urban homes (and parents) and sent to live with families in safer parts of the country. When there was no immediate bombing, many returned home before Christmas 1939, but once the Blitz began (see 13.13) evacuation started again, and many children spent most of the war away from their parents.

13.12 Rationing

Food, petrol and raw materials were in short supply because of government control of materials and German attacks on **convoys** of food-importing ships. This led to the rationing of petrol (September 1939), with only those who could prove a need getting a petrol ration book. Food rationing began in January 1940, so that everyone was entitled to a small amount of meat, sugar, butter, fats and other basic foods including sweets. Less basic foods were rationed by a system of 'points', while clothing was rationed by giving everyone a supply of 'coupons'. Lord Woolton, as Minister of Food, controlled the rationing system and, with the Ministry of Agriculture, persuaded people to 'grow more food' and to use food wisely.

13.13 The Blitzes

After losing the Battle of Britain (see 12.3) the Germans turned to bombing towns and cities. They hoped to disrupt industrial production, to force Britain to seek peace and to ensure that people and materials had to be used to repair bomb damage rather than on producing munitions.

Most bombing was done at night with tons of high-explosive bombs, incendiary bombs which started fires, and parachute mines which could destroy a whole street.

The whole population was partially protected by Anderson shelters, set in earth and covered with soil, by Morrison shelters, which were indoor steel boxes, by communal shelters in town and city streets, and in London by taking shelter in Underground stations.

Heavy damage and many casualties led to some panic and criticism of the Government, but they also led to a greater communal spirit and an increase in the number of volunteers willing to serve in voluntary services, for example fire watching, the Women's Voluntary Service, and St John's Ambulance.

Coventry was raided three times in November 1940, Merseyside was bombed for eight successive nights in May 1941, and other cities and towns suffered in much the same way.

Churchill appointed Air Marshall Arthur ('Bomber') Harris to head Bomber Command and prepare a huge bomber force to attack German towns. After May 1942 'Halifax' and 'Lancaster' bombers attacked German cities by night, with 100 bombers flying in the attacks. After the USA entered the war, they used 'Fortresses' and 'Liberators' to undertake daytime bombing of German towns and cities. Not everyone agreed with the later stages of this bombing of Germany.

13.14 Towards a new Britain

Examiner's tip

i. Note that World War Two had both *short-term* and *long-term* effects on the British people.

ii. Make lists of key words for each heading shown in this chapter and think about which were the most important effects of the War on British people.

Lloyd George had promised to build a new Britain after 1918 'fit for heroes to live in.' He never did. During the Second World War, the Government deliberately planned the creation of a better Britain than the one in which many people had lived in the depressed 1930s. Plans were drawn up and policies were produced which were meant to ensure that, in peacetime, there would be full Employment, a National Health Service, Family Allowances, New Towns and adequate housing.

The most important, and best-selling document was the **Beveridge Report** (December 1942), which set out detailed policies for the attacks needed to destroy 'Five Evil Giants' (Fig. 13.2) WANT (or lack of family income), IGNORANCE (or lack of education), DISEASE (or lack of health care), SQUALOR (or poor housing) and IDLENESS (or unemployment). This was the basis for the post-war Welfare State. The most important war-time legislation was the **Butler Education Act** (1944), which abolished fee paying for secondary (grammar) schools, promised to raise the school leaving age to fifteen in 1947, and to 16 as soon as there were enough teachers to go around.

Fig. 13.2 A cartoon of the time depicting the 'Five Evil Giants'

Summary

1914–18

1 1914: War was welcomed by the public and politicians said there would be 'business as usual'.
2 1915–16: Politicians were forced to change their attitudes with the Munitions of War Act, Conscription and DORA.
3 Some Liberals opposed these laws. Conscientious objectors opposed the war and were harshly treated by the courts and most of the public.
4 Anti-war poetry was written by soldiers like Owen, Sassoon and Graves.
5 There were new working roles for women in industry and services.
6 Britain was greatly affected by air raids, U-Boat campaigns and rationing.
7 Rising living standards and increased union roles helped to raise hopes for a better post-war Britain.

1939–45

1 There were early preparations for war, e.g. conscription, ARP, gas masks.
2 There were increased government powers over industry, labour and raw materials.
3 Evacuees left the cities to avoid bombing in 1939, returned when there was no early bombing, and left again when bombing began.
4 Rationing of food, petrol, clothes and other goods began early in the war.
5 Blitzes on British cities and towns were followed by the later bombing of German towns and cities by British and US planes.
6 Firm policies for a new Britain were written by the Government, especially the Beveridge Report and Butler Act.

Quick questions

1914–18

1 Name:
   i) a poet who welcomed the war;
   ii) an anti-war poet.
2 Who was Prime minister in i) 1914; ii) 1916–18?

3 Who was the first Minister of Munitions in 1915?
4 When was the first Conscription Act brought in?
5 Name *two* German aircraft that bombed British towns in 1916 and 1917?
6 What was the aim of the Corn Production Act?

1939–45

1 What do the following initials stand for i) ARP; ii) DORA?
2 In which month and year did the British:
   i)   build the first air raid shelters;
   ii) declare war on Germany?
3 Who became Minister of Labour in May 1940?
4 Who became Minister of Aricraft Production in May 1940?
5 why were there fewer cars on the road after September 1939?
6 Name:
   i)   *two* British bombers, and
   ii) *two* US bombers used in attacks on German cities between 1942 and 1945.
7 Which report laid the basis for the post-war Welfare State?

Chapter 14
The United Nations Organisation

14.1 How the United Nations began

The United Nations Organisation was planned between 1941 and 1945. In August 1941 Roosevelt and Churchill signed the Atlantic Charter, which declared that basic human freedoms outlined by Roosevelt in his 'four freedoms' speech (see 12.10) had to be respected. Twenty-six nations signed the Washington Declaration (January 1942), which accepted the Atlantic Charter, and in November 1942 the Allied leaders at the Tehran Conference agreed to set up an international organisation at the end of the war.

At the Dumbarton Oaks Conference, Washington (August November 1944), the Allies agreed the framework for the United Nations Organisation. The leading allies agreed on the United Nations Charter and the organisation of the UN at Yalta (February 1945) (see 12.10). Representatives of 50 nations met in San Francisco (April 1945) to approve the Charter, setting out the aims, rules and structure of the United Nations. The Charter was signed in June 1945 and the United Nations Organisation formally began on 24 October 1945.

14.2 The aims of the United Nations Organisation

The founders of the UNO wanted to replace the League of Nations as a way of achieving world peace. The Charter stated that the peoples of the world were determined 'to save succeeding generations from the scourge of war, uphold human rights, establish justice and promote social and economic progress'.

- The founding members of the UNO agreed to work for world peace (Article 1 of the Charter).
- They stated that all peoples should have equal rights to self-determination, and there was to be no interference in the internal affairs of member states except to enforce measures approved by the Security Council (Article 2).
- In order to achieve world peace, UNO members agreed to increase co-operation between nations in cultural, economic and political matters .
- Members of the UNO could join together against aggression (Article 51). Regional organisations like NATO and the Warsaw Pact were set up under this Article (see 15.5).

14.3 The organisation of the United Nations

The United Nations Organisation has six main parts: the General Assembly, the Security Council, the Secretariat, the Economic and Social Council, the Trusteeship Council and the International Court of Justice. There are also many specialised agencies dealing with social and economic activities.

- The **General Assembly** contains all members of the UN. It normally meets in September, but holds emergency sessions if necessary. Its role is to debate and pass resolutions on political problems. All members have equal voting rights and membership has grown from 50 in 1945 to over 150 today. New members were mainly from Africa and Asia. The Assembly elects non-permanent members of the Security Council and members of other committees. The General Assembly passed the 'Uniting for Peace' resolution which gave it power over the Security Council if the council could not agree about the need for armed force (see 14.4)

- The **Security Council** has five permanent members: Britain, Russia, France, the USA and, from 1971, Communist China (see 16.3). Each of these states has a right of **veto** against decisions they do not support. Without a veto the USA and USSR may not have joined the UNO. The USSR **boycotted** the Council in 1950 when the USA refused to allow Mao's Communist China (see 22.10) to join the Council after the Communists drove out Chiang Kai-shek. During the Korean War (see 14.4) the USSR rejoined the Council.

  In 1945 six other members were elected by the General Assembly to the Security Council, but growing UN membership meant that from 1965 ten non-permanent members, representing the various geographical 'blocs' (e.g. Africa, Asia and Eastern Europe) were elected.

  Permanent members have the right of veto to protect their own interests. The Council has the power to raise an army, which it did in Korea (see 14.4), and impose **sanctions** against offending nations (see 23.6). The Council has the power to investigate problems around the world.

- The **Secretariat** is the UN's civil service. It runs the New York headquarters, implements the decisions of the Assembly and Council, and provides funds for the specialised agencies (see 14.5). The **Secretary General** is appointed by the General Assembly on the recommendation of the Security Council. The first Secretary was Trygve Lie of Norway, who supported UNO action against the USSR in Korea (see 14.4). After the Russians refused to support Lie, Dag Hammarskjold of Sweden became General Secretary. He played an important role in the Suez crisis of 1956 (see 25.4). After Hammarskjold's tragic death (see 14.4) U Thant of Burma became the new secretary, but was angered by failures to bring about peace by the time he was replaced in 1977 by Kurt Waldheim of Austria. Waldheim's Peruvian successor, Peres de Cuellar, also dealt with many difficult disputes. In 1996 the USA tried to remove de Cuellar's successor (Boutros Ghalli) because he had failed to solve disputes in Bosnia and other areas of the world.

- The **International Court of Justice** is the successor to the League of Nation's Permanent Court of Justice (see 5.4). Its 15 judges, who meet in the Hague, only have limited success because few states accept its decisions, so it has less power than the European Court of Justice (see 20.6). In 1966 the Court reversed its 1962 decision over the treatment by the South African Government of its territory in south west Africa.

Examiner's tip

Take care not to be confused between the different roles of the various UN organisations (14.3) and agencies (14.5).

14.4 Attempts of the UNO to keep the peace

The major obstacles to the UN's success have been the lack of troops to control vast areas of land, a shortage of funds, and often an unwillingness of enemies to come to terms.

The Korean War (1950–53) was the first major crisis for the UNO to solve. When South Korea had been invaded by Communist North Korea in June 1950, the Security Council met immediately and asked for the invasion to stop, and for the United Nations members to help stop the war. Two days later the USA sent troops to Korea and the UNO asked other members to do the same. Sixteen countries sent troops and 45 countries sent military aid. The American army, led by General MacArthur, dominated the UN forces. The USA wanted to stop the spread of communism in the Pacific.

In November 1950 the General Assembly passed the 'Uniting for Peace' resolution which stated that if the Security Council could not agree, then the General Assembly could recommend the use of armed force. The USSR had returned to the Security Council in August 1950 (see 14.3) so this resolution was needed to overturn the USSR veto.

After MacArthur's troops entered North Korea, China supported another North Korean invasion, threatening a nuclear war, with the USA fighting Russia and China. President Truman therefore decided to limit the war to containing communism, and in 1953 the new US President, Eisenhower, agreed to an armistice. Korea was divided North–South along the 38th parallel, as it had been before the war began. Both sides had lost 1½ million soldiers. Four million Korean civilians died.

The war had shown the dangers of world war, but also increased the authority of the UNO and the General Assembly, and increased support of member states for the USA's policy of opposing China having a Security Council seat. The USSR accused the UNO and the Secretary General, Lie, of being a tool of the USA.

The UNO was also split over the **Suez Crisis** (see Chapter 25), when the crisis was passed to the General Assembly under the Uniting for Peace resolution (see 14.3). The USA and USSR demanded the withdrawal of British and French troops, and Dag Hammarskjold drew up plans for a United Nations Emergency Force (UNEF) which remained a buffer between Israel and Egypt until 1967 (see 24.6). The Suez crisis also increased the authority of the United Nations and the power of its General Secretary, Dag Hammarskjold. His skills of diplomacy led to the phrase 'Leave it to Dag'.

When Belgium gave independence to the **Congo** (June 1960) **civil war** broke out immediately, so Belgian troops returned. Hammarskjold called a meeting of the Security Council which agreed a resolution to create a UN army, whose task was to restore order and help the Belgians leave the Congo. Three thousand UN troops arrived, but Hammarskjold refused to allow them to attack the province of Katanga which had broken away from the Congo. The Congo's President, Lumumbaba, asked for the help of the USSR which demanded Hammarskjold's resignation, but the smaller nations supported him and the USSR withdrew its demand.

Hammarskjold believed that the Congo was a potential battleground between East and West, as well as between different groups in the Congo. Twenty thousand UN troops were used to keep the peace and help with administration and medical and food supplies. In July 1961 Hammarskjold arranged a meeting between the different groups in the Congo, and in September 1961 UN troops entered Katanga. Hammarskjold was killed in an aircrash while on his way to Katanga and replaced by U Thant (see 14.3).

By 1962 UN operations against Katanga were successful, and in 1964 the UN forces left the Congo. In 1970 the Congo was renamed Zaire, led by President Mobutu who had defeated the Katangese rebels and white mercenaries.

14.5 The agencies of the United Nations Organisation

- The **International Labour Organisation** (ILO) began under the League of Nations and has produced agreements on working conditions, paid holidays, minimum wages and training schemes (see 5.2). The ILO Assembly meets every year at Geneva, where governments send two delegates, and trade unions and employers send one delegate.

Examiner's tip

Be ready to explain whether or not the UN was a success. Revise for this question by making a list of successes and failures with reasons for these successes and failures.

- The **Food and Agricultural Organisation** (FAO) has its headquarters in Rome. It is mainly concerned with world food supplies and agricultural development. The FAO has helped developing nations in the Third World with emergency projects and new programmes, such as irrigation and development of crops.
- The **Educational, Scientific and Cultural Organisation (UNESCO)** is based in Paris and its aim is to help the people of member states to reach minimum levels of literacy and numeracy. Through international educational exchanges UNESCO hopes to foster international understanding.
- The **International Monetary Fund (IMF)** was set up at Bretton Woods to promote world trade and give member states financial aid with balance of payments problems. The IMF also advises states about economic policies. Member states put their own money into the Fund and may draw out four times that amount in gold when in financial trouble.
- The **World Health Organisation (WHO)** has provided medical staff, drugs and medical equipment to member states suffering epidemics. The WHO has also helped to spread knowledge about health and medicine to prevent the spread of disease. It has worked closely with the **United Nations Children's Fund (UNICEF)**to promote the health of children in developing countries.

14.6 Peacekeeping by the UNO in the 1990s

The **Gulf War** (1990–91) began when Saddam Hussein ordered the Iraqi army to invade Kuwait, claiming it as an Iraqi province. The UN Security Council passed a resolution calling for Iraq's withdrawal and when Saddam refused, the UN (mainly USA) forces invaded Kuwait and expelled Iraq's forces. The USSR supported the USA in the UN debates, which she would not have done before her defeat in the cold war (see 16.7–9).

When Iraqi forces left Kuwait the war ended, since Muslim member states would not have supported an invasion of Iraq. Trade **sanctions** against Iraq imposed by the UN remained in place in May 1996 because Iraq has not fully complied with UN demands on Iraq to destroy its nuclear and chemical weapons factories.

The UN was not willing or able to stop Saddam's cruel persecution of the Kurds or to punish him for war crimes. The human and financial cost of war, and lack of support among Iraq's neighbours for a new war were the main reasons. The USSR, which supported the USA in the war over Kuwait, also opposed continued fighting in Iraq.

The UN had many difficulties in stopping the **Yugoslavian civil war**, which began after the fall of the Communist Government in 1990 (see 19.6). The war was fought between the mainly Catholic Croats, the mainly Muslim Bosnians and the Orthodox Serbs. These national groups demanded the right to have their own state, and were guilty of massacres of minority races in their territory ('ethnic cleansing'). The Cyrus Vance–David Owen peace plan, agreed by the UNO, failed to win the agreement of all three sides who each demanded more territory.

A peace agreement was signed between the three warring factions in 1995 after the USA committed troops to the United Nations Peacekeeping Force. Yugoslavia was divided on ethnic lines.

14.7 Problems caused by the United Nations Aid policies

Although the UNO agencies have done much valuable work, some of the aid provided to the Third World has caused more problems to the people of these poorer states. Many countries providing aid have insisted that the recipient country spends money on the donor country's military weapons or other goods. Much of the aid has been spent on wasteful 'glamorous' projects such as sports stadia. There have also been cases of western international companies interfering in the political affairs of the country, such as in Latin America. Aid has also sometimes discouraged countries from adopting self-help projects and becoming independent.

14.8 Comparison between the UNO and the League of Nations

There are several differences between the UNO and the League of Nations. The aims of the UNO and the League differ in that the UNO's aims are wider than the mainly political aims of the League. The USSR and the USA were founding members of the UNO, but the USA did not belong to the League of Nations, and the USSR did not join until 1934. No member of the General Assembly has the veto in the UNO, unlike in the League. The UNO's Security Council is in permanent session, while under the League it was called only in emergencies. The League had no power to raise an army to stop aggression, while the UNO has. The UNO has become more representative of world opinion than the League was, as the 'new' nations are included in the UNO, e.g. countries from Africa and Asia following the break up of overseas empires. These new nations have been very keen to join the UNO because it gives them some influence and security .

There are similarities between the UNO and the League. The aims of both organisations are about the keeping of world peace. The different organisations of the UNO (see 14.3) are similar to those of the League (see Fig. 5.1) The ILO was begun under the League of Nations. The International Court of Justice is almost identical to the League's Court of Justice.

Summary

1 The Allied nations planned the UNO between 1941 and 1945 so that the world would be peaceful after the war ended.
2 The Atlantic Charter, signed by Churchill and Roosevelt, declared the 'four freedoms' which had to be respected.
3 The Washington Declaration (1942) accepted the Charter, and the Washington conference (1944) set up the framework for the UNO.
4 The UNO Charter was agreed at Yalta and approved formally at the San Francisco Conference (April 1945).
5 NATO and the Warsaw Pact were set up under the terms of the Charter.
6 The UN's Charter aimed to establish world peace by encouraging co-operation and respect between nations.
7 The General Assembly includes representatives from all nations in the UNO, but the Security Council has five permanent members and ten elected members.
8 There are many agencies within the UNO dealing with children, refugees, agriculture, economic development and education.
9 The UN be came involved in the Korean War (1950–53) to stop the Communist takeover of South Korea, in the Suez Crisis (1956) to bring peace between Israel and Egypt, and in the Congo (1960–62) to help end the civil war.
10 During the 1990s the UN supported war to expel Saddam Hussein's Iraqi army from Kuwait, and the UN also worked hard to bring peace between the warring nations of former Yugoslavia.
11 There are many similarities and differences between the UNO and the League of Nations, but the UN is organised differently to the League, and has been more successful.

Quick questions

1 Between which years was the United Nations Organisation planned?
2 Name the politicians who signed the Atlantic Charter.
3 In which year did the Washington Conference set up the framework of the UNO?
4 Where was the UN Charter finally approved?
5 Name the *two* alliances set up under the terms of the UN Charter.
6 How many permanent members are there in the Security Council?
7 Name *two* groups of people who are helped by the UN.
8 Between which years was the Korean War fought?
9 In which year was there a crisis over the Suez Canal?
10 Name the organisation which the UNO replaced.

Chapter 15
International relations 1945–64

15.1 Uneasy Allies: February–August 1945

The cartoon (Fig. 15.1) appeared during the Yalta Conference (see 12.10). There, the three Allied leaders had agreed on how to deal with the world once the war was over. They had, for example, agreed that the peoples of the countries 'liberated' from the Germans would have the right to hold 'fair and free elections', and to choose the constitution they wanted for their various countries.

That was in February 1945. The next, and last Allied leaders' summit was at Potsdam (see 12.9) in July–August 1945. By then Soviet Union troops had driven the Germans from Eastern Europe (see 12.6 and 19.1) and had imposed USSR-controlled governments on each of the liberated countries.

On 4 June 1945, before the Potsdam conference, Churchill had sent a telegram to the new US President, Truman, in which he asked: 'What is to happen about Russia? An iron curtain is drawn down upon their front. We do not know what is going on behind'. In March 1946 Churchill (no longer Prime Minister) gave a speech at a College in Fulton, Missouri, USA in which he said: 'From Stettin in the Baltic to Trieste in the Adriatic, an iron curtain has descended across the continent'. The former allies no longer trusted one another.

"AND HOW ARE WE FEELING TO-DAY?"

Fig. 15.1 A British cartoon from 1945

15.2 The Cold War

The hostile relationships between the USSR and the West after 1945 was described as a 'Cold War'. There was no declaration of war between the USA and the USSR. When

E **xaminer's tip**

In 1946 a US diplomat, George Kennan wrote from Moscow to warn Truman that Stalin's Russia was a ruthless tyranny menacing European freedom as Hitler had done. His letter led to a change in US policy, to his becoming an advisor to Truman, and to the Truman Doctrine (see 15.3). Communist supporters in the West saw his letter as the start of the Cold War.

they did fight, as in Korea in 1950–53 (see 14.4) they did so under 'assumed titles'. There was no real peace. The struggle between the two superpowers was carried on by the build up of armed forces, by **propaganda** inside and outside their own countries, and by trying to win support in neutral countries by offering economic and military aid to their 'friends'. In Chapter 19 we will see why Stalin felt that the USSR had to have control of eastern Europe (19.1) and why he was suspicious of western countries.

Western statesmen had their own suspicions about the USSR's ambitions. They knew that in 1848 Karl Marx had called on 'workers of the world (to) unite' and to overthrow capitalism. They knew that this idea of world revolution was backed by the Communist International (Comintern), which was run by Stalin's henchman, Zhdanov, until 1943. They feared that the USSR's takeover of eastern Europe was only a first step towards the conquest of the rest of Europe. They saw the USSR's support for Mao Tse-tung (see 22.6) as evidence of USSR ambitions to takeover Asia where, later, the USSR did support communist uprisings in Malaya and Singapore, Indonesia and Korea (see 14.4).

15.3 1947: a critical year

In 1946–7 a civil war was fought in Greece between British-supported troops of the Greek King and USSR-backed communist guerrillas. In February 1947 Britain decided she could no longer afford to fight this war and she asked the USA to step in. In March 1947 Truman explained why the USA was going to spend 4 billion dollars to send troops and aid to Greece. This so-called 'Truman Doctrine' was a sign that the USA would not have a policy of 'isolationism' as it had done in the 1920s (see 9.9). US policy was one of 'containment', to stop the advance of communism.

Britain's withdrawal from Greece and from Palestine (see 24.3) was only one sign of Europe's poverty in 1947. All European countries were struggling to recover from the war and to solve serious economic problems. The US Secretary of State (or Foreign Minister) Marshall feared that this poverty would encourage the growth of Communism in Europe. In June 1947 he offered US economic aid to European countries, including the USSR and its **satellites** in Eastern Europe.

Western European states united to apply for this 'Marshall Aid'. Stalin rejected it, claiming that it was a US attempt to interfere in the USSR's affairs. Zhdanov described the Truman Doctrine and the Marshall Plan as the 'twin forks of US **imperialism**'.

15.4 The Cold War becomes even cooler, 1948–9

In 1947 the USSR set up the **Cominform** to control the activities of Communist Parties throughout Eastern Europe, and to ensure the USSR's grip on that 'empire'. Its first important decision (June 1948) was to agree the expulsion of Yugoslavia from Cominform, and the condemnation of Tito, who had refused to accept Stalin's orders on how to run Yugoslavia, which then got aid from the USA, Britain and France.

By this time Stalin's men had taken control of Czechoslovakia (see 19.2). This 'push to the west' extended the **'iron curtain'** beyond its 1945–6 limits and increased western fears of the USSR's ambitions.

Those fears were deepened by the events of 1948–9 involving Berlin. As part of the post-war settlement, Germany had been divided into four zones of occupation, one controlled by each of the Allies – the USSR, the USA, France and Britain. The old capital, Berlin, well inside the USSR zone, was also divided into four zones, with the western Allies having road, rail and air links with their Berlin zones.

In June 1948 the USSR announced that it was closing all the road and rail links between Berlin and the western zones of Germany. Stalin was frightened that the western zones of Germany (and of Berlin) would be rebuilt with Marshall Aid and would become, again, a threat to the USSR.

By blocking access to Berlin, Stalin hoped to force the British, French and the USA out of west Berlin, which depended on supplies from the West for food and, most importantly, for fuel. The western allies organised a massive airlift in which hundreds of planes landed in the three western airfields in Berlin, bringing the essential supplies.

In May 1949 the USSR admitted defeat and reopened the roads and railways. Later in 1949 the three western zones were joined to form West Germany, and the USSR-controlled zone became East Germany.

15.5 Two new alliances

The takeover of Czechoslovakia and the blockade of Berlin made European leaders fear a future USSR advance to the west. They knew that their small armies (totalling 12 divisions) could not expect to hold off the USSR's 250 divisions. US leaders shared those fears, so in April 1949 they helped set up the **North Atlantic Treaty Organisation (NATO)**, in which Britain, France, Belgium, Holland and Luxemburg ('the Brussels Powers') were joined by the USA, Canada, Norway, Iceland, Denmark, Italy and Portugal. Later they were joined by Greece and Turkey (1952) and West Germany (1955). Forces from all these countries came under the command of a NATO supreme commander, the first of whom was US General Eisenhower. Other national leaders commanded NATO fleets and air forces.

In 1955, Russia, alarmed that West Germany had joined NATO, set up its own similar zone, called the **Warsaw Pact**, which provided for a unified military command of the forces of Albania, Bulgaria, Czechoslovakia, East Germany, Hungary, Poland, Rumania and the USSR. Each country agreed to help any other that came under armed attack.

15.6 A new attitude? 1953–56

The death of Stalin (March 1953) and the coming of a new US President (Eisenhower) in January 1953 led to an easing of the tensions between the two superpowers. One immediate sign of this was the signing of the **armistice** in Korea in July 1953 (see 14.4).

Other signs of this 'thaw' in East-West relations were conferences held at Geneva. One (July 1954) saw the Foreign Ministers of France, Britain, the USA, the USSR and China agreeing on the ending of French involvement in Indo-China, and the creation of two new states: North and South Vietnam (see 17.3).

A second **Geneva Conference** (July 1955) was a 'summit' meeting where President Eisenhower met the Soviet leaders, Khrushchev and Bulganin, and the British and French Prime Ministers. These leaders sought a relaxation of Cold War 'tensions', agreed on a series of cultural exchanges between east and west, and agreed that various countries had different and particular problems, especially in the Far East. This summit raised hopes that 'the spirit of Geneva' (peaceful talks rather than military threats) would enable leaders to provide a better world.

In January 1956, Khrushchev, on his way to becoming the real ruler of the USSR, spoke to the Twentieth Party Congress in Moscow. In this speech he attacked the policies of the dead Stalin and, in doing so, helped unleash great unrest in Eastern Europe (see 19.4). Khrushchev also called for **'peaceful coexistence'** between east and west: communism and capitalism would still compete for world control, but would avoid war, because (with nuclear weapons) war would be suicidal. While this angered the Chinese leaders, it suggested to western leaders that the Cold War might be coming to an end.

15.7 Crises and conferences, 1960–61

Examiner's tip

Note the changing relationships between the USSR and the western nations 1953–1964 and the reasons for these changes. Relations improved 1953–60 and worsened 1960–64.

The division of Germany and of Berlin continued to provide a problem for leaders of the East and the West. Many Germans hoped that their country would be unified one day: Some even called for militant action by the West to 'regain' the east. The USSR, for its part, was frightened that a united Germany would, as in the past, be a threat to Soviet safety. Meanwhile, the people of East Germany and of East Berlin were envious of the much higher living standards enjoyed by West Germans, and the USSR feared that this envy might lead them to rebel against their communist masters.

In September 1959 Khrushchev met President Eisenhower at the President's summer 'retreat', Camp David, where he withdrew a threat he had made that the US would be driven from West Berlin. This meeting led to another Summit which was held in Paris (May 1960), where Khrushchev hoped to get the US to agree that the USSR could sign a separate peace treaty with East Germany.

The Summit broke up in disorder. The USSR had shot down a USA U-2 **'spy plane'** which was photographing Soviet military bases. Khrushchev asked Eisenhower to apologise for using such planes for spying. Eisenhower refused to do so, and Khrushchev left the Conference in a great rage.

In June 1961 Khrushchev held another Summit, this time with the new and young President Kennedy. At this **Vienna Summit**, Khrushchev renewed his threat to the US presence in Berlin and said that the US had six months in which to withdraw its forces from Berlin. Kennedy refused to bow to the threat.

This was followed by the building of the Berlin Wall (see 17.1) and an increase in tension. In October 1961 ten Soviet tanks turned their guns on ten US tanks, facing them across one of the crossing points between East and West Berlin. Fortunately nothing happened.

15.8 The fall of Khrushchev, 1964

In October 1962, Khrushchev's Cuban policy brought the world to the brink of war (see 17.2). His retreat in the face of Kennedy's firmness increased criticism of his policies by the Chinese and communists in the USSR.

He had failed to get the West to sign a treaty and recognise East Germany. He had not built up the economy as he had promised he would. In October 1964 while he was away from Moscow on holiday, the Communist Party's ruling body (the Praesidium) agreed to dismiss Khrushchev from all his posts (see 18.4). He was succeeded by Kosygin as Prime Minister, and by Brezhnev as Party Secretary. Brezhnev became the real ruler of the USSR and brought about an increase in tensions between East and West (see 16.1).

Summary

1 Stalin ignored the decisions made at Yalta and Potsdam and imposed communist governments on eastern European states.
2 Western governments feared USSR policy 1945–53.
3 The 'Truman Doctrine' and the Marshall Aid plan were important US policies to save western Europe from communism.
4 Stalin imposed a blockade of Berlin in 1948 which was broken by the Allies.
5 There was a thaw in the 'Cold War' in 1953, seen by the end of the Korean War and the Geneva Conferences.

6 Khrushchev called for 'peaceful coexistence' with the West in 1956.
7 Germany and Berlin were 'flash points' of conflict between East and West.
8 The Summit Conferences of 1955, 1959, 1960 and 1961 had only limited success in bringing about good East–West relations.
9 The building of the Berlin Wall (1961) added to East–West tensions.
10 Khrushchev fell from power in the USSR after his failure to make the USSR more powerful than the USA.

Quick questions

1 Where were *two* conferences held in 1945 to discuss post-war Europe?
2 Name the only Allied leader to be at both Conferences.
3 When were the three Allied zones of Germany united?
4 Where and when did Churchill speak of 'the Iron Curtain'?
5 i) Who was the President of the USA in 1947?
   ii) Who was his Secretary of State?
6 Over which country did the USA make a stand against communism in 1947?
7 What do the initials NATO stand for?
8 What Pact did the USSR form in opposition to NATO?
9 What action did the USSR take in 1961 in Berlin which confirmed the idea of 'an Iron Curtain'?
10 i) Which country's future seemed to be settled at Geneva in 1954?
    ii) Which countries were at the 1954 Geneva Conference?
11 Who was President of the USA from 1953 to 1960?

Chapter 16
Towards détente 1964–95

16.1 Russian expansionism, 1964–82

Brezhnev, the real ruler of Russia during this period, said that 'the class struggle between the two systems (communism and capitalism) will be continued', a sign that he meant to keep an aggressive foreign policy.

USSR troops fought the Chinese along the Manchurian border after 1969. The USSR backed Ho Chi-Minh in his war against the US-backed South Vietnam in its struggle with Kampuchea. The USSR backed Cuban aid to rebels in Angola, and supplied troops and aid to the communist Government of Ethiopia, which gave the USSR a foothold on the strategically important Horn of Africa. The Soviet Union also backed Syria in her anti-Israel campaigns, and Saddam Hussein of Iraq in his anti-Iran campaigns.

16.2 The arms race, 1960–70

Even with the US forces as part of NATO forces in Europe, the USSR had overwhelming superiority in terms of men, tanks, aircraft and artillery. Europeans feared that a non-nuclear Third World War would see USSR forces sweeping through Germany, France and the Low Countries. Therefore, the USA concentrated on producing various forms of nuclear weapons and nuclear-carrying missiles. By 1967 the USA had over 1000 missiles of one sort or another, about three times as many as the USSR had. This did not help the USA in the Vietnam war (see 17.3).

In 1967 the USSR expanded her output of nuclear-carrying missiles, and by 1969 had as many as the USA. This led to talk of 'Mutual Assured Destruction' (or MAD) since each country could destroy the other while itself being destroyed. Both countries were also, by 1970, concerned at the cost of this arms race which led, in the USA to massive inflation, and in Russia to a continual shortage of consumer goods.

16.3 Nixon's new foreign policy, 1968–73

Richard Nixon had become known as a fervent anti-Communist in the early 1950s. As Eisenhower's Vice President he had played a minor part in earlier talks with the USSR (see 15.6 and 15.7), but when he became President (1968) most Americans expected him to have a hardline anti-Communist foreign policy. However, he surprised everyone.

- In 1971 he backed Communist China's claim to China's seat in the UN, then occupied by the Government of Taiwan (see 14.3).
- In 1971–2 he visited both China and the USSR, and so helped to make contact between officials who later brought about **détente**.
- In 1973 he ended US participation in the Vietnamese War (see 17.3) enabling the Communists to take control there.
- In May 1972 he signed the first **Strategic Arms Limitation Treaty** (SALT 1) by which the USSR and the USA agreed to reduce the number of anti-ballistic missiles they had, and to hold further talks aimed at further arms reduction.

16.4 Détente defined

Western statesmen believed that détente would come about because East and West have common interests (in improving people's living standards), and because increased contact between politicians would lead to improved understanding on both sides. They thought that arms reduction was an essential part of the process of détente, while trade and other agreements would forge links between the two sides.

Brezhnev, on the other hand, welcomed the lessening of tension and of the risk of war, but he insisted on keeping up the struggle between 'the two systems' (see 16.1). He welcomed the trade, cultural and other links with the West: the flow of US grain helped avert a famine in Russia; German technology and western capital allowed for the partial modernisation of some Russian industry. However, he rejected the western idea that the West had the right to comment critically on the USSR's internal policies, including its harsh treatment of Jews and of dissidents who opposed Communist rule. Those matters, he said, were nothing to do with the West.

xaminer's tip

Study carefully the policies of Brezhnev's USSR and Nixon's USA. Note the fact that these policies *changed* during the period and the reasons for these changes.

16.5 A more peaceful Europe, 1972–75

In 1972 West Germany signed treaties with the USSR and Poland, which accepted the loss of former German territory to post-war Poland.

Following the signing of the SALT 1 agreements (see 16.3), delegates from the USA, Canada and 33 European states, including the USSR, met at Helsinki. They negotiated the **Helsinki Agreement** (August 1975) which recognised USSR control of Eastern Europe, and ended West Germany's claim to be the only German state (so recognising the existence of East Germany for the first time). The USSR made several agreements:
- to encourage more East-West tourism and to allow western journalists greater freedom when working in the USSR;
- to allow outside inspection of the USSR's records on the treatment of Jews and political dissidents – the inspectors were to be allowed to draw up records of the Government's ill-treatment of opponents.

In return the USA promised to continue to supply the USSR with wheat in return for USSR oil. Business backed détente.

16.6 SALT 2 and human rights

In January 1977 'Jimmy' Carter became US President. A well-meaning 'liberal', he hoped that the USSR would honour the Helsinki Agreement and would improve its record on human rights. Brezhnev replied that this was 'an attempt to interfere with our internal affairs': dissidents continued to be arrested and sent to concentration camps; Jews were still refused exit visas which they needed to emigrate to Israel. Carter chose to ignore the evidence of Brezhnev's hardline policies. Instead he agreed to a second round of SALT negotiations, which led to an agreement by both sides to limit the number of nuclear missiles each had. In 1979 the US Senate refused to ratify (approve) this Treaty, and called for the ending of wheat exports to the USSR. Carter ignored the Senate and called a halt to US rearmament policies, while allowing US farmers to sell their wheat to the USSR.

By the time of the US election, November 1980, many Americans believed that Brezhnev had made the USSR stronger than the USA for the following reasons:

- USSR rearmament went ahead. Better and larger missiles were produced while USA output was checked.
- The USSR gained control or great influence in Angola and Ethiopia.
- On Christmas Eve, 1977, Soviet troops invaded Afghanistan to support hardline rebels opposed to the existing Communist Government there.
- Carter's mild reaction was to call on USA athletes to **boycott** the 1980 Olympic Games which were to be held in Moscow.
- In 1979 the revolutionary Islamic Government of Iran seized the US Embassy in Tehran and held 50 American hostages for over a year. Carter tried economic **sanctions** against Iran, but this had no effect on a government that was prepared to let its oil industry rot rather than submit to the 'wicked West'. He also tried a military raid aimed at rescuing the hostages. Its dismal failure made the USA a laughing stock, and was the single most important reason for Carter's defeat in the election held in November 1980.

16.7 Reagan and the USSR, 1980–84

President Ronald Reagan (1981–8) changed the USA's arms policy. He ordered new, larger and more powerful missiles and missile-carrying weapons, a new heavy bomber and an improved Trident nuclear submarine.

He persuaded European governments to allow the installation of Cruise Missiles in their countries to face the recently installed powerful Soviet SS20 missiles. He discussed the possibilities of a computer-based **Strategic Defence Initiative** (SDI or 'Star Wars') aimed at destroying any missiles attacking the USA.

He also showed that he was prepared to adopt an aggressive foreign policy. In 1983 he ordered US troops into the British Commonwealth island of Grenada in the West Indies to help overthrow a Cuban supported Communist Government, and to restore a democratic one. In 1986 he ordered the bombing of Gadaffi's Libyan capital, Tripoli, as 'punishment' for Gadaffi's support of terrorism.

As a result of Reagan's rearming of western Europe, the USSR offered a reduction in their arms, but only if the Europeans agreed to the removal of the new US weapons. NATO offered a 'zero option', by which both sides would dismantle their short-range (or 'intermediate') missiles, while leaving alone the number of long-range (or 'intercontinental') missiles. The USSR leaders rejected this proposal.

16.8 Reagan and Gorbachev, 1985–88

Mikhail Gorbachev became 'ruler' of the USSR in 1985. He found that the USSR spent 25% more on weapons and defence systems than the USA, while her people had a Third World standard of housing, health, transport and living standards in general (see 18.5).

Reagan and Gorbachev met in Geneva (November 1985) and Iceland (1987) but failed to reach agreement. Gorbachev threatened to match US spending on 'Star Wars' and threatened no further meetings unless the USA halted its SDI ('Star Wars') spending. Reagan refused to halt SDI.

However, the harsh reality of the USSR's economic condition, and Reagan's refusal to give in to the USSR's threats, led to a third Summit in Washington (December 1988) and an agreement by which the USSR withdrew 5000 tanks from Eastern Europe and another 5000 from western Russia. The USSR also withdrew 800 aircraft, 50,000 men and 85,000 pieces of artillery. This still left the Warsaw Pact states with twice as many tanks as NATO states, three times as much artillery and five times as many missiles.

Gorbachev also cut military spending outside the USSR. The USSR withdrew from Afghanistan ('Russia's Vietnam'), from Angola, Kampuchea and Eritrea where it had supported the Ethiopians against the Eritrean nationalist rebels.

Examiner's tip

i. Students often get confused about the meaning of terms such as Détente, the Helsinki Agreement, SALT 2 and SDI. Take care with revision on these topics.

ii. You will find it useful to make a timeline showing the fast-changing events of 1977–1991.

iii. Be ready to show the examiner that you realise that there were times of great east–west tension (1977–1986) followed by more understanding.

iv. Study carefully the reasons for these changes and the roles of Gorbachev, Bush and Reagan.

16.9 More arms reductions, 1989–95

President Bush succeeded Reagan in January 1989. Bush negotiated with Gorbachev (until Gorbachev fell from power in December 1991), and then with Yeltsin who succeeded him (see 18.6). Bush benefited from the collapse of the USSR and of Communism in Eastern Europe. He was able to get agreements for much wider and deeper arms cuts than had previously seemed possible.

Nuclear stocks in the USA and USSR were partially dismantled, which the **Campaign for Nuclear Disarmament (CND)** had campaigned for in vain. Both sides removed missiles from central Europe, and the USA withdrew Cruise Missiles from Britain. The Cold War had ended at last.

Summary

1 Brezhnev followed an aggressive foreign policy in Manchuria, Vietnam, Angola, Ethiopia, Syria and Iraq.

2 The USSR's superiority in conventional (non-nuclear) weapons led the USA to seek nuclear superiority.

3 The arms race was very costly to the USA and the USSR.

4 Nixon searched for peace with China, the USSR and Vietnam.

5 Détente and lessening tensions led to increased trade, cultural and other contacts and, the USA hoped, a better deal for Russian Jews and other political dissidents.

6 The Helsinki Agreements (1972–5) saw the settlement of the eastern borders, and Soviet agreement to improve human rights.

7 Carter made vain attempts to persuade the USSR to accept the need to improve her human rights record.

8 SALT 1 and SALT 2 saw the USSR gain nuclear equality with the USA. The USSR also gained greater influence in Africa, Afghanistan and Iran (1977–80).

9 President Reagan adopted a more vigorous policy on American arms, Libya and Grenada.

10 Gorbachev and Yeltsin agreed to Russian disarmament because of her economic and social collapse. They made agreements with American President Bush on massive reductions in nuclear and conventional forces.

Quick questions

1 Who was in charge of Soviet policy in i) 1964–82; ii) 1985–91; iii) 1991–95?
2 Name i) *two* African and ii) *two* Arab states where Soviet influence grew in the 1960s and 1970s.
3 Why did the USA feel that it had to have nuclear superiority over the USSR in the 1960s?
4 What do the initials MAD stand for?
5 Name *two* countries visited by Nixon in 1971–2.
6 What do the initials SALT stand for?
7 What did i) Russia and ii) western countries hope to gain by signing the Helsinki Agreements of 1975?
8 Who was the President of the USA in i) 1977–80; ii) 1981–8; iii) 1989–92?
9 What do the initials SDI stand for?
10 Where were the hostages held prisoners in 1979–80?

Chapter 17

Three international case studies

17.1 The Berlin Wall, 1961–89

E xaminer's tip

Study carefully the reasons why the status of West Berlin was important to both the USA and the USSR.

Khrushchev was anxious to get the western countries to recognise East Germany as an independent state and to end their control of West Berlin. This would have allowed an East Germany government to end travel from West Berlin to West Germany, and so end the flow of millions of refugees from East Germany to the West via West Berlin, which created a labour shortage in east Germany.

In 1958–9, 1960 and 1961 Khrushchev tried to get Eisenhower and, later, Kennedy to accept the need to leave Berlin, threatening that if they did not it might lead to war (see 15.1). These threats led to an increase in the number of refugees.

After the failure of the Kennedy-Khrushchev Summit in June 1961 (see 15.7), Khrushchev planned the building of the Berlin Wall. On 13 August 1961 two divisions of Soviet tanks were ordered to prepare to combat resistance in East Germany. Truckloads of East German Police (Vopos) lined the boundary between the Soviet and Allied zones of Berlin. On 17 August workmen began to build a wall across Berlin, giving the 'iron curtain' (see 15.1) a physical force.

Berlin was a symbol of the Cold War (see 15.4 and 17.1) and, in 1989, a major outward sign (in the pulling down of the Wall) of both the end of that War and of Communism.

About 60,000 East Berliners lost the jobs they had had in West Berlin. The flood of refugees was halted and the few who tried to escape had to take great risks. Many were killed in the attempts. The wall remained a symbol of the Cold War. Its destruction on 10 November 1989 was one outward sign of the collapse of the Communist system in East Germany and in Western Europe generally (see 19.6). After this, many thousands of refugees moved freely into West Berlin, and so on into West Germany. This was, for the refugees, the symbol of the triumph of capitalism over Communism.

17.2 The Berlin Wall – a case study

Study the Introduction and Sources A to E and then answer *all* parts of the question.

Introduction

'In 1945, when the Second World War had ended, Germany and Berlin were divided. After this the Superpowers often argued about Berlin. The most serious dispute was the blockade and airlift of 1948–49. Twelve years later, on 13 August 1961, a wall was built to separate West Berlin from the German Democratic Republic (East Germany).'

Source A

'The Western powers use West Berlin as a centre of activities aimed against the German Democratic Republic. There are more centres of spying in West Berlin than anywhere else in the world. These centres smuggle their agents into the German Democratic Republic. Their job is to commit sabotage, to recruit spies and to set up disturbances.

The government's plans will stop all this activity. Effective control will be established around West Berlin including its border with democratic Berlin. Protecting ourselves will contribute to peace.'

> From a statement made on 10 August 1961 by the
> Government of the German Democratic Republic.

A British cartoon drawn by Ronald Searle in late August 1961.
At this time American, Soviet and British representatives
were meeting to discuss nuclear disarmament.

Source C

East Germany and the Soviet Union thought of West Berlin as an island of Western influence. Most important of all, it was an exit to the west. East Germans took full advantage.

For twelve years, from 1949 to 1961, they escaped at the rate of 20 000 a month. This showed how bad the East German system was. It was also a drain on East Germany's economy and had to be stopped.

In early August 1961 Warsaw pact leaders met in Moscow, Krushchev, the Soviet leader, agreed to the East German demand to close the border.'

From *The Coming of the Wall*, (1969) by John Mann, a British historian.

Source D

A photograph of the Berlin Wall, taken in about 1967.

Source E

When the East Germans built the Berlin Wall in 1961, they claimed that by closing the Berlin border they had saved the peace. It happened at the time of Nikita Khrushchev. A rush of people to the West was threatening to cause the collapse of the East German state. That collapse would have brought the two Superpowers into violent collision.'

From an article by Neil Ascherson in *The Independent*, a British Newspaper, (10 November 1989).

E xaminer's tip

Remember to give *balanced* answers in document questions. Give your view, but weigh up both sets of arguments.

To answer the questions, use the information given in 17.1 and Sources. In your answers, you should refer to the Sources by their letters.

(a) The Berlin Wall was built soon after the East German government made the statement in Source A. Does this statement prove that the East German government had good reasons for building the Wall? Explain your answer (6)

(b) 'As Source B was drawn at the time of the Berlin Crisis of 1961, it is very useful as evidence.' Do you agree or disagree with this statement? Explain your answer. (5)

(c) In Source C John Mann says the Wall was built to stop East Germans escaping to the West. Does the photograph, Source D, prove that he was right? Explain your answer. (5)

(d) 'Source E was written 28 years after the Berlin Crisis of 1961. Therefore it is more reliable than source C.' Do you agree or disagree with this statement? Explain your answer. (6)

(e) In Source A the East German government claimed that the building of the Berlin Wall would 'contribute to peace'. Does the evidence of the Introduction and Sources B, C, D and E support this East German claim? Explain your answer. (8)

For suggestions on answers see page 196. *SEG 1993*

17.3 The Cuban Crisis, 1962

In 1958 Fidel Castro's small band of guerillas overthrew the US-backed government of Cuba and attacked US-owned capitalist enterprises which Castro blamed for the inequalities in Cuban life.

The US Government refused to recognise Castro's Government and refused to trade with Cuba, from which she had previously bought most of the sugar crop. The US took in and supported anti-Castro refugees. Castro then took over (nationalised) more US investment in Cuba.

The USSR bought the sugar crop and became Castro's major supporter. The USSR, Castro and the USA saw the new Government as a model Communist government in the Caribbean, which other Latin American countries might imitate by setting up Communist and anti-US governments.

In April 1961 the new US President, Kennedy, allowed a US-supported invasion of Cuba by anti-Castro Cuban refugees based in Florida. This **'Bay of Pigs'** invasion was a disaster, which increased US hostility while encouraging Castro's supporters.

The Bay of Pigs (April 1961) (the Bahia de Cochinos) saw 1500 anti-Castro men failing to win local support and being quickly overrun by Cuban forces. Kennedy had just come to office and felt that he had to let this planned invasion go ahead.

In October 1962 US **'spy planes'** brought back photographs showing that there were USSR missiles based in Cuba. Kennedy announced a naval blockade meant to prevent further USSR shipments to Cuba. He also demanded that the missiles be removed from Cuba. He said that if a missile were launched, the US would retaliate: the Cold War got very hot. Khrushchev claimed that the missiles were meant to defend Cuba and not to threaten the USA. He claimed that they were no different to the US missiles based in Turkey. Kennedy rejected this argument. He put the US air force and the fleet of Polaris nuclear submarines on to a war footing. As a USSR convey sailed towards Cuba (22–28 October 1962) people did not know whether it would challenge the US blockade and risk nuclear war, or whether the USSR convoy would turn back.

On 28 October Khrushchev ordered the ships to turn round, except for an oil-tanker which Kennedy decided could be let through. Khrushchev then announced that the missiles would be removed from Cuba. Kennedy promised that the USA would never invade Cuba.

17.4 The Cuban Crisis – a case study

Study sources A, B, C and D and answer the following questions.

Look at Source A.

(a) Does Source A fully explain why President Kennedy opposed the setting up of military bases on Cuba by the USSR? Use the source *and your own knowledge* to explain your answer.

Study Sources B and C and *use your own knowledge.*

(b) These two sources give different interpretations of the result of the Cuban Crisis. Why do you think they differ in this way?

Study Source D and use your own knowledge.

(c) How accurate is the view of the Cuban Crisis shown in Source D?

Source A

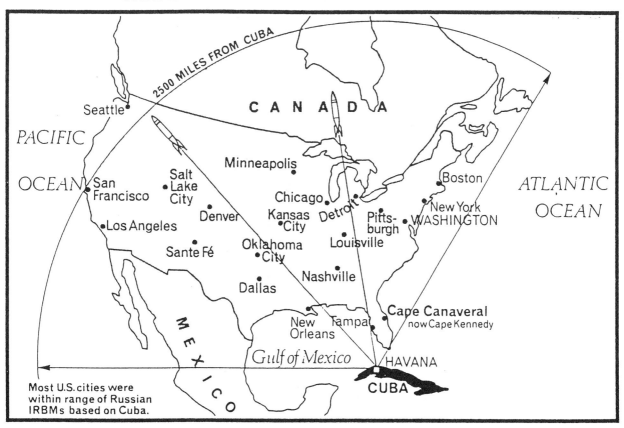

The range of Soviet missiles in Cuba.

Source B. A member of the American State Department writing in 1982 about events in 1962.

The Cuban Crisis was a real test for Kennedy. If he did nothing, then the Russians would finish the missile sites and have us at their mercy. If he attacked Cuba, he risked a nuclear war with Russia. But he did neither. He told Khrushchev that the US navy was going to blockade Cuba to stop any ships carrying weapons there. Luckily Khrushchev was as scared of nuclear war as we were and he agreed to do what President Kennedy wanted.

We were careful not to boast about our success and Khrushchev talked about a victory for common sense. But the whole world knew he had had to back down.

Source C. From '*Khrushchev Remembers*', the memoirs of the Soviet leader, Nikita Khrushchev.

I decided to install missiles with nuclear warheads in Cuba, without letting the United States find out they were there until it was too late to do anything about them. The missiles would stop the United States from taking military action against Cuba. The Americans had surrounded our country with military bases and threatened us with nuclear weapons, and now they would learn just what it feels like to have enemy missiles pointing at you.

We sent the Americans a note saying that we agreed to remove our missiles and bombers on condition that the President gives us his assurance that there would be no invasion of Cuba. Finally Kennedy gave in and agreed to make a statement giving us such an assurance. It was a great victory for us, a spectacular success without having to fire a single shot.

Source D. A cartoon published in 1962.

'Khrushchev and Kennedy engage in a trial of strength over the issue of Cuban missiles.'

For suggestions on answers see page 196.   *NEAB*

17.5 Vietnam, 1960–75

In 1954 the Geneva Agreement (see 15.6) ended the French effort to hold on to their empire in Indo-China. The former colonies of Laos and Cambodia were given their independence, while Vietnam was divided in two along the 17th parallel of latitude. The North was governed by a Communist Government led by Ho Chi-minh, while a government friendly to the West controlled the South. Hanoi became the capital of the North and Saigon became the capital of the South.

The Geneva Agreement said that elections were to be held in 1956 to choose a government for a united Vietnam, but the USA refused to sign this part of the Agreement, fearing that the Communists would win such an election. Eisenhower's Secretary of State (Foreign Minister) was Dulles. He had a Domino Theory – that if one state (e.g. Vietnam) became Communist-controlled, other neighbouring states would also fall under Communist control, perhaps from internal revolution, perhaps from external aggression.

The Vietcong forces were controlled by general Giap Vo Nguyen, a French-educated lawyer who had led the army which defeated the French (1945–54) and then forced the US to withdraw in 1973. He wrote *'People's War, People's Army'*, a book which became a textbook for revolutionaries.

So, from 1955 onwards the USA became involved in supporting the government of the South, which came under attack from a Communist organisation called the Vietcong based in the south. In 1957 the Vietcong (VC) started a guerrilla war against the Southern government. In this they were backed by aid and men from the North. At first US help consisted of a small number of military and technical advisers to the Government of the South.

However, under Kennedy (1961–63) and Johnson (1963–68) there was a rapid increase in the number of US soldiers and airmen taking part in a full-scale and terrible war against Vietnamese Communists, North and South. The Vietcong terrorised southern villagers and forced them to support the Communists. The US aircraft dropped high explosive bombs on towns in the North and on Vietcong bases in the South: more bombs were dropped in Vietnam than were dropped during the Second World War. Napalm (fire) bombs were used against people, and chemicals were used to destroy forests where the VC might be hiding and destroy crops on which they depended. Vast numbers of Vietnamese men, women and children were killed or maimed. To try to stop supplies reaching the VC from the North, US planes bombed trade routes in Cambodia, so extending the war.

The American people saw the horrors of the war on their television sets. By 1968 over half the American people – and well over half of the young people – opposed US participation in the war, and there were many protect marches and demonstrations. President Nixon (1968–1974) hoped that the South Vietnamese themselves would play an increasing role in the war against the Northern communists. But like Chiang's men in China in 1947–49 (see 7.10), they had little stomach for a fight. In January 1973 the USA and North Vietnam agreed a ceasefire: US troops were withdrawn, although fighting between Vietnamese forces continued. In May 1975 the VC forces took Saigon and created a united Vietnam which was admitted to the UNO in 1977.

17.6 Vietnam – a case study

Use the sources, and *your own knowledge*, to answer the following questions.

Study Sources A and B.

(a) *Use your own knowledge* and sources A and B to explain why the USA became involved in South Vietnam in the 1950s and 1960s. (6)

Study Sources C and D.

(b) These two sources suggest that there was widespread opposition to the Americans in Vietnam from the Vietnamese people. *Use your knowledge* and sources C and D to explain how reliable they are in helping you to understand the extent of this opposition. (9)

Study Sources E, F and G.

(c) How useful are sources E, F and G in helping you understand why there was opposition in the United States of America to the Vietnam War? *Use your own knowledge* of the events in Vietnam after 1954 to help you to answer the question. (10)

Study Source H.

(d) This source is an interpretation that tries to explain how and why President Nixon and Henry Kissinger brought the war in Vietnam to an end.

Use your own knowledge and source H to explain how far you agree with this interpretation. (10)

You should use *your own knowledge* to answer the following question.

(e) Why did the communists in Vietnam use guerrilla tactic in the Vietnam war? In giving your answer you may wish to use the following as a guide:

Imbalance of military forces
Theory of Guerrilla warfare
Guerrilla tactics, 1965–1973 (20)

Source A: From a US foreign policy statement in 1952.

'US foreign policy should prevent the countries of south-east Asia from passing into communist influence. It should assist them to develop the will and ability to resist communist and should help them to contribute to the strengthening of the free world.'

Source B: From President Johnson's message to Congress in August 1964.

'The threat to the free nations of south-east Asia has long been clear. The North Vietnamese government has constantly sought to take over South Vietnam and Laos . . . The USA will continue its basic policy of assisting free nations of the area to defend their freedom.'

Examiner's tip

Make a time line showing the key events in the three case studies of the Cold War. Note the periods of greater hostility and greater warmth between the Superpowers.

Examiner's tip

Students sometimes fail to use their own knowledge properly in document questions. Revise the key points carefully. You should show the examiner that you can compare what the sources, say, with what actually occurred.

Source C: From a North Vietnamese woodcut.

We will fight and fight from this generation to the next

Source D: From a speech made in 1964 by Pham Van Dong, the founder of the Vietminh.

'The US can go on increasing aid to South Vietnam. It can increase its own army personnel. I hate to see war go on, develop and intensify. Yet our people are determined to struggle . . . The struggle of our people exceeds the imagination.'

Source E: Graph showing the American people's opposition to the Vietnam War. The graph was taken from an American high School textbook.

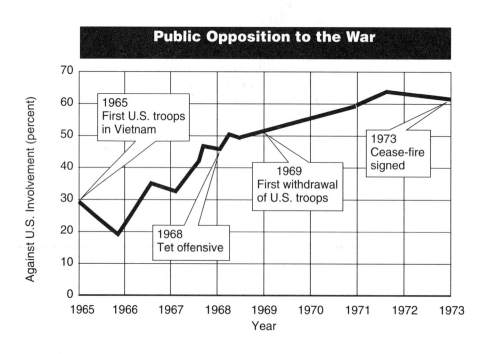

Source F: American students demonstrating against the war. The photograph was taken in 1967.

Source G: Photograph of a wounded American marine at the battle of Hue, 1968.

Source H: A modern historian's view of the end of the Vietnam War taken from a book written in 1979.

'The new President's way of ending the war involved secret negotiations between the North and Henry Kissinger, Nixon's chief advisor. These secret negotiations resulted in an agreement to end the war.

A few days before the Presidential election of November 1972 Kissinger announced that "peace was at hand" in Vietnam. Nixon didn't just win the election: he buried the Democratic candidate, George McGovern, in an electoral landslide.'

For suggestions on answers see page 197.   *NEAB*

Chapter 18
Russia 1953–95

18.1 Khrushchev succeeds Stalin

Stalin was succeeded by Khrushchev as Party Secretary, and Malenkov as Prime Minister. Khrushchev used his position to promote his own supporters to the Central Committee. After he criticised Khrushchev, Malenkov was replaced by Bulganin (1955) who in turn was dismissed in 1958. Khrushchev became Prime Minister while staying on as the Party Secretary. As supreme ruler Khrushchev wanted to modernise the USSR, but also to rule more humanely than Stalin had done (see Chapter 6).

18.2 De-Stalinisation

Between 1953 and 1956 the use of persecution and terror against innocent people was lessened: many prisoners were released; Beria, the head of Stalin's secret police was executed; the powers of the secret police were reduced; controls over writers and artists were loosened, and foreign tourists were allowed to visit the USSR.

At the **Twentieth Congress of the Communist Party** (February 1956), which western observers were allowed to attend, Khrushchev made a massive attack on Stalin and his methods of rule. He condemned Stalin for the murders of his rivals, and blamed Stalin for Kirov's death (see 6.9), and he said that many innocent communists had been tortured into making the show trial confessions. He said that Stalin's purges of the leaders of the armed forces led to the early defeats by Hitler (1941–2), and he condemned Stalin's self-glorification and misuse of power. Khrushchev also said that the USSR could live peacefully alongside the West. Other Party leaders also attacked Stalin. These speeches helped the USSR to become a freer country and the terror was ended. Statues of Stalin were removed.

18.3 Modernisation of industry and agriculture

Khrushchev realised that industry and agriculture were inefficient due to over centralisation under Stalin, so in 1957 he divided the USSR into regions with the power to plan their own industry. Factories were encouraged to make profits and change production to meet demand. Production of industrial goods rose.

More resources were devoted to consumer goods, because Khrushchev wanted living standards to rise so that the people would support Communism now that Stalin's terror policies had been ended.

Grain production rose from 82 million tons in 1953 to 147 million in 1962, but in 1963 production fell to 110 million and grain had to be bought from the USA.

Although Khrushchev tried to improve the agriculture by paying the collective farms higher prices and providing machines and fertilisers, the collective farms remained inefficient. The newly ploughed lands were infertile, farms were mismanaged and 40 million workers in the USSR produced less than 4 million in the USA. The small private plots of land produced much more than State collectives.

18.4 The Fall of Khrushchev 1964

xaminer's tip

You could revise this topic by making two lists showing the successes and failures of Khrushchev's government of the USSR, and the differences and similarities between Khrushchev's rule with Stalin's rule.

Opposition to Khrushchev within the Communist Party grew from about 1961 for many reasons. Food remained in short supply, so prices rose. He lost face in the 1962 Cuban missile crisis (see 17.2) and his quarrel with China (see 22.9) worried many. Khrushchev had been rude to many Party men who worried that he was becoming dictatorial. In October 1964 Khrushchev was sacked by the Central Committee (see 15.8) and was replaced by Kosygin as Prime Minister and by Brezhnev as Party Secretary. Between 1975 and 1982 Brezhnev led the USSR on his own.

Despite his faults, Khrushchev had left his country a better place than he had found it in 1953 in both the eyes of the world and of most Soviet citizens.

18.5 The decline of Communism in the USSR 1964–85

Russian industry and agriculture fell further behind the West every year. Kosygin and Brezhnev realised that the State-run firms had to improve workers' productivity and technology. Although bonus payments to efficient workers were introduced and modern machinery was imported from the USA and Germany, the economy did not really improve. Soviet people still suffered low living standards. People had to put up with long queues for food, poor housing and rising infant mortality. The primary diseases polio, diptheria, scarlet fever, measles and whooping cough were out of control in many areas. Many Communist Party leaders realised that the people of the USSR would not tolerate this for ever.

Defence spending was 25% higher than that of the USA, which enabled the USSR to control Eastern Europe (see Chapter 19) and to fight the Cold War (see Chapter 15), but there was not enough money to pay for improved technology in agriculture and industry. The USSR was ahead of NATO in the nuclear arms race in 1980.

There were continuing tensions with the western 'capitalist' states led by the USA:

- Brezhnev used force to keep Czechoslovakia under Soviet control, fearing the West would attack Eastern Europe (see Chapter 19).
- Angola and Afghanistan also fell under the USSR's influence (see 16.1).
- Western governments were angry that Brezhnev thought that the Helsinki agreement on Human Rights was just a scrap of paper (see 16.6).

Due to these tensions the USSR could not get the trade agreements that she needed to improve the people's living standards.

In the 1980s President Reagan of the USA (see Chapter 21), and Margaret Thatcher, the British Prime Minister, increased the West's nuclear spending to catch up with the USSR (see 16.7). When Mikhail Gorbachev became the Soviet President in 1985 (see 16.8) he realised that the USSR could not afford to continue the arms race and remain the enemy of the West.

The Government of the USSR was a group of old men who did not have the energy to deal with these serious long-term problems. Brezhnev had developed the 'cult of the personality' which had been favoured by Stalin and Khrushchev, and put his own cronies into positions of power. Government officials and managers of the State firms were often corrupt and incompetent. Writers and scientists like Solzhenitsyn and Sakharov who criticised the Government were imprisoned in psychiatric hospitals or exiled. This further increased the hostility of the west towards Soviet Communism. When Brezhnev died (1982), his two elderly successors, Andropov (1983–4) and Chernenko (1984–5) were unable to solve the problems of the communist system.

18.6 Mikhail Gorbachev and the collapse of Communism, 1985–90

Gorbachev had already visited the West before he was elected Party Secretary by the leading communists. He was determined to force the USSR to break from the past. He called for **'perestroika'** – restructuring of the economy to solve the problems described in 18.5, and **'glasnost'** – openness to new ideas. Agricultural reform was attempted by giving farm workers larger private plots on which they could grow food for sale in private markets. Some collective farms were broken up and tenants were given long leases. Five percent of land was privately owned, but produced 30% of the country's food, which showed that 'privatisation works'. Industrial managers were given more freedom to plan production and sell to local markets.

Corrupt and incompetent local and national leaders were sacked and replaced by young, ambitious and more able men. Gorbachev's new Constitution (1988) allowed elections at local level and election for his own post as President in 1993. In March 1989 the first free election to the Soviet Parliament resulted in a real opposition to Communist rule. A leading opponent of Communism, Andrei Sakharov, called on Gorbachev to increase the pace of reform by granting a democratic constitution and ending Communist Party control over the country, while at the same time privatising industry and reducing government spending. Sakharov warned that the army or hardline Communists could try to dismiss Gorbachev.

The Communist governments of Eastern Europe began to collapse between 1988 and 1990 (see 19.6) as the people realised that the 'liberal' Gorbachev would not send troops to crush their democratic and nationalist revolutions.

Millions of Soviet TV viewers watched the collapse of Communism abroad, and many of them thought that if the people of Poland, Czechoslovakia, East Germany and the Baltic States could have democracy, then so should the USSR. They also watched the debates in the new Soviet Parliament where anti-communist ideas were being debated.

Gorbachev realised that he needed to get support from the West for the Soviet economy, so he did not attempt to stop these movements for freedom. He also supported moves to reduce the nuclear arms race (see 16.8), since the USSR could not afford its defence spending and because Gorbachev appreciated, unlike his predecessors, that the West did not trust the USSR which had superiority in the number of nuclear arms.

Many Russian people also thought that Gorbachev should make more changes in the economy, which was continuing to fall further behind the West. Gorbachev's economic reforms had failed to improve living standards. Poor transport of food and other goods, malnutrition, inflation, strikes and failing factory machinery were getting increasingly worse.

Western governments were unwilling to provide much help until Communist Party control was ended, as Gorbachev discovered when he met the US President Bush and leaders of the European Union.

18.7 The fall of Gorbachev

Hardliners complained that 'glasnost' encouraged the republics of the USSR, such as the Ukraine, Georgia, Armenia and the Baltic States to try to break away from the

USSR, but Gorbachev realised that he could not force these republics to remain in the Soviet Union. In June 1990 Gorbachev proposed the ending of the USSR by calling for elections in the 15 republics, which Gorbachev hoped would stay together as the USSS (Union of Sovereign Soviet States). He wanted to keep foreign and defence policies under his control, but many republics did not want any control by Moscow.

Boris Yeltsin was elected as President of the Russian republic against Gorbachev's nominee. Yeltsin became the leader of those demanding total democracy. He had been elected to his position of President, but Gorbachev had not been elected to his position as Party Secretary. Yeltsin led the resistance to the attempt by some hardline Communists and army officers to remove Gorbachev and his 'liberal' government in August 1991. Gorbachev was kept prisioner in his holiday home. When he returned, Yeltsin demanded that he sign a decree abolishing the Communist Party's control of the USSS.

On 12 December 1991 Gorbachev resigned his position as Head of the USSS, when Yeltsin and Presidents of the Ukraine and Belorussia agreed to create the **Commonwealth of Independent States**. They called on the other former republics of the USSR to join the CIS.

Yeltsin accepted the advice of leading economists and introduced economic reforms such as cutting government spending, ending price controls and beginning the privatising of State farms and industry.

These reforms caused many hardships for Russian people, who suffered greater unemployment and hardship as the State withdrew subsidies for rents and inefficient factories. Many people wanted a return to Communist rule, while others argued that economic reforms should go further along the capitalist road. In 1995 the value of the rouble, the Russian currency, began to rise as some Russian firms became more efficient, and foreign companies began to invest in Russia.

Yeltsin struggled to control the racial groups within the Russian Republic who wished to break away from Moscow's control. The war with the mainly Muslim Cherchnaya was costly in money and human life.

In spite of these problems Yeltsin won the Presidential Election (May 1996) which showed that the Russian people accepted the need to abandon communism.

Examiner's tip

i. You will find it useful to revise the *reasons for* Gorbachev's fall and *the effects* of his fall.
ii. Be ready to explain whether or not Gorbachev was a successful leader of the USSR.

Summary

1 Stalin was replaced by Khrushchev as Party Secretary, and Malenkov as Prime Minister, but by 1958 Khrushchev was in control of the USSR.
2 At the 20th Party Congress Stalin was condemned by Khrushchev .
3 Khrushchev tried to modernise Soviet farming and industry by giving farms and factories greater freedom to plan their production.
4 Grain production rose under Khrushchev, but there were still food shortages and the State farms were badly mismanaged.
5 In October 1964 the Communist Party leaders dismissed Khrushchev, replacing him with Brezhnev.
6 The USSR continued to produce less food and industrial goods that the West, so the people suffered ill health and poverty under Communism.
7 Brezhnev tried to rule as a dictator, and his Government of old men became more corrupt.
8 When Gorbachev became leader of the USSR he started to modernise it with the ideas of 'perestroika' and 'glasnost'.
9 As the Communist states of Eastern Europe collapsed, the people of the USSR began to demand the fall of Communism in their country.
10 Gorbachev called elections for the 15 separate Soviet republics, and Yeltsin was elected as the Russian President.
11 Yeltsin brought many western-style market reforms to Russia, which caused much hardship, but by 1995 living standards for some people began to rise.
12 The CIS was formed, with the republics of the former USSR joining together as equal partners.

Quick questions

1 Who replaced Stalin as Communist Party Secretary in 1953?
2 At which Party Congress was Stalin condemned by Khrushchev?
3 Were the State farms badly managed under Khrushchev's rule?
4 Which part of the world did the USSR fall further behind industrially under Khrushchev?
5 Who replaced Khrushchev as Communist Party leader in 1964?
6 What sort of people were in charge of the USSR in Brezhnev's days?
7 When did Gorbachev become the leader of the USSR?
8 Write down *two* ideas which Gorbachev tried to implement in the USSR.
9 Who became the leader of the USSR after Gorbachev fell from power?
10 What organisation did the republics of the old USSR form?

Chapter 19
Eastern Europe 1945–95

19.1 Stalin's European Empire

Soviet troops freed most of Eastern Europe from the Germans in 1944–45. At Yalta (see 15.1) Stalin promised that Poland would get a 'free and independent government'. In March 1945, he invited the sixteen leaders of Poland's **guerrilla** army to Moscow where he imprisoned them. He then appointed a Moscow-trained henchman, Gomulka, to form a government. Much the same was done in Rumania, Bulgaria and Hungary, in defiance of promises made by Stalin when he signed the Atlantic Charter (see 12.10) in January 1942. In all three states, Red Army forces installed Moscow-trained leaders to head what one leader called 'Popular Democracies'.

They were, in fact, neither popular (never having been elected) nor democratic (for they used Stalin's methods to crush opposition, control the media and education, limit the power of the Churches, and to keep themselves in power).

In Albania and Yugoslavia, communist guerrilla forces drove out the Germans and set up communist and dictatorial governments without USSR control. Stalin wanted this USSR-controlled empire to be a buffer between the USSR and the capitalist west. He remembered how the western states had aided the Whites during Russia's Civil War (see 6.6). The West had treated the USSR as a 'leper' until allowing her to join the League of Nations in 1934, had ignored her when dealing with Hitler at Munich in 1938 (see 10.7), and had seemed unwilling to open a Second Front while German troops were hammering the USSR in 1941–43. He feared that after the war, the West might well launch an anti-Russian crusade.

19.2 1948: Stalin's gains and losses

Cominform was set up in 1947 to allow the USSR to control the **satellite** states of Eastern Europe (see 15.4). When Tito of Yugoslavia refused to obey Stalin's orders, he was expelled from Cominform in 1948. At that time the Czechoslovak Communists were only minor partners in a Coalition Government led by Masaryk, the son of the founder of the new state in 1919 (see 4.4 and Fig. 4.2). He and President Benes were democrats and nationalists, and refused to allow Communists to develop their influence. On 10 March 1948 Masaryk 'fell' from the window of his Ministry and died: one obstacle was removed. Soon afterwards, in May 1948, the Communists, led by the Stalinist Gottwald, seized power. Opposition leaders were arrested and either imprisoned or executed.

19.3 Extending Stalinist power

Stalin was alarmed by Tito's 'rebellion'. He feared that others might imitate this example in a Red view of the 'Domino Theory' (see 17.15). In Czechoslovakia, Slansky, the Party Secretary, called for the acceptance of Marshall Aid (see 15.3). He and other like-minded Czech Communists were arrested and executed. In Poland, Gomulka claimed that 'Our Polish democracy is not the same as the Soviet system'. So he was also driven from power, and 75,000 Communists were expelled from the Party.

Nagy, the nationalist-minded Communist head of the Hungarian Government, was on holiday in Switzerland when he had a 'phone call telling him he was dismissed from power. In each of the satellite states earlier leaders were replaced by lesser-known men, put in power by Stalin to whom they would be loyal. Only in Berlin was Stalin unsuccessful in 1948–9 (see 15.4).

19.4 Anti-Soviet movements, 1953–56

Stalin's death in 1953 was the signal for uprisings by discontented workers in East Berlin and the Soviet zone of Germany, and by car workers in the Skoda works in Pilsen, Czechoslovakia. All such risings and demonstrations were brutally crushed by USSR tanks, military forces and their police, their leaders being imprisoned or executed.

Khrushchev's condemnation of Stalin and Stalinism in January 1956 (see 18.2) sent shock waves through Eastern Europe. On 28 June 1956 Polish car workers went on strike for better wages and living conditions. They got the support of the general public which, in many towns, held anti-Soviet demonstrations and fought pitched battles with police, troops and tanks.

Khrushchev was forced to make concessions: Gomulka was restored to power and allowed to form a more 'liberal' economic and social policy. However, even he was careful not to break with the USSR and Cominform, nor to withdraw from the Warsaw Pact (see 15.5). News of the Polish rising led to a similar one in Hungary, where demonstrators called for a better standard of living, the removal of the Stalinist Rakosi as head of government, and the abolition of the secret police. In July 1956 the USSR sacked Rakosi and restored Nagy (see 19.3) to power. Nagy negotiated with the USSR, which withdrew its tanks and troops from Budapest (26 October) after they had killed over 600 people.

Nagy then passed laws giving new freedoms to press, radio and TV, and allowed politicians to form non-Communist parties. Statues of Stalin were smashed and hundreds of secret policemen were lynched by anti-Communist demonstrators who continued their anti-Soviet campaigns.

Nagy then announced that Hungary would withdraw from the Warsaw Pact and become 'neutral' between East and West. The USSR then sent troops and tanks back into Budapest to crush the Revolution. On 14 November Budapest was bombed from the air. Artillery and tanks fired on the rebel-held radio station, newspaper offices and university. About 20,000 Hungarians were killed in ten days of fighting, while another 200,000 fled to Austria and the West.

Nagy surrendered to Khrushchev's puppet, Kadar. Nagy was taken to the USSR and executed, having been promised his freedom. Kadar ruled Hungary for more than twenty years. He and Khrushchev had a Stalin-like attitude towards some dissidents.

19.5 Czechoslovakia, 1968

Examiner's tip

Take care not to get confused between the events in Hungary, Poland and Czechoslovakia. Study these different areas of conflict carefully.

Under a hardline President, Novotny, Czechoslovakia was a Stalinistic state. Then in 1967 a 'liberal' Communist, Dubcek, became Party Secretary and, as such, the head of the Government. In 1968 his popular policies on a greater output of consumer goods, a freer press and the end of censorship gained him the support which helped drive Novotny from office. A 'liberal' President, Svoboda, succeeded him. He and Dubcek then brought in a series of liberal reforms:

- public and political meetings were allowed;
- political prisoners were freed;
- the activities of the secret police were limited.

When Dubcek began negotiations with West Germany for a peace treaty, the USSR sent in troops and tanks (20 August) backed by forces from other Warsaw Pact states. They crushed the resistance in Prague and other cities, and arrested Dubcek who was taken to Moscow. He and Svoboda were forced to negotiate with the Soviet Government and to give up most of their reforms. Soviet troops stayed in Czechoslovakia, and Dubcek's supporters were removed from office. In 1970 a hardline government under Husak was put in power. Brezhnev, like Khrushchev and Stalin, had no time for dissidents and liberals.

19.6 Poland, 1970–80

In December 1970 there was widespread rioting when Gomulka's government announced huge increases in the prices of food, fuel and clothing. Gomulka was forced from power and replaced by Gierek. He negotiated with the Church and other leaders of the opposition, and cancelled most of Gomulka's price increases. Gierek also allowed wide-ranging and open discussions about what was wrong with Polish society. This led to demands for democratic freedom and, on the Government's side a series of reforming measures. Younger, non-Communist people were given positions of power; industry was given greater freedom; firms were allowed to borrow money from western banks to enable them to modernise. There was some improvement in living standards as real wages rose and industrial and agricultural output rose.

In October 1978 the Archbishop of Krakow became Pope John Paul II, the head of the Catholic Church. This encouraged workers to form trade unions under the general banner of **Solidarity**. It was this Solidarity movement which led the campaigns for greater workers' freedom, higher wages and better working conditions (1978–80).

Some in the Solidarity movement extended their aims beyond wages and working conditions. They demanded free elections and the right to form non-Communist parties. These demands, together with the growing power of the Church, led the USSR to step in. Gierek was dismissed and a Polish General, Jaruzelski, was appointed to head the Government. He imposed martial law and arrested or forced into hiding many leaders of Solidarity which was banned.

Examiner's tip

i. You will find it useful to revise this chapter by making a time line showing the key events shown in this chapter.
ii. Make a list of reasons for the revolts against Soviet power in Poland, Hungary and Czechoslovakia, and why they were successful in the end.
iii. Write down the key actions of people like Tito, Khrushchev, Nagy, Walesa, and Dubcek.

The discontented Poles resented the Jaruzelski Government, but feared even more the danger of the USSR intervening as she had done in the past (see 19.3). The Government tried, but failed, to deal with the economic problems that were common to the USSR and all Communist governments in the 1980s: inflation, shortages of goods, unemployment and huge overseas debts.

The Catholic Church provided the focus for the discontent, which was also voiced by the outlawed Solidarity movement. Finally, in 1989 Jaruzelski held talks with **Walesa** and other Solidarity leaders. The talks led to Solidarity being legalised. The press and opposition were given greater freedom and the Church was allowed to run its own schools and papers. A date was set for free elections (June 1989). These changes were able to take place because of the 'liberal' attitudes of Gorbachev, the Soviet leader (see 18.6).

As a result of the elections, the first non-Communist government in Eastern Europe took power in August 1989, with Walesa becoming President. The end of Communism in Poland was the first step on the road to the end of Communism in Hungary (March 1990), East Germany (March 1990), Rumania (May 1990) and Czechoslovakia January (1990).

Summary

1 Stalin created a satellite Empire in Eastern Europe after 1945.
2 1948: Stalin lost control of Yugoslavia, but took control of Czechoslovakia.
3 Stalin was ruthless with Communist Party leaders who showed independence.
4 1953: There were workers risings in East Germany and Czechoslovakia.
5 1956: After Khrushchev's denunciation of Stalin there was a successful rising in Poland and the Hungarian rising was crushed.
6 1968: Dubcek led Czechoslovakia into a new era of freedom, but was crushed by the USSR.
7 1970 onwards there was the growth of freedom in Poland. Freedom increased again after the election of the Polish Pope.
8 The Solidarity Movement was formed, then banned, then legalised.
9 1989–90: Communist rule in Poland and the rest of Europe ended.

Quick questions

1 Name *four* countries liberated by the Red Army, 1944–5.
2 Name *two* countries where local Communists freed their own countries.
3 Which Communist leader refused to obey Stalin in 1947–8?
4 Name *two* non-Communist leaders in Czechoslovakia from 1947 to 1948.
5 Name:
   i)   the first Communist 'ruler' of Czechoslovakia, 1948;
   ii) the Polish Communist who was dismissed from power in 1949, but brought back by Khrushchev in 1956.
6 Name:
   i)   the Hungarian Prime Minister overthrown by the USSR in 1956;
   ii) his successor.
7 What are the capital cities of i) Hungary; ii) Czechoslovakia?
8 Name the 'liberal' Communist leader of Czechoslovakia, 1968.
9 What was (and is) the general name of the Polish free trade union movement?
10 Name the Polish general who controlled Poland from 1978 to 1989.

Chapter 20

Western European integration

20.1 Why the European nations came closer together after 1945

When World War II ended in 1945, Europe was a devastated continent. 25 million people lived in refugee camps or bombed out buildings. European industries, trade and transport had been almost totally destroyed. Politicians knew that no country could rebuild on its own, and they agreed with Winston Churchill who said: 'We must build a kind of United States of Europe'.

The 'Europeans' who wished to build a united Europe had four main reasons.
- Europe had 10% of the world's population which, if they joined together, would become a powerful trading area.
- They wanted to avoid another war between European nations, especially between France and Germany.
- The Europeans wanted to form an alliance which would resist threats from the powerful USSR (see 15.2–5).
- They believed the USA would be more willing to listen to them if they united.

20.2 The beginning of European co-operation

In 1943 the **UNRRA** (United Nations Relief and Emergency Rehabilitation Administration) was set up to provide relief to countries liberated from Germany (see Chapter 12). UNRRA existed from 1944 to 1947. In 1947 the USA offered aid to the European states on condition that they produced a plan for how the aid was to be used (see 15.3).

The Benelux countries (Belgium, Holland and Luxemburg) formed a customs union in 1947, and developed ever closer ties between them. In 1948 the **OEEC** (Organisation for European Economic Co-operation) was set up by sixteen European states and the three German zones to plan how the Marshall Aid from the USA was to be used. When the OEEC nations met they developed the idea of Western European Co-operation.

The OEEC helped to bring about the rebirth of Europe which individual countries acting alone could not have done. Specialist advisory committees on such matters as fisheries, transport and power supplies helped nations to rebuild. Each decision of the OEEC had to be approved by individual governments and parliaments.

The Council of Europe was set up in May 1948 by political leaders from ten European states. The Council was not much more than a debating chamber. Nations sent representatives to Strasbourg three times a year, but the Council had no powers to make laws. Some European politicians wanted the Council to be a European Parliament elected by the peoples of Europe, but Britain objected as it might want to control the British Parliament and Government.

20.3 The European Coal and Steel Community (ECSC)

Due to the success of the OEEC and Benelux Union, the leaders of the European states decided to pool their coal and steel resources together. Konrad Adenauer, the West German Chancellor and Robert Schuman, the French Foreign Minister who had originally been a German citizen and fought in the First World War, were the driving forces in the founding of the ECSC. They agreed that the ECSC should be a controlling authority which would enforce a 'common market' with no trade restrictions in coal and steel. The European nations saw that the ECSC would create a bigger market for coal and steel and encourage greater efficiency. They also realised that co-operation would help to prevent war between Germany and France.

The British Labour Government refused to join the ECSC because it did not want Europeans having a say over what happened to British coal and steel. The Europeans were disappointed because Britain's coal and steel industries were very large and Britain was highly regarded after the victory over Hitler (see Chapter 12).

Six countries approved of the ECSC plans. France and West Germany were joined by Italy, Belgium, Holland and Luxemburg who signed the Treaty of Paris (1951), setting up the ECSC with headquarters in Luxemburg. The ECSC was controlled by a nine-member executive, the High Authority, which in turn was controlled by an Assembly of delegates from member countries. The first President of the High Authority was Jean Monnet, the 'Father of Europe'. Winston Churchill, who was again British Prime Minister, refused to allow Britain to join, though he had earlier called for the creation of a United States of Europe.

20.4 The European Economic Community (EEC), 1957

The Coal and Steel Community was very successful. Production and trade within the ECSC rose quickly and the member states decided to allow free trade in all industries. They knew that free trade encouraged efficiency and increased output, leading to lower prices, more jobs and higher living standards.

In June 1955 the six members of the ECSC met at Messina, Sicily to plan a closer union of these states. Britain sent a junior civil servant to be an observer at this meeting. He told them the plan for greater union could not work and left the meeting early. A committee under the Belgian Foreign Minister, Spaak, drew up the **Treaty of Rome** which founded the **European Economic Community** (EEC). On 25 March 1957 the 'Six': France, West Germany, Italy, Holland, Belgium and Luxemburg signed the treaty.

The EEC aimed to abolish all tariffs by 1967, and to have low tariffs on goods coming into the EEC from outside. The member states agreed to work towards creating a fuller union so that eventually a United States of Europe would be set up. The British Conservative Government refused to join because it did not wish to give up its sovereignty (control of its affairs) to the Europeans.

The founders of the EEC agreed that a **European Commission** should oversee the working of the community to make sure that tariff policies were carried out equally in all countries. The Commission, meeting in Brussels, had to answer to the **European Parliament** which had representatives from each member state. Parliament could only advise the Commission about policy.

Each nation sent a minister to the **European Council of Ministers** which discussed matters of common interest like farming, fisheries and foreign affairs. The Council of Ministers voted on the recommendations made by the European Commission. On important matters there had to be unanimous agreement in the Council of Ministers. Ministers could **veto** proposals that they did not like, but on minor matters majority voting was to be allowed.

E **xaminer's tip**

i. You should study the reasons why European politicians wanted to create a European Community.
ii. Study the *stages* by which the European Community was created.

The EEC was very successful in raising the living standards of its members because free trade increased trade, production and employment. Britain, having refused to join in 1957, changed its mind about the EEC.

The Conservative Prime Minister, Harold Macmillan applied to join the EEC in 1961–2, but General de Gaulle of France vetoed the application. In 1967 Harold Wilson, the Labour Prime Minister, applied to join because by now all the political parties understood the advantages of being in the EEC. De Gaulle, vetoed the second application. He thought that Britain was too dominated by the USA and too interested in the Commonwealth to be a reliable member of the EEC.

20.5 The EEC grows and becomes the EC

In 1973 Britain, under Ted Heath, did persuade the EEC to admit her, along with Denmark and Eire, so that 'The Six' became 'The Nine'. Greece, Spain and Portugal joined in 1986 after they became democracies. The 'Nine' became 'The Twelve', some of whom were very wealthy (Germany) and others relatively poor (Greece).

In 1978 the European Parliament (see 20.4)became more powerful when direct elections were held for it. Large countries like Britain, Germany and Italy had 81 Members of the European Parliament (MEPs). Smaller countries had fewer representatives. The European Parliament began to demand control over the Commission and Council of Ministers, and the MEPs sat as Liberals, Socialists and Conservatives rather than in their national groups. The Maastricht Treaty (see 20.7) increased the power of Parliament to block decisions made by the Commission.

As a result of Inter-Governmental Conferences (IGC) at Milan and Luxemburg (1987), the EEC became the European Community when members signed the **Single European Act**. The Act stated that Europe would become a single market in 1992. This meant that there was to be free trade and free movement of people and money within the community. Most European politicians believed that a single market meant that each country would have to have the same levels of taxation, subsidies for industry, the same welfare and trade union policies, and above all a common currency. The power of members of the Council of Ministers to **veto** proposals was reduced, and majority voting grew. This meant that individual nations had less power over policy than before. The European leaders welcomed this, but the British Government, led by Margaret Thatcher, did not fully explain to the British people that the Government had agreed to an increase in the powers of the European Union over Britain.

20.6 The development of the European Union

The powers of the Commission and the European Court grew as laws made in Europe had to be enforced in individual countries. Most of the European laws have not proved controversial, but laws protecting part-time workers and forcing Britain to accept metrication have angered some people in Britain. Once the single market began in 1992 member states began to plan for a single currency for all of Europe by 1999. Jacques Delors, the President of the European Commission, led the moves towards the single European currency which he believed would help to make the single market work.

In 1992 Denmark, Sweden, Austria and Portugal joined the European Community. Norway voted in a referendum to stay out, and Switzerland also remained outside the EC. All other Western European nations belonged to the EC.

20.7 The Treaty of Maastricht, November 1993

At Maastricht the leaders of the member states agreed to create the **European Union (EU)**. They agreed on co-operation between governments on foreign and security policy, and in the fields of justice and home affairs. In practice the treaty led to ever closer union between states. This union included moves towards **European Monetary Union (EMU)** which would lead to a single currency and a European Central Bank (ECB). The treaty included a 'Social Chapter' extending the rights of employees throughout the union on matters like working hours, dismissal procedures for part-time workers, and parental leave. The European Court of Justice gained increased powers to fine member states who do not obey EU law.

Most European politicians wanted the members of the EU to grow closer to one another politically, and they were happy with the increased powers of the European Court and the European Commission.

The treaty also stated the principle of 'subsidiarity', which meant that each individual country should keep as much control of its affairs as possible. This clause pleased the British Government, which was opposed to the creation of a United States of Europe which the other members of the European Union supported. By 1996 it seemed that the dreams of the founders of the ECSC and EEC, for a United States of Europe (see 20.4) were close to being fulfilled.

20.8 Britain and the EEC

After Britain finally joined the EEC in 1973 (see 20.5) the British people voted in a Referendum in 1975 to stay within the Community. Britain continued to be divided on the question of whether she benefited from membership. Most members of the Labour Party opposed membership during the 1980s, until the Party accepted that Britain could not withdraw. In the 1990s the Conservative Party was divided about whether to accept closer integration into the European Union.

The **Common Agricultural Policy** (CAP) angered many people in Britain. Farmers receive a guaranteed price for their produce which is fixed by the annual review by the Ministers of Agriculture of the member states. This encouraged farmers to produce too much food which had to be stored or sold cheaply outside Europe. The CAP was designed to please the farmers of France, Germany and Holland who formed the majority of voters in the 1950s, when the EEC began (see 20.4). In the 1990s the CAP was reformed so that farmers were paid to 'set aside' land instead of growing food. This reduced the 'food mountains'.

As Britain is a food-importing country, most British tax payers resented the high food prices and subsidies for farmers, but the CAP does ensure a guaranteed food supply which the founders of the EEC were anxious to do (see 20.1). In 1984 Mrs Thatcher insisted that the European Commission agree to pay back some of Britain's contribution to the EEC budget because the amount that Britain paid was the highest in Europe. The amount that each country had to pay into the European budget was related to the level of imports from outside of Europe and Britain's level was the highest in the European Community.

The **Common Fisheries Policy** also caused anger in Britain, because European fishermen were allowed to fish in 'British' waters, and all fishermen were limited in what they could catch. Many British fishermen lost their livelihoods.

Britain benefited in many ways from membership of the European Community.
● Increased trade produced more jobs.
● Countries outside Europe, such as Japan, invested in Britain because Britain belonged to the European Union.
● Britain's regions such as Wales, Scotland, the North East and North West of England have received large grants to encourage new industries to grow in place of older industries, such as coal mining and steel making which have died.

The Treaty of Maastricht (see 20.7) caused much controversy in Britain. John Major's Conservative Government won an 'opt out' clause of the movement towards a single European Currency, since this would lead to a Central European Bank and take away powers of the British Government to control economic policy.

The Government also 'opted out' of the **Social Chapter** giving workers increased rights at work since, the Government argued, this would cause higher unemployment because employers' costs would rise and businesses would not be able to compete with the new 'tiger' economies of Asia and the Pacific. The Labour Party was undecided about the single currency, but supported the Social Chapter.

Britain's failure to join Europe in the 1950s (see 20.1–2) meant that by the time Britain joined the European 'club' many of the rules by which Europe operated were fixed in ways unfavourable to Britain (e.g. the CAP and the budget policy). This caused Britain problems in accepting the growth of the European Union. Many Europeans accused Britain of always being too late in getting on board the European train.

Britain benefited from the single European Act (see 20.6) because her efficient industries helped British companies to increase their exports to Europe. Britain had one of the lowest rate of unemployment in the EU in 1996. Some people believed that Britain gained from the opt-out from the Social Chapter because this meant that employers were freer to make decisions than they were in Europe. British wage costs were among the lowest in the EU, so employers could afford to take on more workers.

E **xaminer's tip**

i. You should summarise the key points of the following key European institutions and laws: the Commission, the Council of Ministers, the Single European Act, EMU and the Common Fisheries and Agricultural Policies.
ii. Note the increasing speed with which European nations came closer together.
iii. Revise carefully the advantages and disadvantages for Britain of the European Union, and the reasons why some British people opposed membership of the European Union.

Summary

1 The effects of World War II encouraged the European leaders to co-operate together. Many of them wanted to form a United States of Europe.
2 The early forms of European co-operation were the OEEC, ECSC and the Benelux Union.
3 The 'Six' met at Messina to draw up plans for the EEC, which was created by the 1957 Treaty of Rome.
4 The EEC was led by the European Commission and representatives were sent to the European Parliament.
5 Britain refused to join the EEC, but applied to join in 1961 and again in 1967. General de Gaulle vetoed the applications on both occasions.

6 The increased trade in the EEC helped the economies of the 'Six' to grow much faster than Britain.

7 In the 1980s the EEC became the European Union, with fifteen members and some former Warsaw Pact nations hoping to join. The EU's ruling body was the European Commission.

8 The Single European Act and the Maastricht Treaty helped Europe along the road to becoming the United States of Europe which the EEC's founders wanted.

9 Britain benefited from being within Europe because of increased trade, but many people resented the CAP and the threat of a single currency.

10 The powers of countries to veto proposals in the Council of Ministers was reduced in the 1990s, and the power of the European Court was stronger than those of British Courts in some cases.

Quick questions

1 Name *three* early forms of European co-operation.
2 where did the 'Six' meet to draw up plans for the EEC?
3 When was the Treaty of Rome signed?
4 In which *two* years did Britain try and fail to join the EEC?
5 Which organisation was put in charge of the EEC?
6 By the end of the 1980s how many countries had joined the EEC?
7 Name the Treaty which helped Europe to become a closer union.
8 Which law made Europe a single market?
9 What does CAP stand for?
10 In which group do the leaders of each member state meet?

Chapter 21
The USA 1945–97

21.1 The effects of World War Two on the USA

The USA was the 'arsenal of democracy' because it supplied the planes, tanks and other equipment to Britain and Russia in the war with Germany (see Chapter 12). The USA also helped the Chinese in their war with Japan (see Chapter 7). Sixteen million US servicemen fought around the world during the war.

Unemployment fell from 9 million in 1939 to almost nothing in 1943 as factories took on workers making military equipment. US workers' incomes increased and they spent money on 'consumer goods' produced by American factories. The war was therefore more effective than the New Deal (see 9.7–8) in increasing living standards and putting people back to work. Due to the shortage of workers the trade unions became stronger and were able to force employers to increase their wages.

Farmers incomes increased 400% as they sold their food to Britain and to US soldiers and factory workers. Black people found work more easily and became more self-confident and conscious of the need to end discrimination (see 21.3).

The federal Government's powers increased. Prices were fixed, public transport was controlled, and factories were converted to produce war material. Conscription was introduced in 1940, the first time this was done in peacetime. President Roosevelt was the leader of the 'Free World', and when the war ended the USA continued this role, fighting Communism (see 15.2–3).

The USA became the richest country in the world as foreign gold was exchanged for military equipment. The USA's bankers became the world's bankers, arranging loans to the Allies. American companies won British markets during the war, so exports grew, bringing more money into the USA.

The war effort also led to massive technological advances, for example in electronics, science and engineering, so the USA was able to lead the world's economies after the war ended. The invention of the atomic bomb (see 12.8) showed how advanced the USA had become.

The war did leave the USA with major problems to overcome. When price controls were ended inflation rose, due to high government wartime spending and shortages of goods. Trade unions demanded higher wages and called nation-wide strikes, which often became violent. There was also pressure to 'bring the boys home', so unemployment rose as soldiers returned from the war. Roosevelt's successor, President Truman (1945–53) therefore became unpopular. He tried, but failed, to extend the New Deal (see 9.7) with his own 'Fair Deal', which would have given civil rights to black people, as well as better social security for the poor. Tax payers did not want to pay more taxes to help the poor, and most white people did not want to allow black Americans to have equality with them.

E **xaminer's tip**

Note that World War Two had both positive and negative effects. You should be ready to explain whether or not the positive effects outweighed the negative effects.

21.2 McCarthyism

During World War Two, many people began to fear that Communism was spreading to the USA. After the war these fears worsened. Mao's Chinese Communist Revolution, the 'Cold War' between East and West (see Chapter 15), and knowledge about Stalin (see Chapter 6) made people frightened of Communism. Many Americans joined in the hunt for communists in government service, and President Truman set up loyalty checks on government employees in 1949.

In 1950 Hiss, a high ranking State Department official was found guilty of spying for the Russians in the 1930s. He had been Roosevelt's advisor at Yalta (see 15.1), and had advised the UNO at the San Francisco Conference (see 14.1). At the same time Julius and Ethel Rosenberg were caught betraying atomic secrets to the USSR.

Congress passed the **Internal Security Act** (1950) which restricted Communist activity and banned the entry of those known to be Communists. Congress overrode Truman's **veto** on this Act. Truman thought the Act went against American's basic freedoms, but the majority of US voters seemed to support McCarthy's anti-Communist **propaganda** and witch hunt.

Senator Joseph McCarthy became famous in 1950 when he accused the State Department of knowingly harbouring eighty-one communists. He took over the **Un-American Activities Committee** which had been set up to investigate Nazis. Now the committee was used against communists, socialists and liberals. Leading teachers, artists, scientists and politicians were accused of being 'commies' and 'traitors'. The Republican Party had accused Truman of allowing Stalin to take over Eastern Europe (see Chapter 19). They also accused US communists of helping Mao's Communist Revolution in China (see Chapter 22).

McCarthy was hoping that his anti-Communist campaign would help him to become the Republican Party leader and then President of the USA. He managed to organise censorship of films and burning of 'subversive' literature. His bullying tactics made him popular with many Americans, especially when President Truman sacked General MacArthur (1951) for campaigning for an attack on China during the Korean War (see 14.4).

McCarthy rarely proved his accusations, but he helped the Republican General Eisenhower to become President (1952). McCarthy's powers declined in 1954 when the Senate removed him from the Committee of Permanent Investigation. TV journalists had exposed the fact that McCarthy was a bully and a liar. He died in 1957. The success of McCarthy's campaigns showed that the USA was a divided country.

21.3 The campaign for civil rights before 1960

During the 1860s slavery was abolished, but America's black people were second class citizens. In the southern states, where black people form a large proportion of the population, white politicians passed state laws preventing them from having social, political and educational rights.

Black people had to take the lowest jobs and the worst housing. They could not use the same toilets, buses, beaches and park benches as white people. Black children could not attend the same schools as white children, and the state governments spent much less on the schools of black children than they did on the white children. Even during the war there was **segregation** in the army, with separate units for black servicemen. In northern cities black people lived in overcrowded slums or ghettos, and had fewer job opportunities and poorer schools.

The Ku Klux Klan (see 9.4) frightened black people from taking advantage of laws passed by the federal Government which benefited black people. Lynching of black people by mobs of hooded men with fiery crosses was a frequent event. Poorer white people often supported the KKK because they feared that black people would take their jobs. Some Christian Churches believed that the Bible taught that black people were inferior to white people. Many young white people grew up not knowing about the idea that everyone should have equal rights, which the writers of the American Constitution had agreed. These people were angry when, in 1954, the Supreme Court declared that compulsory segregation of schools was illegal.

In 1957 the State Government of Arkansas encouraged the white mobs who tried to stop nine black children from enrolling at an all white school. President Eisenhower sent federal troops to enforce the law and allow the children into school. Other states refused to stop **segregation**, and many black parents were frightened to take their children to all-white schools.

Desegregation of buses in Montgomery, Alabama, began to take place when black people refused to use the public transport system in 1955. Café sit-ins forced the start of the removal of segregation. Martin Luther King became the leader of the peaceful **Civil Rights Movement** which persuaded Congress to pass the 1957 **Civil Rights Act**, giving equal voting rights to black people. In 1960 King campaigned for federal supervision of elections so that white mobs could not stop black people voting. Many black people moved to the northern cities from the south to get away from KKK violence, but this flight to the north added to the problems suffered by many black people in the north: overcrowded slums, unemployment and crime.

21.4 Civil rights under Kennedy and Johnson, 1960–68

The National Association for the Advancement of Coloured People (founded in 1909) was joined by new groups, such as the SNCC (Student Non Violent Coordinating Committee) and CORE (Congress of Racial Equality). These groups campaigned for civil rights and desegregation. Martin Luther King became the leader of these protesters. His deep Christian faith and passionate speeches made him a hero among blacks and white reformers, but he was hated by white racists. In 1963 he was gaoled for leading a protest march in Birmingham, Alabama. King preached that whites and blacks could live together side by side. He argued that protest should be non-violent so that white people could be persuaded to change.

President Kennedy (JFK, 1960–63) tried to respond to these protest movements. He appointed the first black judge, ambassador and army commander, and his brother Robert, the Attorney General, used legal powers and the army to help black people use their voting rights. The army was sent to Oxford, Mississippi when whites rioted after a black person tried to enrol at an all-white school. The State Governor had refused to use his troops against the rioters, probably because he feared he would not be re-elected if he supported the rights of black people.

Congress stopped Kennedy passing a law to clear the slums because taxes would have had to rise. His health service reforms were also blocked by Congress. Kennedy's civil rights laws were held up in Congress by Republicans and southern democrats who represented white voters. His murder in Dallas (1963) was applauded by many conservative Americans opposed to black emancipation. Many people think that if Kennedy had won a second term as President he would have been more successful. The **Warren Commission**, which investigated Kennedy's death, suggested the CIA and FBI may have been involved in a conspiracy to kill him.

President Lyndon Johnson (1964–8) tried to build the 'Great Society' by passing more civil rights laws and social reforms, which would have benefited black people because they were amongst the poorest in the USA. Laws were passed providing money for slum clearance, educational expansion and aid for the unemployed. Medicare was provided for the elderly. The minimum wage was raised and extended to more industries. The 1965 Civil Rights Act gave black people equal rights of entry to the cinema and shops. They were also guaranteed the right to vote. Despite the reforms by Kennedy and Johnson, black people still suffered injustice. White mobs in many southern states attacked them when they went to vote, and when they went into 'white' shops. Basic inequality remained in jobs, schools and housing.

When Martin Luther King was assassinated (April 1968) many younger black people argued that peaceful protest was not enough, so more people joined the Black Power Movement. The murder of Robert Kennedy (June 1968) also led blacks to believe that white people did not want to help.

Stokey Carmichael taught that 'Black is beautiful', believing that 'Black consciousness' would help his people rise out of oppression. He believed that black people would not be really freed by 'white liberals' like Kennedy and Johnson.

Malcom X, the militant leader of the Black Muslims, demanded a separate state for black people, where black people would help themselves. He supported violent action against white property and people. Many black converts to Islam refused to fight in the Vietnam war (see 17.3) on behalf of a country which oppressed them, and against the non-white poor people of North Vietnam.

Cassius Clay, the world boxing champion, called Muhammad Ali after his conversion, refused to go to war. He was gaoled and lost his title. Impatience with the lack of real reforms led to urban riots (1967–9), causing injuries and deaths to thousands and destruction of property worth £15m.

The **Vietnam war** cost the USA billions of dollars and wrecked Johnson's plans for slum clearance, social security and educational advancement. Violent anti-war protests by (mainly white) university students, caused great divisions in America and took attention away from civil rights for blacks (see 17.3). Many white people opposed the taxes necessary to pay for Johnson's reforms. Poorer whites liked to feel superior to black people, and resented programmes to help them. Johnson was exhausted by his failures and decided not to seek re-election in 1968. In that year a Republican, Richard Nixon, was elected on the promise to slow down the Kennedy-Johnson reforms and to cut taxes.

Examiner's tip

i. Students often mix up the events of the Civil Rights campaign. Make sure you revise carefully the events of the KKK riots, the 1950's Civil Rights movement and the policies of Presidents Kennedy and Johnson.
ii. Study carefully the differences between the various black civil rights campaigners.

21.5 From Nixon to Clinton

Black militancy died down in 1969 as a number of the leaders were in prison, and many black people were tired of the deaths and destruction of their own neighbourhoods. In 1969 the Supreme Court ruled that desegregation of schools should begin immediately, and in the 1970s there was a big expansion of black students attending college. Black people began to elect their own leaders to Congress and State legislatures. Many black people found well paid jobs in the professions.

Racism still existed, and millions of black people were very poor, but Martin Luther King's ideas about peaceful change seemed to be working for some black people. Nixon was re-elected in 1972, easily defeating the left-wing Democratic candidate, George McGovern.

Nixon's Presidency is most remembered for the scandal of **'Watergate'**. During the 1972 Election, the Democratic Party's headquarters in the Watergate building was burgled. Eventually, after a running battle with the courts, Nixon was forced to hand over the tape-recordings of conversations he had held in the White House, with his chief advisors, during the election period. The tapes proved that Nixon was guilty of covering up the plot to burgle the building. The tapes showed that Nixon was foul-mouthed as well as a crook, and the American public were very embarrassed. Nixon was forced to resign in August 1974 to avoid arrest. He was succeeded by **Gerald Ford**, the Vice President who saved Nixon from prison with a Presidential pardon.

The Watergate affair distracted attention from the fact that Nixon's policy of easing tensions with China and the USSR was successful (see 16.3). Congress realised that since Roosevelt (see Chapter 9), the USA had been ruled by very powerful Presidents who had taken power away from the Congress. The Democratic President, **Jimmy Carter** (1976–80), was unable to control Congress, which wanted to increase its powers over the President.

President Carter was an unsuccessful President. His policy towards the USSR seemed to be weak (see 16.6) and he increased taxes to try to help the poor. As a result he was succeeded by the Republican, **Ronald Reagan** (1980–88). Reagan reduced government spending on the poor, which pleased most voters, and his foreign policy helped to begin the process of nuclear disarmament (see 16.7–8).

President George Bush (1988–92) continued the policy of **détente** with the Communist states (see 16.9) and led the United Nations war effort against Iraq (see 14.6).

Bill Clinton (1992–7) also pursued peace with the new Russia (see 18.6). He failed to persuade Congress to pass laws to introduce health and social reforms which Truman, Kennedy and Johnson (see 21.4) had also failed to introduce, and in August 1996 Clinton accepted the law, passed by the Republican-controlled Congress, greatly reducing aid to the poor and unemployed.

21.6 The development of youth culture

After World War Two most young people became more prosperous and better educated due to the economic progress made by the USA (see 21.1). They had more money to travel and to buy consumer goods such as cars, radios, and from the 1950s, televisions. They also had money to buy records and attend pop concerts. So many young people attended their concerts, that pop musicians like Buddy Holly and Elvis Presley became 'superstars'. The era of **'Rock and Roll'** was seen by most older people as a threat, since young people's tastes in clothes, music and sexual behaviour became more 'liberated'. A great deal of money was spent on drugs, and people spoke about the 'generation gap', because older generations seemed to be unable to understand younger people.

Music was also used as a way of protest. Bob Dylan's songs such as 'Blowing in the Wind' and 'With God on our Side' were anthems of anti-Vietnam War protest marchers (see 17.5). Many university students campaigned violently against the war policies of Johnson and Nixon. Generally, poorer black young people were attracted to jazz and reggae music. In the 1960s and 1970s British pop groups such as the Beatles and the Rolling Stones became very popular. These two groups were not politically motivated, but they did offer young people values which rejected their parents values about sexuality, obedience and hard work.

The **'Hippie'** movement, which began in San Francisco, attracted young people who wanted to reject the conventional lifestyle of America. Many of these people who 'dropped out' of society, were children of well-off parents, unlike the poorer people who were 'drop outs' because of circumstances rather than out of choice. It must be remembered, however, that most Americans were not rebellious. Nixon's victory in 1968 (see 21.4) was based on his appeal to the conservative 'silent majority' of Americans.

During the Vietnam war (see 17.5) television and radio, as well as the newspapers, brought news about the fighting. They showed the American public pictures of young babies being attacked by American planes, stories of massacres of villages by American soldiers, as well as pictures of the bodies of dead American soldiers. The images in the media helped to persuade Nixon's Government to 'bring the boys home' and end the war. During the war with Saddam Hussein's Iraq, President Bush had to promise his people that the war would 'not be another Vietnam' (see 14.6). Some people said that the USA lost the Vietnam war in 'the drawing rooms of America'

Examiner's tip

Study the effects of the Vietnam War and economic change on society in the USA.

Summary

1 During World War Two the USA was the 'arsenal of democracy', making equipment for Britain and Russia.

2 Most Americans prospered during the war, and the USA became a richer, more powerful country.

3 As a result of the war, trade unions became stronger and black people began to demand their civil rights.

4 Senator McCarthy led a 'witch hunt' for Communist traitors after Alger Hiss was caught spying for Russia in the State Department.

5 The Ku Klux Klan led white racist attacks on the black civil rights movement, which was led by Martin Luther King.

6 Presidents Kennedy and Johnson passed civil rights laws and social reforms, but millions of people still suffered poverty and discrimination.

7 The Black Power movement supported violent revolution against the whites. Malcom X was a leader of the militant blacks.

8 President Nixon's rule is best remembered for the 'Watergate affair', when the Democratic Party's headquarters were burgled by Republicans.

9 Young people developed their own culture from the 1950s onwards, and musicians like Dylan and Presley became heroes.

10 The mass media played a big part in spreading new values and publicising the horrors of the Vietnam war.

11 Older people were horrified by the Hippie movement's ideas of dropping out, free love and the use of drugs.

Quick questions

1 Name the USA Presidents during World War Two.
2 Which senator led the anti-Communist campaign during the 1950s?
3 Which organisation was feared by black people in the USA?
4 Name the most important leaders of the black people's civil rights movement.
5 Which *two* USA Presidents passed civil rights laws and social reforms?
6 Name *two* militant black leaders of the 1960s.
7 Which Republican President was responsible for the 'Watergate' scandal?
8 Name *two* famous American musicians.
9 Which war led to the growth of the 'peace movement' in the USA?
10 Name the young people's movement which horrified many older people.

Chapter 22
China 1949–95

22.1 How Mao Tse-tung faced the problems of China in 1949

China was devastated by the long war against Japan in the 1930s and 1940s, and the civil war (1945–9) (see Chapter 7). Railways, roads and canals were destroyed, and there were major food shortages due to the rising population and China's backward agricultural system. Mao studied the methods used by Stalin in modernising the USSR (see 6.10–11). He was prepared to experiment by trial and error to find the methods that would best work in China.

Mao tried to keep the support of the middle-class non-communist intellectuals and officials who had supported him against the KMT Government (see 7.10). Former owners of the major industries and banks were compensated.

The Communist Party 're-educated' people in the ways of communism. A war was waged against corruption, waste and government inefficiency, and at least a million opponents of communism were executed.

22.2 Agricultural reform

In 1949 the grain harvest was only 108 million tons, 32 million tons less than in 1935. Mao needed to increase grain output to feed the people and for export. Under the first stage of Mao's agricultural modernisation (1950–52) land was taken from large landowners and given to the 300 million landless peasants. Mao hoped the peasants would then grow more food. Communist Party officials (cadres) distributed the land, which won the support of the peasants, but a million landowners were executed for resisting the loss of their land.

The second stage of agricultural modernisation (1953–6) took place when Communist Party cadres 'persuaded' peasants to join together in collective farms (co-operatives). These larger units (APC's) could then use bigger machines and experiment with fertilisers and animal breeding. By 1956 about 95% of all peasants were in these collectives, which owned the farm and equipment, and consisted of between 100 and 300 families. Grain production rose to 163 million tons in 1952, and 170 million in 1957, but the population had risen to 647 million in 1957, from 590 million in 1952.

22.3 'The Hundred Flowers Campaign', 1957

Mao decided to allow discussion about China's future. He said 'Let a hundred flowers bloom and a hundred schools of thought contend'. The Communist Party was attacked in these discussions, so Mao stopped the campaign. Critics of the Communists were purged and Mao decided to launch his 'Great Leap Forward' to make China more Communist.

22.4 The Great Leap Forward, 1958

Mao wanted the peasants to work in factories when they were not harvesting or sowing, and he wanted the unemployed town workers to work on projects such as canal building and steel furnaces. Ninety percent of the peasants were reorganised into 24,000 **communes**, with an average population of 30,000. The commune was controlled by the Communist Party and was meant to replace family life. It elected its own local council, which controlled local affairs such as schools, hospitals and local army unit.

Peasants had to work on projects such as canal building and irrigation schemes, or to work in small workshops like 'back yard steel furnaces'. City dwellers were sent to work in the communes, in the 'labour-intensive' factories which produced industrial goods for export (e.g. steel) and for use in the farms (e.g. tractors).

22.5 Retreat from the Great Leap Forward

Mao was surprised that the 'Great Leap Forward' had many failures.
- Food production fell (1958–62) since the peasants did not own their land and had no incentive to sell food that they did not eat themselves.
- Natural disasters made the situation worse, and the Chinese Government was forced to buy food from Canada and Australia.
- Rationing was reintroduced to avoid famine, which caused the Party leaders to fear another uprising.
- Most 'backyard steel' was useless since it had been made quickly by untrained peasants.
- Managers of the factories falsified figures to gain favour with the Communist Party.
These problems caused Mao to step down from being head of state. He concentrated on being Chairman of the Communist Party. Liu Shao-chi became head of state and Chou En-lai became Prime Minister.

Chou and Liu knew they had to abandon Maoist Communism in order to save the economy. To encourage more food production, they allowed the peasants to own their own land again and they were not forced to work in the factories. The day-to-day running of the commune was given to teams which ran individual villages. This reduced the power of the Communist Party over the peasants, some of whom became rich in the new freer system.

22.6 Industrial modernisation: the five-year plans

Mao's first five-year plan (1953–7) concentrated on the development of heavy industry (electricity, coal, iron, steel and chemicals). China received help from the USSR in money, advisers and equipment. Mao wanted strong industries for defence and for producing the machines which would harvest the crops and house the workers. The diagram below (Fig. 22.1) shows the success of the plan, which was similar to Stalin's plans in the USSR (see 6.10).

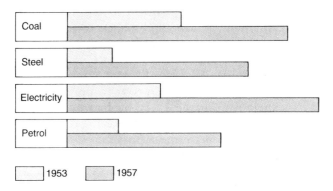

Fig. 22.1 China's first five-year plan

After the second five-year plan, which was part of the 'Great Leap Forward' (see 22.4), the third five-year plan (1962–7) was targeted at new industries such as machine tools, aircraft and electrical equipment. Although the USSR withdrew her technicians and aid to China's industries, China became the world's second largest coal producer, and her steel production equalled that of the USA and USSR. A railway network linked China's industrial centres and ports, and China's industries produced advanced military weapons. In 1964 China became a nuclear power.

To achieve these successes Chou En-lai encouraged a new class of expert managers to run the factories instead of Party cadres. Skilled workers were paid more to encourage hard work and talent, and this angered the 'Maoists' who saw that pure Communism was being abandoned. In the towns, as in the countryside (see 21.5), differences in wealth between the successful and the average Chinese person grew.

22.7 The impact of industrial and agricultural modernisation

By 1965 the Chinese were better fed, housed and educated than in 1949. Chinese workers had full employment, and inflation was avoided. China remained a mainly agricultural country with some industrial areas. The factories relied more on human labour than on machinery, so industrial goods were cheap to export. The industrial advances enabled the Chinese armed forces to become stronger, so there was less danger of defeat by the Japanese or Russians (see Chapter 7).

Most people in China were proud of China's new found strength and security. Women were emancipated by Communism. They participated in the commune elections and benefited from public nurseries provided by the communes. Many young Chinese people seem to have been inspired by Mao's idea of the commune as the basic unit of society and industry, and there was less inequality and corruption in Communist China than before (see 7.10)

However, these gains were at the cost of great repression by the Communist Party. Millions of anti-Communists were executed or imprisoned and tortured, and the Churches were crushed out of existence because the Party did not want any criticism to be expressed.

Examiner's tip

i. Make a list of the advantages and disadvantages of Mao's policies up to 1966.
ii. Study the evidence to help you to assess whether Chou and Liu were more important than Mao in China's modernisation policies.

22.8 The Cultural Revolution, 1966–71

After Mao resigned as Head of State in 1958 (see 22.4–5) he became angry that his successors, Chou En-lai and Liu Shao-chi, were becoming 'right wingers' and abandoning Communism, giving way to protests against the 'Great Leap Forward'.

Mao used his position as Chinese Communist Party Chairman to rouse up Communist students and soldiers to attack the 'right wingers' for trying to make China a capitalist country. Mao's supporters, the **Red Guards**, took over factories, trains, newspapers and schools all over China and forced everyone to listen to lectures about Mao's **'Little Red Book'**. Mao was supported by the army chief Lin Piao.

Government Ministers were humiliated and forced to resign. Liu Shao-chi was expelled from the Party he had helped to victory in 1949. Deng Xiaoping, the Communist Party Secretary, was forced to resign. Businessmen fled the country and little work was done in the factories, as workers were forced by Mao's Red Guard to discuss politics. The Red Guards fought against the workers and soldiers who opposed Maoism.

Eventually Lin Piao, whom Mao had named as his successor, realised that Mao's **Cultural Revolution** was leading to chaos and civil war. He tried to get the army to stop the Cultural Revolution which he had helped to start. Mao discovered Lin's 'treachery' and turned on him, and Lin was killed in an 'accidental' aircrash while escaping to the West.

Eventually the army leaders decided to end the Cultural Revolution. Army commanders opposed to the Cultural Revolution fought pitched battles with the Red Guards and drove them back to their classrooms.

Chou had the backing of the army and civil servants, so he became China's Prime Minister. Mao was Party Chairman until his death in 1976. Deng Xiaoping became Deputy Prime Minister in 1973 and was the real ruler of China, responsible for economic reform. This was the sign that the Cultural Revolution was over.

22.9 Communist China and the USSR

China had many quarrels with the USSR – they shared borders, and China was suspicious that the USSR wanted to seize Manchuria. Mao also thought Khrushchev wanted the USSR to become too westernised, and was angry when Soviet aid to China was cut off in 1960. In 1962 Mao accused Khrushchev of cowardice during the Cuban crisis (see Chapter 17). Mao was angry that Khrushchev opposed an international Communist revolution, and he refused to sign the 1963 **Test Ban Treaty**, calling Khrushchev a 'paper tiger'. Khrushchev called Mao an 'Asian Hitler'.

During the cultural revolution (see 22.8) the USSR was even more hostile to China, since Brezhnev (see 18.5) feared the chaos would spread to the USSR. There were skirmishes between the USSR and China on the Mongolian border (1965–9).

In the 1980s and 1990s both China and the USSR tried to talk through their differences and increase trade between the two nations. Gorbachev (see 18.6) criticised China's refusal to reform Communism.

22.10 Communist China and the USA

China and the USA were enemies until the 1970s. The USA refused to recognise Communist China and vetoed China's entry to the UN. The USA was angry with Mao's support for North Korea (see 14.4), and his support for North Vietnam in the Vietnam war (see 17.3).

In 1971 relations with the USA improved greatly. President Nixon allowed China to join the UN Security Council (see 16.3) in place of non-Communist Taiwan. China allowed USA table tennis teams to come to China. Nixon visited Peking, and many western leaders followed in the 1970s and 1980s, anxious to promote peace with China.

The West wanted to sell its goods to the huge Chinese population, and the Chinese Government knew that its 'cold war' with the West was expensive. The Chinese Government wanted access to western markets and also to attract western capital for China's industrial development.

22.11 Communist China and her neighbours

Mao and his successors were ruthless with **Tibet**. Tibetan moves to independence were crushed, and the Dalai Lama was forced to flee. Tibet was declared a self-governing part of China from 1965.

China also seized areas in **Burma** and the Himalayas, which India also claimed. China won the war with India in 1962, seizing 39,000 square kilometres of land.

In 1983 Britain and China began to negotiate over **Hong Kong**. They agreed that China should take control of the colony in 1997. China agreed to allow Hong Kong to develop as a privileged part of China, but opposed Hong Kong's desire to become democratic. In the 1980s and 1990s the Chinese Government came to see Hong Kong as an important point of access to the West. The Communist Government did not try to seize the nearby areas of Kowloon or Macao from Britain and Portugal, since China wanted to improve relations with the West for economic reasons.

China was still hostile to Taiwan, but under Deng Xiaoping, China encouraged a better relationship with the island. Taiwan was very rich due to its private enterprise system. Deng knew Taiwan could provide money for China's industrial development.

China could be regarded as a 'Superpower' due to its ability to produce nuclear weapons, its industrial development and enormous population. Western and Russian politicians and businesses became increasingly anxious to be on good terms with China. They knew that as the billion people in China became richer they would be able to buy more western-made goods.

22.12 The modernisation of China after Mao

After the deaths of Mao and Chou En-lai in 1976, Deng Xiaoping became China's real ruler. Madam Mao and other leading Maoists were imprisoned for their part in the 'Cultural Revolution', which had caused great misery and chaos in China.

Deng Xiaoping, and the leaders of China from 1976 onwards, wanted to reform China's economy and create 'Free Market Socialism'. Many old leaders were forced to retire, and they were replaced by younger pragmatic men who did not believe in Mao's ideas (see 22.4).

The most important reformer of China's economic policies was Hu Yaobang. Hu, and his successor Zhao Zi Zang, encouraged the peasants to grow and sell food privately, and after 1980 many peasants grew rich. These incentives caused food output to grow. Foreigners were encouraged to invest in China. Japan, in particular, took advantage of the tax free zones set up around the main ports, and in the 1990s businesses from Europe and the USA also invested in China. These countries hoped to sell their products to China's huge population.

Successful Chinese businessmen also became rich as they took advantage of the freedom to develop private companies.

22.13 Opposition to the 'modernising' Deng Xiaoping

Many town workers resented the new wealth of the richer peasants, and objected to inflation which grew with the increase of bank credit. Many workers lost their jobs if their businesses were inefficient, so these unemployed people were also angry with the 'new' China.

Maoists, led by Li Peng, opposed the new private enterprise methods. They were angry about the gulf that grew between the clever, richer peasants and workers and the rest of the population. This inequality showed that Communism was being abandoned in the new private enterprise economy. They also hated the increase in corruption and crime which the new wealth was encouraging.

22.14 Tiananmen Square

Examiner's tip

i.   A time line will help you to revise the key points in this chapter.
ii. List the reasons for and effects of the Cultural Revolution.
iii. Revise carefully the roles of Deng Xiaoping and Hu Yaobang in China's modernisation policies.
iv. Study the differences and similarities between the policies of the 'new' communist leaders and those of Mao and his supporters.
v.   Note that China under Mao began to change before his death in 1976.

Many university students, writers and business people thought that Deng and his reformers had not reformed China enough. In 1989 they organised a series of pro-democracy demonstrations in Peking and other cities. They all gathered in Tiananmen Square and demanded press freedom, free speech, release of anti-Communists, and moves towards democracy. The demonstrators were joined by workers angry about inflation and unemployment.

The Government ordered the demonstrations to stop, because Gorbachev (see 18.6) was coming to China, but they refused. The police and the Peking army unit were unwilling to break up the demonstration. After Gorbachev left, the students demanded Deng's removal, and many went on hunger strike. People around the world watched the demonstrations on television and many people thought an anti-Communist revolution was taking place.

On 4 June 1989 Li Peng and Deng sent 'loyal' troops to crush the demonstrations. Thousands of 'dissidents' were arrested and many were killed – the massacre of Tiananmen Square shocked the West. Universities, schools and writers were put under Communist Party control again.

After the Tiananmen Square incident, Deng's Government continued to encourage private enterprise. Many peasants and workers grew richer. In 1991 foreign trade was worth $135 billion, 30% of China's output. Old Maoists were still angry about growing inequality, corruption and the end of true Communism. Some pro-democracy students still campaigned 'underground' for political freedom, which Deng and the rest of the Communist Party leadership refused to accept.

Summary

1 China was devastated by the war with Japan and the civil war with the KMT.
2 In the first stage of Mao's agricultural modernisation, the peasants were given land to encourage them to grow food.
3 In the second stage of agricultural modernisation, the peasants' farms were collectivised, and these larger units produced more grain.
4 After the 'Hundred Flowers Campaign', the 'Great Leap Forward' forced the peasants into communes causing famine and bloodshed.
5 Mao resigned as Head of State in 1958, and the new leaders of China allowed peasants and workers to own some of their own property.
6 The Cultural Revolution was started by Mao to force China back on to the road of true Communism.
7 After the bloodshed of the Cultural Revolution the Chinese leaders continued to introduce capitalist ideas into the economy.
8 The 'modernising' leaders Deng Xiaoping and Hu Yaobang were criticised for these reforms by both Maoists, who thought there was too much change, and by many students who thought there was not enough democratic change.
9 The massacre at Tiananmen Square crushed movements towards democracy, but economic change continued to give peasants and workers more private wealth.
10 China had conflicts with the USSR over her borders and the future of Communism.

10 Relations with the USA improved after 1971. Western countries wanted to trade with China. They ignored China's crushing of Tibetan dissidents.

Quick questions

1 With which country did China go to war in the 1930s, to devastating effect?
2 What were the peasants given to encourage them to grow food (1950–2)?
3 What happened to peasant holdings during the second stage of modernisation?
4 When did Mao resign as Head of State?
5 Who started the 'Cultural Revolution'?
6 Name *two* modernising Chinese leaders criticised by Mao and his supporters.
7 Where were many students massacred in June 1989?
8 Name a country which had several border disputes with China.
9 In which year did the USA become friendlier with China?
10 Name the country that was crushed by Communist China in the 1960s.

Chapter 23
South Africa 1945–95

23.1 The origins of apartheid

The Union of South Africa was created in 1910 under British control. Power remained in the hands of the white population though they formed only 17% of the total population. In the Cape Province, Africans (70% of the population) were forbidden to vote. The other ethnic groups, the 'Coloureds' and the 'Asians', were only allowed to vote for white MP's. There were two main groups of white people: the Afrikaners who descended from the Dutch 'Boer' settlers, and the English speakers.

In 1948 the mainly **Afrikaner Nationalist Party**, led by Dr Malan, won the general election promising the white voters to rescue them from the 'black menace'. The Afrikaner Nationalist Party had split from the more 'liberal' English-speaking **South Africa Party**, led by Smuts.

Although parliament had voted narrowly to support Smuts' alliance with Britain against Germany during World War Two, there was sympathy among the Afrikaners for the racist policies of Nazism and Fascism. The Dutch Reformed Church believed that black people should be servants of white people, and that the whites were the 'master race'. The whites were frightened by the granting of independence to India and Pakistan (see Chapter 11) in 1947, and by new ideas of racial equality which World War II helped to promote. They feared that their black and Asian employees would demand better wages and social conditions if they gained political power. The whites were afraid that a Communist system of government, which the ANC (see 23.5) seemed to favour, would emerge, and in the 1960s they also saw that many African states like Zaire (see 14.4) and Uganda were chaotic and ruled by vicious dictators.

23.2 How the apartheid system worked

Malan and his successors passed a series of laws which created the system of apartheid (separate development). Presidents Verwoerd (1958–66) and Vorster (1966–78) strengthened apartheid. **Segregation** and discrimination had always existed in South Africa, but now the oppression of Africans and Asians was made systematic.

- The **Population Registration Act** (1950) classified all people into racial groups from birth. Only white people were regarded as citizens of South Africa.
- The **Group Areas Act** (1950) forced black people out of areas listed as 'whites only', and their former homes were demolished as they moved to townships (below) or tribal reserves.
- The **Bantu Self-Government Act** (1959) set up eight self-governing regions

called Bantustans, based on the tribal reserves. These covered 14% of South African land, but held 80% of the South African population.

- In the cities blacks had to move to separate townships, and there was complete segregation in public places such as in transport, schools, churches, beaches and sports grounds. Africans' homes could be pulled down at any time.

23.3 How apartheid was enforced

- The **Pass Laws** enforced this system. All 'non-whites' had to carry their passes so that police could control their movement.
- Marriage and sexual relations between whites and non-whites was forbidden, so that the purity of the white race could be maintained.
- There were no black or Asian MPs, and non-whites had no right to vote. The High Court of Parliament was controlled by pro-apartheid judges.
- The **Suppression of Communism Act** (1950) allowed the government to crush attempts by Africans or whites to protest against apartheid. Arrests without charge, rigged trials, torture and imprisonment were used to repress protests.
- Black workers were forbidden to strike, and protesters could be flogged.
- **Bantu Education Acts** ensured that African children only had a low level of education, since they were meant to have low-paid jobs. The Government hoped that, if they were uneducated, the black people would not expect a better way of life.

23.4 The impact of apartheid on the Africans and the whites

E **xaminer's tip**

Revise carefully the details of the various apartheid laws and the reasons for, and effects of, the setting up of Apartheid.

Africans and other non-whites suffered appalling living conditions. Their slum housing in the townships lacked basic water and electricity supplies, and the schools lacked text books, teachers and furniture. Many African families broke up because the men had to live in work hostels as migrant workers, while their families stayed in the townships and Bantustans.

A vicious cycle of poverty, crime, and drunkenness set in. **Soweto** became the best known of these townships, where there were frequent riots and massacres by police, as well as fights between different African tribes and political groups (see 23.5).

Most white people did not think the system should be changed, for reasons we have looked at in 23.1, but increasingly white employers realised the need for better educated black workers, since there was a shortage of skilled white workers. Some of the taxes that white people paid went to the army and police which were needed to oppress the Africans, the majority population so many white people lived in fear of. Increasingly white people realised that the apartheid system would have to change for economic reasons, but they were frightened of making these changes because their power over the majority population would be removed.

23.5 Opposition to apartheid within South Africa

The **African National Congress** and the **South African Indian Congress** tried to oppose apartheid non-violently, influenced by the tactics of Gandhi and Martin Luther

E **xaminer's tip**

Mandela, Sisulu and other leaders of the ANC were lawyers, part of that educated group (see 11.4) who were 'half satisfied' (see note 1.3).

King. Non-whites tried to break the **segregation** and pass laws by bus **boycotts**, protest marches and peaceful demonstrations. In March 1960, at Sharpeville, about seventy Africans were shot, and many more were wounded in the anti-pass law demonstrations.

This massacre led to national rioting and world-wide protests. The ANC (African National Congress) and the **Pan African Congress** (PAC) who had organised the protests were banned, and the leaders like Nelson Mandela, Jo Slovo and Walter Sisulu were arrested and held in prison until February 1990. The ANC then adopted a policy of 'armed struggle', which frightened white liberals abroad and in South Africa.

The ANC opposed the Black Consciousness movement, led by **Steve Biko** who was killed in prison after breaking a police order confining him to his Bantustan. Like Malcom X and Stokey Carmichael in the USA (21.4), Biko's followers believed that the Africans should rely on themselves and seek self-rule. Mandela disagreed with this, believing that the whites should be persuaded of the need to create a multi-racial South Africa which would belong to whites and blacks. The ANC regarded the PAC's aims as too narrow because the PAC was anti-Indian and anti-Communist, and not as disciplined as the ANC. The ANC was also rivalled by the Zulu **Inkatha Party** led by Chief Buthelezi, and there were often bloody confrontations between them in the townships. The ANC accused Inkatha of being used by the white Government as spies and provokers of riots. Inkatha feared the ANC would set up a dictatorship.

23.6 Opposition to apartheid outside South Africa

The UNO condemned apartheid and called for the unbanning of the ANC and Mandela's release. Pressure for change also came from the Commonwealth and the African states. International pressure for abolition of apartheid came in the form of trade boycotts, sporting bans, diplomatic pressure, campaigns to release Mandela by musicians, and pressure by most national leaders. In Europe many shoppers boycotted businesses connected with South Africa.

Reforms by President Botha (1978–89), who abolished the pass laws, marriage and segregation laws, were regarded as 'too little too late' inside and outside South Africa. Botha warned his white voters that they had to 'adapt or die'.

23.7 The movement to majority rule

In the 1970s the opposition of white (mainly English speaking) South Africans to apartheid started to grow. They hated the boycotts of their sports teams and the international hatred of apartheid. They watched foreign television programmes criticising South Africa. More Africans were getting skilled jobs, yet they lacked civil rights. Policing apartheid also cost a lot in taxes and human life. 'Liberals', like the journalist Donald Woods and the Progressive Party leader Helen Suzman, persuaded other white people of the need for change. When white politicians met Mandela in prison they were impressed by his desire for peace and reconciliation between whites and blacks.

The Christian Churches in South Africa and throughout the world attacked apartheid, and eventually the Dutch Reformed Church ended its support for apartheid. Archbishop Desmond Tutu led the Churches' campaign for a new South Africa, and tried to persuade white South Africans to accept that the system of apartheid was evil. Tutu also argued for Mandela's release, and non-violence between the African groups and between black and white South Africans.

When President Botha called whites-only elections in August 1989 the results showed that a majority of whites wanted apartheid to be totally abolished, and following an illness he resigned. De Klerk became President, and in February 1990 he freed Mandela who called off the 'armed struggle' in August 1990. Mandela and De Klerk set up a **Convention for a Democratic South Africa** in which the different parties would write the new Constitution. The hardline whites who opposed change resigned from the National Party and set up the Conservative Party. Other extremists had already set up a neo-Fascist Afrikaner Party. De Klerk called a whites-only referendum on the changes and 70% of them voted to support them.

23.8 Nelson Mandela becomes President of the new South Africa

Examiner's tip

i.   A time line showing the key events in the protests against Apartheid will help you revise this topic.
ii. Take care not to confuse the various individuals and groups who led the opposition to Apartheid. List their actions briefly under a series of headings.
iii. Be ready to explain which individuals played the most important role in the abolition of Apartheid.

The Convention voted on 3 June 1993 to call elections for the new South African National Assembly, to be elected by 'one-man-one-vote' for the first time. The elections, held on 27 April 1994, were won by the ANC who got 62% of the vote, with the National Party the second largest party. Inkkatha and the Conservative party refused to take part, which Mandela regretted.

On 10 May 1994 Nelson Mandela was installed as the President of South Africa. De Klerk joined him as Vice President in a **Government of National Unity**. The new Government set about the task of solving the many problems of Apartheid: poverty, violence, racial tension between blacks and whites and between the black tribes. Mandela also had to win the confidence of white business leaders and foreign investors, so that the economy would be strong.

In April 1996 the South African Parliament approved the new Constitution which established majority rule. De Klerk's National Party left the Government to become the opposition to the ANC. Apartheid was dead.

Summary

1 The system of apartheid was begun officially in 1948 by the national Government, led by Malan and developed further by his successors.
2 Most white people wished to maintain their control over the Africans, Asians and Coloured peoples by a series of laws which made the 'non-white' majority inferior in status to the white people.
3 The white population feared a loss of economic, political and social power if the majority ruled in South Africa.
4 The Government oppressed the opponents by ruthless use of the army, arrests and the pass laws.
5 The Bantustans and townships were overcrowded and lawless places, where different groups fought amongst themselves as well as against the Government forces.
6 The ANC, led by Nelson Mandela, adopted violence against the Government after the Sharpville massacre.
7 The ANC was more moderate and disciplined than other groups, such as the PAC and Inkatha.
8 Pressure for abolition of apartheid grew outside South Africa during the 1960s and 1970s in the form of demonstrations, sporting and trade boycotts and diplomatic pressure.
9 Within South Africa, many white people began to want change, due to the pressures mentioned in point 8 and the need for a happier, better off African and Asian population.

10 President Botha started to get rid of 'petty' apartheid rules such as segregation, and De Klerk released Mandela and unbanned the ANC. The whites–only referendum supported these reforms, but some Afrikaners left the National Party.

11 In April 1994 the ANC won the first all–South African General Election, and Mandela became President. De Klerk and Mandela won the Nobel Peace Prize for their work for peace.

Quick questions

1 When was the apartheid system started?
2 Which Church supported the apartheid system?
3 Name the South African leader responsible for the introduction of apartheid.
4 When were the following Acts passed:
    i)   Population Registration Act;
    ii) Bantu Self-Government Act and the Bantu Education Act;
    iii) Group Areas Act;
    iv) Suppression of Communism Act.
5 Name *two* white South African Presidents who helped to abolish apartheid.
6 Name the leader of the ANC, released from prison by President de Klerk in February 1990.
7 When was the first all-South African election held?

Chapter 24
The Middle East

24.1 Important features of this region

The Suez Canal, opened in 1869, was a short and relatively easy **trading route** between Europe and Asia and Australasia. From 1875 to 1956 the Canal was run by a Company, with Britain as a major shareholder. Since the Canal runs through Egypt, Britain wanted good relations with Egypt: she governed that country from 1882 to 1922, and after that kept troops stationed along the Canal until 1954. Conflict over control of the canal led to an international crisis in 1956 (see 25.6)

About one-third of all **oil supplies** come from countries around the Persian Gulf: Iraq, Kuwait, Saudi Arabia, the Emirates, Bahrain and Iran. In 1973, and again in 1978–9, the **Organisation of Petroleum Exporting Countries** (OPEC) sharply increased the price of oil and so caused economic problems for the industrial world, which had to pay higher prices for the imported and essential fuel (see Chapter 25).

Three of the world's main **religions** have their origins in this region: Judaism, Islam and Christianity. The creation of the State of Israel, and the rise of Arab (mainly Islamic) nationalism led to a series of wars and crises after 1945.

24.2 Palestine and the Middle East

Britain and France gained **mandates** in Syria, Lebanon, Palestine and Mesopotamia (Iraq) in the 1920s (see 4.7). We have also seen (4.6) that Britain made contradictory promises to both Jews and Arabs about the future developments of the areas it controlled.

In the 1920s and 1930s there were anti-British riots in Egypt and Iraq, forcing Britain to give up control of these countries (1922 and 1936 respectively), though Britain still had a great deal of influence behind the scenes.

Palestine was the main source of trouble in this period. Balfour's promise of a 'National Home' for Jews in Palestine (see 4.6) angered the Arabs there, who made up 93% of the population. Many Jews arrived in Palestine in the 1920s. This led to anti-British and anti-Jewish riots by militant Arabs, led by their religious leader, the grand Mufti of Jerusalem. Britain imposed limits on the number of Jewish immigrants (1933) just when Hitler began his persecution of Jews (see 8.11). In spite of this, by 1939 Jews made up about one-third of the population of Palestine. Their hard work, technical skills and aid from abroad helped the Jews to make the 'desert bloom'. They bought land from the Arab landowners, and the Arab riots against the Jewish settlements led the British to propose (1937) the division of Palestine into Jewish and Arab states. The Arabs rejected this proposal.

24.3 Palestine, 1945–47

In 1945 there was a world-wide demand that the British should allow the survivors of the Holocaust free entry into Palestine. The Labour Government refused to do this because it was aware of Britain's need for friendship with the Arab rulers of the oil-producing states, where British companies had major investments.

Britain's policy led to the smuggling of illegal Jewish immigrants, the turning back of immigrant ships by the Royal Navy, fighting between British and Jewish forces, and between British and angry anti-Jewish rioters.

In 1947 Britain ended its part in the Greek civil war (see 15.3) and also announced that it was ending its mandate in Palestine. It handed that problem to the UNO on 14 May 1948.

24.4 The first Arab-Israeli War, 1948–49

Examiner's tip

Revise carefully the different views of the Jewish settlers in Palestine, the Arabs and the British Government.

As Britain ended its mandate, Ben Gurion, head of the Jewish Agency in Palestine, declared that a new state, Israel, was formed, with himself as Prime Minister. At the same time, the UN proposed that Palestine be divided (or partitioned) between Arabs and Jews (see the map on page 183). The Arabs refused to accept both the existence of Israel and the UN proposal for partition. Egyptian armies and Jordanian troops invaded the new state. Other members of the Arab League (Saudi Arabia, Iraq, Syria and the states of North Africa) promised to send help. Few of them did, and those that did sent few troops. The surrounded and outnumbered Jews appealed for world help, but got none. The UN tried to mediate a truce to end the fighting, but the mediator, Count Bernadotte, was killed by Jewish terrorists.

The Jews, led by British-trained officers (who had fought in the 1939–45 war), were determined to fight to the bitter end. The Arabs, on the other hand, were divided: Jordan wanted to gain the land on the West Bank of the River Jordan, including Jerusalem, for herself; Egypt wanted to extend its lands northwards; other Arab states were unwilling to risk their own men in fighting for the interests of Egypt and Jordan.

In February 1949, the fighting ended after a series of ceasefires between Israel and various Arab states. Israel gained more land than had been offered in the UN plan: she had extended her holdings in the north and linked together the lands given by the UN there; she also took more land in the Negev area in the south, although she failed to take the Gaza Strip.

24.5 An uneasy peace, 1949–56

A UNO commission had helped to negotiate the end of the fighting, and a UN force was sent as a Supervisory Commission to police the frontiers between Israel and its Arab neighbours. Relations between Israel and those neighbours were hostile for several reasons.
- Both Israel and Jordan wanted to control all of Jerusalem.
- Both Egypt and Israel wanted the Gaza Strip.
- Terrorist attacks on Israel were launched from Gaza with Egyptian support.
- The USSR had originally supported Israel, seeing her as an anti-Arab (and hence anti-western state). In 1948–9 the USSR saw Israel as a client state of the USA, so she turned to supporting the Arab states.

- Many thousands of Arabs fled from the lands that the Israelis now controlled. They became refugees in Jordan and other neighbouring Arab countries, where they lived in badly organised refugee camps. The rich oil-producing Arab states did not build them homes and 'make the desert bloom' as Israel did for their people. The Arabs seemed to prefer to keep their refugees in poverty, as a reminder of past suffering, as a stimulus to young Arabs to join terrorist organisations, and as a constant reminder of Israel's existence and growth.

- Nasser saw himself as a reformer who would develop Egypt, and as the leader who would unite all Arabs in an Arab Union. His ambitions frightened other Arab leaders, as well as the USA, Britain and France.

His anti-Israeli policies led him to blockade the Israeli ships using the Suez Canal. To help develop Egypt, he planned the building of a large dam on the Nile at Aswan to provide water for irrigation and for the generation of electricity. The USA promised to help finance this scheme, but withdrew its offer when Nasser bought modern weapons from Czechoslovakia and accepted Soviet military and economic aid.

The **second Arab-Israeli war**, the Suez Crisis, is covered in the case study in Chapter 25.

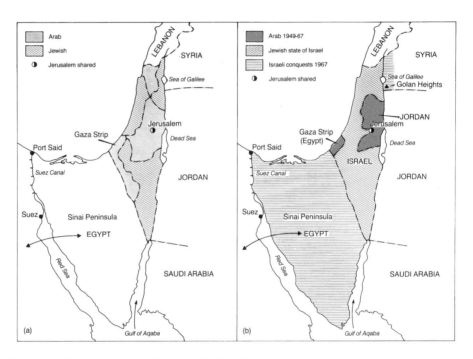

Fig. 24.1 The expansion of Israel, 1949–67

24.6 An uneasy peace, 1956–57

The UN peacekeeping force (see 14.4) cleared the Suez Canal, kept peace on the Israel-Egypt border, and had a post at the entrance to the Gulf of Aqaba to ensure that Israeli ships could get through to the port of Eilat.

Nasser, more popular than ever with Arabs, formed a United Arab Republic with Syria, which shelled Israeli settlements from military posts on the Golan Heights. In Lebanon, Iraq, Aden and the Yemen, pro-Nasser and anti-Israeli governments seized power.

The **Palestinian Liberation Organisation** (PLO) was set up in 1964 to bring together various Palestinian Arab groups. It was soon dominated by one group, Al Fatah, led by Yasser Arafat who was supported by the Syrian government. Many groups inside the PLO waged guerrilla and terrorist tactics inside Israel and against Israeli people and businesses world wide. There were also constant terrorist attacks by the Egyptian-controlled Gaza Strip on Israel.

There were some challenges to Nasser's domination of Arab affairs. In 1961 Syria left the United Arab Republic; Iraq's leaders claimed Iraq to be the leading Arab state; Saudi Arabia helped anti-Nasser forces in the Yemen and claimed leadership of the less radical Arabs.

Nasser felt it necessary to act in order to regain his former position among Arab states. On 4 June 1967, the PLO groups inside Jordan forced the King of Jordan to sign a military pact with Nasser, who then ordered the UN peacekeeping forces to withdraw from the border areas. He meant to attack Israel with help from Syria and Jordan.

24.7 The third (Six Day) Arab-Israeli War, 1967

On 5 June 1967 Israel launched its own attack ('the best form of defence'). Its airforces destroyed the airforces of Jordan, Syria and Egypt. Its troops conquered the Sinai, destroying the Egyptian army, drove the Jordanians from the West Bank and routed the Syrians on the Golan. On 8 June Hussein of Jordan capitulated, and on 11 June both Syria and Egypt surrendered.

Israel refused UN pleas for a return to the old borders. She occupied the Sinai right up to the Suez Canal, occupied part of Syria including the Golan, and kept the West Bank up to the River Jordan (see Fig. 24.1).

24.8 Tension and terrorism, 1967–73

The failure of the Arab states to 'drive the Jews into the Mediterranean', led to increased support for the terrorist groups inside the PLO. These drew attention to their cause and to the plight of the refugees by their frequent raids into Israel, by hijacking Israeli aircraft, and by murderous attacks such as the gunning down of 100 people at Israel's Lydda airport.

In September 1970 the PLO, backed by the refugees, challenged King Hussein of Jordan, who had the loyal support of his army and people. Hussein turned against Arafat and the PLO, drove them and their organisation from his Kingdom, and forced them to seek refuge in Syria. Some extremists saw this as a **'Black September'**, and gave that name to a new terrorist group which was responsible for the kidnapping of Israeli athletes at the 1972 Olympic Games – the athletes were killed in a gunfight between the terrorists and the German police.

Nasser died in 1970 while trying to negotiate peace between Hussein and the PLO in Jordan. His successor was Sadat.

24.9 The fourth Arab-Israeli War, 1973

Sadat wanted to get back the Sinai: Syria wanted to get back the Golan. On 6 October (the Jewish holy day of Yom Kippur) Syria, aided by Jordan, Iraq and Saudi Arabia, and with tanks and other weapons received from the USSR, drove into the Golan in a surprise attack. The Egyptians attacked across the Canal and broke through the Israeli defences in the Sinai.

On 8 October the Israelis counter-attacked. In the west they drove the Egyptians from the Sinai, crossed the Suez Canal and drove on the Suez-Cairo road towards the

Egyptian capital. In the Golan, they recaptured land lost on 6 October, drove down into Syria itself and reached a point some 35 miles from the Syrian capital, Damascus.

On 24 October the UN arranged a ceasefire, but it was March 1974 before Israeli and Egyptian forces finally disengaged along the Canal, and May 1974 before a UN force was stationed between Syrian and Israeli forces on the Golan Heights.

24.10 1974–76: more crises

The Arab oil-producing members of **OPEC**, angered at the success of Israel, pushed up oil prices so that in 1974 they were four times as higher than they had been in 1972–3. They also cut off oil supplies to nations which had supported Israel, Holland being the first victim.

This 'oil weapon' led to increased fuel prices in the western world, which led to rising inflation, and a slow down in world trade as countries stopped importing non-oil goods so that they could afford the new and higher oil prices.

In 1975–6 a civil war between Muslims and Christians in Lebanon saw the PLO supporting the Muslims. Arafat hoped to find a new base for himself in a Muslim-controlled Lebanon. Syrian forces, which had once supported Arafat, invaded Lebanon to restore peace there and fought against the ambitious PLO forces.

In March 1976, Arafat led a PLO delegation to the UN General Assembly in New York, where he was allowed to take part in a debate on conditions in the Israeli-occupied West Bank. He asked for UN help so that this territory could be handed to Arabs for the creation of a Palestinian state. He ignored the fact that Arabs could have had that region in 1948 (see the map on page 154) and that Jordan had seized it in 1948–9.

In June 1976 PLO terrorists hijacked an Air France plane containing many Jewish passengers, and forced it to fly to Entebbe in Uganda. The dictator, Idi Amin, allowed the PLO to use the old airport as a prison, where they kept the Jews as hostages while demanding the release of PLO terrorists held in Israeli prisons. The Israelis mounted a rescue operation, flying in an airborne force which rescued nearly all the hostages, and killed most of the hijackers and the Ugandan guards placed around the airport by Amin.

24.11 Egyptian-Israeli peace, 1977–79

Sadat wanted to cut down on military spending so that he could spend money on Egyptian social reform. In November 1977 he offered to go to speak to the Israeli Parliament (the Knesset). Menachem Begin, Prime Minister of Israel, but once a leader of Jewish terrorists against British rule 1945–8 (see 24.3) accepted the offer. Sadat's visit and speech (1921 November) was the first time an Arab Head of State recognised Israel.

24.12 Israel and Lebanon, 1976–82

The PLO took advantage of the continuing civil war in Lebanon to set up bases in South Lebanon. From here the PLO launched attacks on Israeli settlements across the border, and organised terrorist activities which led to assassinations of leading Israelis in London, Paris and elsewhere.

In 1982 Begin's government launched attacks on PLO bases in South Lebanon, advanced towards the Lebanese capital, Beirut, and fought Syrian forces for the control of North Lebanon.

This invasion succeeded in so far as, with Syrian help, the PLO was driven from Lebanon and Arafat was forced to withdraw his forces. However, the invasion failed because Syria and other governments in the world could not allow Israel to occupy Lebanon. By 1984 Israel was forced to withdraw its forces to South Lebanon where it kept some forces with the co-operation of the Christian Government of that area.

24.13 Israel and the Arab uprising, 1987–89

Israeli politicians, and Israelis in general, remained badly divided over what to do about making peace with the Arabs, and over what to do about the West Bank lands taken in the 1967 war and in 1973.

The Labour Party, led sometimes by Peres and sometimes by Rabin, wanted to try to reach a peaceful agreement with the Arabs, and was prepared to make some moves towards Palestinians living in the West Bank having some control over some parts of that region.

The Likud Party, led by former anti-British terrorists like Begin and Shamir, or by former military commanders like Aron, tended to take a harder line. They claimed the occupied lands were, in fact, part of the Biblical area of Judea and Samaria, and so were part of historic Israel. They supported the building of new Jewish settlements in these occupied lands as a way of cementing Israel's claim.

The invasion, and later occupation, of Southern Lebanon divided both the political parties and the people. In December 1987, Palestinians in the West Bank occupied lands rose in what seemed to be a spontaneous uprising (*intifadah*). Children attacked Israeli troops and offices with stones and petrol bombs. Arab workers went on strike, and Arab traders closed down their businesses. The Israeli army was sent in to restore order, leading to well-publicised pictures of soldiers beating children and firing on crowds of young people, some of whom were killed.

Examiner's tip

i. Study the reasons for and the effects of PLO terrorism against Israel.
ii. Prepare answers to the questions about why peace between Israel and the Arabs was hard to achieve.

24.14 The USA peace plan, 1991–93

In November 1988 the Palestinian National Council, of which the PLO was a leading member, made a major decision. It announced that it would recognise the state of Israel (as Sadat had done in 1977), and the PLO agreed to renounce and condemn terrorism against Israel, with whose leaders it proposed to negotiate a plan for peace.

In May 1989 the right-wing government of Israel announced that elections would be held in the West Bank and Gaza. This alarmed more extreme members of the Likud Party, as well as the Jews settled in the West Bank, who clashed with police and Israeli troops as they rioted against the Government.

In 1991 the US Government (on which Israel depends for military and economic aid) forced Shamir, leader of Likud, to agree to attend an international conference on the Palestinian issue. This opened in Madrid and was attended by statesmen from the USA, Britain, France, most Arab states, and by Palestinian representatives.

It was soon clear that Syria and Israel were at loggerheads. The conference later moved to Washington while, in Israel, a Labour government, led by Rabin, took power. In 1993 Rabin, with Peres as his Foreign Minister, signed an accord with Yasser Arafat. President Bill Clinton acted as an 'honest broker' in bringing the two sides together.

Following that agreement, elections were held in the Gaza Strip and in some parts of the West Bank, which enabled Palestinians to form their own Government with Arafat as President. It is still (1997) not clear how successful this Government will be in tackling the social and economic problems of its people.

It is clear that many Arab extremists have rejected the Washington agreement as a 'final settlement' of the Palestinian problem. One group, Hezbollah, has set up bases in

Lebanon from where it has launched rocket and other attacks on Israeli settlements. The Israeli response has been to bomb Hezbollah camps in Lebanon where, not surprisingly, many innocent people have been killed by these bombardments.

Summary

1 The Middle East region was important due to the Suez Canal, the oil and the religions represented there.
2 1919–39: Arabs fought Jews for control of the British mandate. Both groups fought the British, and the Arabs rejected British partition proposals, 1937–9.
3 1945–7: both legal and illegal Jewish immigration increased. Arab and Jewish terrorism increased and Britain handed its mandate back to the UN, 1947–8.
4 May 1948: The UN proposal for partition of Palestine was rejected by the Arabs.
5 1948: The new state of Israel was formed, leading to the first Arab-Israel war in which Israel extended her borders beyond limits suggested by the UN. Jordan took the West Bank.
6 1949–56: Arab-Israeli hostility grew. Nasser became the leader of the Arab world.
7 1956: The Suez crisis led to the second Arab-Israeli war. The UN intervened.
8 The PLO was formed and there were divisions among Arab states.
9 1967: The third ('Six Day') war led to further extensions of Israel's territory.
10 1967–72: Arab-Israeli tensions led to the Munich massacre (1972).
11 1973: The fourth ('Yom Kippur') war was won by Israel after initial Arab successes. Israel took the Golan and Sinai.
12 1973–6: OPEC raised the price of oil; there was a Lebanese Civil War; Arafat went to the UNO, but there was PLO terrorism at Tel Aviv and Entebbe.
13 1977: Sadat started the process towards the Egypt-Israel peace settlement.
14 1982: Israeli opinion was divided on her invasion of Lebanon.
15 The Intifadah began against Israel's occupation of the West Bank.
16 1991–3: The US peace plan led to the Washington Agreement with the PLO.

Quick questions

1 When did the UN take control of former the British mandate in Palestine?
2 Name the first Israeli Prime Minister.
3 What territory did Jordan seize in 1948–9?
4 Who 'ruled' Egypt from 1954 to 1970?
5 Where did Egypt build a Dam in 1956?
6 Name the area from which Syrian troops bombarded Israeli towns.
7 What do the following initials stand for: i)OPEC; ii)PLO?
8 When did King Hussein expel the PLO from Jordan?
9 Where and when were Israeli athletes kidnapped by Arab terrorists?
10 Name *four* Arab states which united against Israel in 1973.
11 In which country is Entebbe?
12 Name the *three* statesmen who negotiated the Egyptian-Israeli peace settlement of 1979.
13 When did Israel invade Lebanon?
14 What is the Arab word for the 'uprising' of 1987–9?
15 Name the *two* Jewish and *one* Arab leader who signed the Washington Accord in 1993.

Chapter 25
The Suez Crisis: a case study

25.1 The background to the crisis

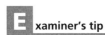

Examiner's tip

Study the different policies of the anti-Egyptian Allies in the Suez Crisis.

- Israel was angered by guerrilla (*fedayeen*) attacks from Egyptian-controlled Gaza and by Nasser's blockade of the port of Eilat.
- France was angered by Nasser's help to Algerian rebels fighting for their independence from France.
- Eden, the British Prime Minister, thought that Nasser was 'a modern Mussolini' who had to be stopped before he got too powerful. Eden said 'He must be destroyed'.

25.2 The course of the crisis, 1956

On 19 July the USA and Britain (21 July) cancelled the aid they had promised to help Nasser build the Aswan Dam (Source A).

26 July, Nasser announced the nationalisation of the Suez Canal Company. He would use the income from the Canal to finance the building of the Aswan Dam. Egyptians welcomed this anti-British and anti-colonial move (Source B).

27 July, Nasser was condemned in the British Press (Source C), and by the British Parliament, where the Labour opposition backed Eden (Source D). Eden set up a small Egyptian Committee to plan a war on Egypt (Source F).

31 July, in a friendly letter, President Eisenhower warned Eden against the use of force, although his Secretary of State (Foreign Minister) Dulles seemed to support the need for force: 'Nasser must be forced to disgorge'.

In August, Dulles organised various attempts to negotiate with Nasser, who rejected every attempt.

10 September, Dulles and Eden agreed on the use of force (Source G).

11 September, Eisenhower denied a promise about using force (Source H).

1 October, The USSR warned Britain about the use of force.

11 October, Eisenhower seemed to back Eden again.

22 October, Britain signed a formal agreement with France and Israel about the coming campaign.

29 October, Israeli forces invaded the Sinai.

30 October, Britain and France declared a war 'to separate the warring parties'.

31 October, an angry letter was sent to Eden from Eisenhower, and the USA led the condemnation of Britain and France by the UN (Source K).

5 November, the British Chancellor Macmillan, who had called for war, now told Eden that the pressure on the pound (£) was so great that the war had to be called off.

7 November, the British and French advance down the Canal was halted and the war was ended.

25.3 The results of the war

- Nasser was made to look a successful hero among the Arabs, and he grew more popular among Arabs generally, though not among the ruling families in Arab states.
- The Canal remained blocked by Nasser's Egypt.
- France and Britain were humiliated by the failure of 'the Empires' last fling'.
- The USSR gained more influence in the region, and with the UNO distracted by the Suez Crisis (Source K), the USSR had a free hand in Hungary (see 19.4).
- A UN force replaced the so-called peacekeeping armies of Britain and France.

25.4 Interpreting and evaluating sources

a) Study Sources A to D and answer the following questions:
   i) How can *each* of these Sources be used to explain why war came in 1956?
   ii) How fully do these Sources explain why war occurred in 1956? Explain your answer.
b) Study Sources E to J. Do the Sources show that politicians were confused over the Suez Crisis? Explain your answer.
c) Study Sources C and K. Do you agree that these cartoons are useless as evidence for historians writing about the Suez Crisis? Give reasons for your answer.

xaminer's tip

i. Remember that all sources are useful to historians to an extent, depending on what uses historians wish to make of the sources.

ii. Questions such as 'how fully do these Sources explain' should lead students to refer to their knowledge in deciding how useful the sources have been.

Source A. A British Cabinet Minister on the Aswan Dam loans, July 1956

In July Dulles announced that the USA would not give financial aid for the Aswan Dam. Within a few days Britain followed suit. For Nasser the Dam was a symbol of the rebuilding of Egypt, of Arab nationalism. The withdrawal of aid was a stinging personal insult.

(The Earl of Kilmuir, *Memoirs*, 1956)

Right (picture): **Source B. Nasser welcomed by Egyptian crowds after nationalising the Canal**

Source C. A British reaction to the announcement

Source D. A Labour leader backs Eden's condemnation of Nasser, July 1956
This pocket dictator does not consult his Parliament. There is no discussion with us or other parties to the Treaty. This action is morally wrong and to be condemned.
(Herbert Morrison, House of Commons, 27 July 1956)

Source E. Eisenhower and Dulles differ in their attitudes
During July–September Eisenhower and Dulles were not on the same wavelength. Eisenhower was opposed to force. Dulles shared the British fear that Nasser could not be trusted, and that force might have to be used. He conveyed this to his Allies, but he maddened them at critical moments by suddenly changing his views so as to avoid a public difference with his President.
(T. Hooper, *The Devil and John F. Dulles*, 1974)

Source F. The Suez campaign planned, 10 September 1956
The first phase . . . a sudden air attack on the Egyptian Air Force to take a few days. This would show the Egyptians that they were now unprotected and unable to resist other pressures we might bring.
   The second phase . . . air attacks on chosen targets, the main one being the oil supply to Cairo.
   The third phase . . . the move of a land force into Port Said to restore order and to re-open the Canal.
(Minutes of the British Egypt Committee, 10 September 1956)

Source G. An Anglo-American agreed statement, 10 September 1956
. . . if the Egyptian Government should seek to interfere with the operation of the (Suez Canal Users Association) then that Government will be . . . in breach of the (Canal) Convention of 1888. In that event, Her Majesty's Government and others concerned will be free to take such further steps as seem to be required, either through the UN or by other means for the assertion of their rights.
(Statement issued at the same time in London and Washington, and repeated in the Commons by Eden, 12 September 1956)

Source H. Eisenhower denies a US promise to use force, 11 September 1956
I don't know what you mean by 'backing Britain and France'. We will not go to war while I am President unless there was an unexpected attack on this country.

(Press Conference, 11 September 1956)

Source J. Eisenhower seems to back Eden, 11 October 1956

The Soviets are playing hard to get a dominant position in the area, and have quite a hold on Nasser. I know that Dulles is working closely with Selwyn Lloyd at the UN and I deplore suggestions in the Press here and abroad that you and we are at cross purposes.

(Letter to Anthony Eden, 11 October 1956)

Source K. A cartoon on the Suez Crisis
In November 1956, Punch showed a stern-looking UN Secretary General Hammarskjold punishing the 'culprits' in the attack on Egypt: the pugnacious Ben Gurion, of Israel, and Eton-jacketed Selwyn Lloyd, of Britain, have the French leader between them. A triumphant Nasser looks on, while Khrushchev takes advantage of 'teacher's' concern over Suez to beat Hungary into submission.

For suggestion on answers see page 202.

Examination questions

1 International relations 1870–1914

This topic is covered in Chapter 2.

(a) Questions (i) to (v) relate to the events in the table below.

1878	The Treaty of San Stephano
1878	The Congress of Berlin.
1908	The annexation of Bosnia-Herzegovina by Austria-Hungary

    (i)   Give *one* reason why the Congress of Berlin was held in 1878.   (2)

    (ii) In what ways did the Congress of Berlin change the situation in the Balkans?   (4)

    (iii) Why did Austria–Hungary annex Bosnia-Herzegovina in 1908?   (5)

    (iv) Why did that annexation increase tension in the Balkans in the years 1908 to 1913?   (6)

    (v)· Why did the assassination of Archduke Francis Ferdinand lead to the outbreak of a European War in the summer of 1914?   (8)

(b) This is an essay question about German foreign policy, 1870–1914.

    (i)   What were the aims of Bismarck's policies towards France in the 1870s and 1880s?   (5)

    (ii) In what ways did German foreign policy change after Bismarck's resignation in 1890?   (8)

    (iii) Why did rivalry develop between Britain and Germany in the years 1890 to 1910?   (12)

ULEAC

2 The First World War

This topic is covered in Chapter 3.

Look carefully at Sources A to E which refer to the Battle of Passchendaele (3rd Ypres), 31 July to 12 November 1917. Then answer all the questions.

Source A. An entry dated 19 June 1917 from the diary of Field Marshal Haig, Commander-in-Chief of British forces on the Western Front. He had met the War Cabinet in London to discuss a new offensive.

    'The members of the War Cabinet asked me many questions, all tending to show that each of them was more pessimistic than the other. Lloyd George seemed to believe the decisive moment of the war would be 1918. Until then we ought to do little or nothing except support Italy with guns and gunners. I strongly argued that Germany was nearer to her end than they seemed to think. I stated that Germany was within six months of the total exhaustion of her available manpower if the fighting continues at its present level on the Western Front.'

Source B. An extract from an account of the Battle of Passchendaele published in 1931 and written by General Gough. Gough was a British general during the battle.
'The state of the ground was frightful on 17 August. the task of bringing up supplies and ammunition, or moving or firing the guns, which had often sunk up to their axles, was a fearful strain on the officers and men. When it came to an infantry attack across the water-logged shell-holes, movement was so slow and tiring that only the shortest advance could be considered. I informed the Commander-in-Chief that success was not possible, or would be too costly, under such conditions, and advised that the attack should now be abandoned.'

Source C. A photograph taken in the battle area on 1 August 1917

Source D. Two differing views of the battle
(i) An extract from the diary of an important New Zealand officer whose men fought in the battle. It was written after the battle.
'My opinion is that the generals who direct these battles do not know of the conditions, mud, cold, rain and lack of shelter for the men. The Germans are not so played out as our High Command think. Exhausted men struggling through mud cannot compete against dry men with machine-guns.'
(ii) A telegraph sent from Lloyd George to Field Marshal Haig on 16 October 1917.
'The War Cabinet desires to congratulate you upon the achievements of the British Armies in the great battle which has been raging since 31 July. Starting from positions in which the enemy had every advantage and despite being hampered by most unfavourable weather, you and your men have nevertheless driven the enemy back with skill and courage and have filled the enemy with alarm. I am personally glad to pass this message to you, and to your gallant troops, and to state again my confidence in your leadership.'

Source E: A comment on the Battle of Passchendaele taken from a German history of the war published in the 1920s.
'Above everything else the battle had used up Germany strength. Losses had been so high that they could no longer be replaced and the fighting strength of battalions was further reduced. Our enemies were well-prepared, greater in number and brave. However they had been able to achieve little, partly because of the bad weather conditions which made movement extremely difficult. But water and mud were no less a disadvantage to the defenders. These conditions, more

than the bloody fighting, led to a rapid wearing out of the troops.'
(a) Look at Source C.
   Why were there so much mud in the battle area? (2)
(b) Read Source D(ii).
   State two advantages which German soldiers had in the battle. (2)
(c) Read Source A.
   In what ways may Haig's account of his meeting with the War Cabinet be biased? Explain your answer. (6)
(d) Read Source D(ii) and Source E.
   Which of these two sources gives the more reliable view of the battle? Explain your answer. (8)
(e) Look at all the sources.
   In his war memoirs written in the 1930s Lloyd George called Passchendaele 'the senseless campaign'.
   Do these sources show his view to be true? Explain your answer fully. (12)

3 Peacemaking 1919–23

This topic is covered in Chapter 4.
Study Source A and then answer all parts of the question.

Source A. The Treaty of Versailles

The peace conference in 1919 was a conference of victors, at which the main treaty of peace with Germany, the Treaty of Versailles, was worked out and presented to the German delegates for their signature on 7 May. They had hoped that they would be allowed to debate the terms and protested strongly at the severity of the terms ofered them. The Allies allowed no discussion and treated the German delegates like prisoners in the dock. After a change of government in Germany, the final act was staged. In the Hall of Mirrors in the Palace of Versailles, on 28 June, the German delegates, cowed and pale, signed the Treaty.

(From *Britain between the Wars, 1918–1940*, C. L. Mowat, 1966)

(a) The Germans later described the Treaty as 'a diktat'. How does Source A support that view? (4)
(b) What territorial changes were made by the Treaty in Central and Eastern Europe? (8)
(c) Why were the majority of German people angered by the terms of the Treaty? (8)

4 The League of Nations

This topic is covered in Chapter 5.
Study the source carefully, and then answer the questions that follow.

A Punch cartoon of 10 December 1919

(a) What is the cartoonist saying about the League of Nations? Explain your answer, referring to details in the cartoon. (5)

(b) What did the Great Powers want to achieve when they set up the League of Nations? (5)

MEG

5 Russia 1914–53

This topic is covered in Chapter 6.
Look carefully at Sources A to E which refer to the New Economic Policy (NEP), then answer all the questions.

Source A. Lenin introduces the NEP at the Tenth Party Congress, March 1921

'Our large factories have been so ruined that it will take a long time to restore them. We must therefore help to restore small industry. This will mean the revival of private profit and capitalism. The workers are in no danger as long as they firmly hold power over the most important parts of the economy. This is a retreat, but only for a new attack.'

Source B. Two views of NEP

(i) Bukharin, one of Lenin's economic advisers, spoke of the future in 1922

'Poor, starving old Russia, Russia of primitive lighting and the meal of a crust of black bread, is going to be covered by a network of electric power stations. The NEP will transform the Russian economy and rebuild a broken nation. The future is endless and beautiful.'

(ii) Kopelev, a former Soviet Communist Party member, spoke in a British television programme in 1990.

'We thought at the time that the NEP was a retreat, that maybe it was necessary, but it must be ended as quickly as possible. The NEP meant the recovery of capitalism. I was about 15 years old and I wrote a poem called 'The NEP' where I said things like how awful it was, but at some point it would come to an end because there were still true Bolsheviks alive. We were lads in 1927. We thought that stealing from an NEP man was not a sin; to steal sweets or beer, that was part of the class struggle.'

Source C. A British historian in 1985 noted these comments about the NEP

'In 1925 the Soviet Commissar for Finance admitted that the pay of miners, metal workers and engine drivers was still lower than it had been before 1914. This in turn meant that workers' housing and food were poor. The factory committee of a cement works in Smolensk reported, for example, in 1929: "Every day there are many complaints about apartments; many workers have families of six or seven people, and live in one room"'

From *A History of the Soviet Union*, G. Hosking, published by Harper Collins Ltd.

Source D

(i) A Soviet painting of 1927 entitled 'Forward Heavy Industry'

(ii) A poster advertising the new film 'October', 1927

Source E. A graph that shows production under the NEP

The lines on the graph show the change in production of four basic commodities compared with 1913. The graph was compiled from statistics taken from Russian Sources by a British historian in the 1990's.

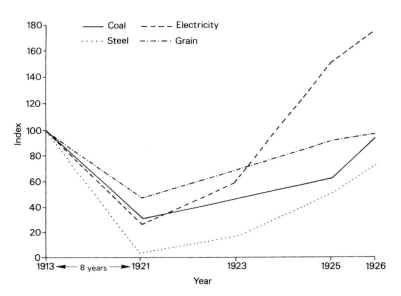

(a) Look at Source E. Give two reasons why production fell between 1913 and 1921. (2)

(b) Read Source B ii). Why did Kopelev think that stealing from a NEP man was 'part of the class struggle'? (2)

(c) Read Source B i). What evidence is there that Bukharin's statement is propaganda? Explain your answer. (6)

(d) Look at Sources D i), D ii) and E. Do the illustrations or the graph give the more reliable view of the achievements of the NEP? Explain your answer. (8)

(e) Look at all the Sources. 'NEP was abandoned in 1927 because it was failing'. Do these Sources show this view to be true? Explain your answer fully. (12)

Essay question

(i) Explain how Stalin set up a personal dictatorship in Communist Russia after death of Lenin. (15)

OR

(ii) Explain how Russia's involvement in the First World War brought an end to the rule of Nicholas II. (15)

ULEAC

6 China, 1914–49

This topic is covered in Chapter 7.

Study Sources A, B, C and D which relate to the Long March, and then answer questions a) to d) which follow.

Source A. Adapted from a book about the Long March written in 1971

'The 'historian' of the Long March, Hsu Meng-chui, said "We lost nearly all our official documents in the Grasslands and in crossing rivers. We also burned many documents that could not be conveniently carried." Much weight had therefore to be put on the memory of the men involved, and that is only too human. General Pen Teh-huai was once explaining how they planned a breakthrough in one of the Encirclement campaignments, when he paused suddenly. He had made a mistake. The battle he was describing was a quite different one, in Szechuan, several hundred miles away. "There were so many battles", he remembered.

Since 1935 there has been a gradual process of 'tidying up' history on the part of the Chinese Communists, whose interest lies in portraying the Long March as a fully successful result of perfect decision-making on the part of the present leadership.'

Source B. From a description of his experiences in the Long March by Tung Pi-wu. Here he remembers the Great Snow Mountain

'So we started straight up the mountain, heading for a pass near the summit. Heavy fogs swirled up, there was a high wind and half way up it began to rain. As we climbed higher and higher we were caught in a terrible hailstorm, and the air became so thin we could hardly breathe at all. Speech was completely impossible and the cold so dreadful that our breath froze and our hands and lips turned blue. Men and animals staggered and fell into chasms and disappeared forever.

Those who sat down to rest or relieve themselves froze to death on the spot. Exhausted political workers encouraged men by sign and touch to continue moving, indicating that the pass was just ahead.'

Source C. From a speech made by Mao Zedong [Mao Tse-tung] in 1935

'We say that the Long March is the first of its kind ever recorded in history ... For twelve months we were under daily reconnaissance and bombing from the air by scores of planes; we were encircled, pursued, obstructed and intercepted on the ground by a big force of several thousand men; we encountered untold difficulties

and great obstacles on the way, but by keeping our two feet going we swept across a distance of more than 20,000 li★ … Well, has there ever been in history a long march like ours? No, never. The Long March also … proclaims that the Red Army is an army of heroes, and that the imperialists and their jackals, Chiang Kai-shek and the like, are perfect non-entities. The Long March also has sown seeds in many provinces, which will bear fruit and yield a crop in future.'
★20,000 li = 6,000 miles

Source D. A picture showing an incident from the Long March

Study sources A, B and C.
(a) (i) Using the sources and your own knowledge, explain the causes of the Long March. (5)
(ii) Use the sources and your own knowledge to explain the effects of the Long March on the conflict between the Communists and the Guomindang (Kuomintang). (5)
(b) Study source A.
According to the author of source A, what are the difficulties facing the historian studying the Long March? (3)
(c) Study sources B and C.
To what extent do these sources demonstrate the difficulties referred to in source A? Refer in detail to each source in your answer. (4)
(d) Do you think that source D is of any value to historians studying the Long March? Explain your answer. (3)
ULEAC

7 Germany 1919–39

This topic is covered in Chapter 8.
Study the Source below and then attempt all the questions.

Seats held by the Nazi Party in the Reichstag (Parliament) 1920–32		Unemployment	
1920	0		
1924	32 (May)		
1924	14 (December)		
1928	13		
		1929 (September)	1.3 millions
1930	107		
		1931 (August)	4.0 millions
1932	230 (July)	1932 (February)	6.0 millions.

From official figures

(a) Hitler made his first attempt to seize power in November 1923. Why did this seem to be a good time to choose such an attempt? (7)
(b) Why did the Nazis make very little progress between 1923 and 1929? (6)
(c) Between 1929 and 1932 support for the Nazis increased enormously and they became the largest party in the Reichstag. Why did this change come about? (7)

(d) 'These statistics provide solid facts and are therefore of great use to historians in explaining the rise of the Nazis' Do you agree or disagree with this view? (5)

SEG 1991

8 The USA 1919–39

This topic is covered in Chapter 9.

Source A. A flow chart explaining the New Deal

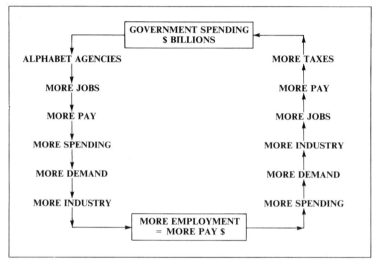

Source B. A cartoon published during the New Deal

Source C. An American businessmen remembers the New Deal

'The New Deal hurt us. The President was a rich man's son and he betrayed his own class by wasting billions of dollars of our money on his schemes. He didn't understand that when you give to people you hurt them. We had the soup lines and the depression because people lost confidence in themselves. Welfare kills a man's spirit because it makes him lose the will to fend for himself. If you want a dog to hunt you have to let him go hungry. If you want a man to be successful, he needs to face the setbacks of life. You're free to eat if you can pay for your food and free to starve if you don't pay for it.'

Source D. A reporter talking about the New Deal in 1936
'Everyone is against the New Deal except the voters.'

(a) According to Source A, what action needed to be taken by the government to overcome the depression? (1)

(b) Explain Source A and show how the New Deal was meant to end the depression. (6)

(c) What were the Alphabet Agencies mentioned in Source A? Explain how successful they were in dealing with the depression. (6)

(d) Explain whether the cartoonist in Source B is for or against the New Deal. Give reasons for your answer. (3)

(e) Would the writer of Source C have agreed or disagreed with the cartoonist of Source B? Give reasons for your answer. (2)

(f) Explain in your own words the arguments used by the writer of Source C against giving welfare to people. (3)

(g) Explain the statement in Source D. (3)

NEAB

9 International Relations 1935–39

This topic is covered in Chapter 10.
Study Source A and then answer all parts of the question.

Source A. A photograph taken in March 1939

The photograph shows Czechs giving the Nazi salute as German troops march into Prague, the capital of Czechoslovakia.

(a) Describe the ways in which Germany broke the terms of the Treaty of Versailles in the period 1935–38 (8)

(b) 'The Czech people welcomed the arrival of German troops in Prague'
Does Source A support this view?
Explain your answer (4)

(c) In September 1938 Britain and France were ready to make an agreement with Germany. In September 1939 Britain and France declared war on Germany
Explain why this change came about. (8)

SEG (specimen) 1998

10 The Second World War, 1939–45

This topic is covered in Chapter 12.
(a) Study this picture, which shows Hiroshima after the dropping of the atomic bomb, and then answer questions (i) to (v) which follow.

   (i)   Write a sentence to explain the term 'ultimatum'. (2)
   (ii) Write a sentence to explain the term 'kamikaze'. (2)
   (iii) Write one or two sentences to explain why the USSR declared war on Japan in August 1945 (3)
   (iv) Write a paragraph to explain why the USA dropped an atomic bomb on Hiroshima. (4)
   (v) Write a paragraph to explain why the Japanese did not surrender directly after the attack on Hiroshima. (4)
(b) Essay questions
   (i)   Why were Japanese forces successful in gaining so much territory in the years 1941–2? (15)
or
   (ii) 'The main reason for the defeat of Germany in the Second World War was the involvement of the USA on the side of the European allies.'
        Do you agree with this statement? Give reasons for your answer. (15)

ULEAC

11 The United Nations

This topic is covered in Chapter 14.
Study the Sources below and then answer the questions which follow.

Source A. A Cartoon published in 1950

'Come on, your help is needed in Korea.'

Source B. Statement by the US Secretary of State in 1951

'The attack on Korea was a challenge to the whole system of collective security and a threat to the independence of all nations. The decision to meet force with force was essential. The authority and very survival of the United Nations was involved. The operation in Korea has been a success. The Soviet plot for a communist takeover of Korea from the North has been stopped, and the attempts by the North Koreans and the Chinese communists to drive out the United Nation forces have failed.'

Source C. From an historian writing in 1953

'The so-called UN action in Korea is a fraud. It is almost entirely an American Imperialist operation in support of a puppet dictatorship. The Security Council resolution recommending military intervention is illegal because neither the USSR nor the People's Republic of China were present when it was passed. The wanton American aggression into North Korea is clear proof that the real intention of the USA was to destroy communism in the whole area. Only the valiant and heroic actions of the Chinese volunteers have stopped this evil plan.'

Source D. Two maps of the Korean War

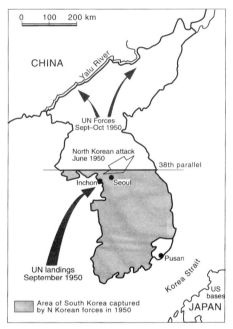 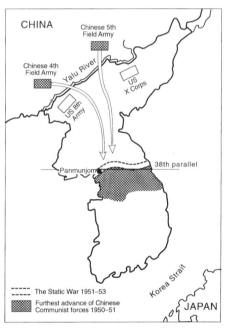

War in Korea up to October 1950   War in Korea, October 1950–1953

(a) What position did the man shown in the cartoon in Source A hold? (1)

(b) Explain the cartoon in Source A. (5)

(c) Explain the reasons given in Source B for the action of the USA in Korea. (4)

(d) Do the views expressed in Source A agree or disagree with the views expressed in Source B? Give reasons for your answer (4)

(e) 'Source C is biased and therefore of little value to an historian writing about the war in Korea.' Give reasons why you agree or disagree with this statement. (8)

(f) Source C says that neither the USSR not the People's Republic of China was present when the Security Council passed its resolution recommending military intervention in Korea. Explain why these two powers were not present at this time. (2)

(g) Using the information in Source D and your knowledge of the period, say how far you think that the action of the United Nations in Korea was a success. (4)

NEAB

12 International relations 1945–64

This topic is covered in Chapter 15.
Study Sources A, B, C and D, which are about United States economic aid, and then answer questions a) to e) which follow.

Source A. From a speech by President Truman, 1947

One way of life is based upon the will of the majority. It includes free institutions, representative government, free elections, guarantees of individual liberty, freedom of speech and religion, and freedom from political oppression.

The second way of life is based upon the will of a minority forced upon the majority. It relies upon terror and oppression, a controlled press and radio, fixed elections, and the suppression of personal freedoms.

I believe that it must be the policy of the United States to support free peoples who are resisting attempted take over by armed minorities or by outside pressures. Our help should lmainly come through economic and financial aid.

Source B. From a speech by US Secretary of State, George Marshall, June 1947

Our aid policy is direct not against any country or doctrine but against hunger, poverty, desperation, and chaos. Its purpose should be the revival of a working economy in the world.

Source C. From a British school history textbook, 1965

Alarmed by the possibilities of a complete economic breakdown in Europe, the United States came forward with the most magnificent offer to help that history records. That it was not inspired merely by fear of a spread of communism is shown by the fact that the offer was made to all countries needing help in their recovery. In the first year of the Marshall Plan a total of 1,325 million dollars was paid out by the US which asked only for slight trade concessions in return. US aid became the basis of the economy of most of the free countries in Europe.

Source D. British cartoon of 1948 on the USA's European Recovery Plan, the Marshall Plan

THE WIND FROM THE WEST
"And now get down to it"

Study Source A.
  (a) What does Source A tell you about the reasons why the United States was anxious in 1947 'to support free peoples'? (3)

Study Sources B and C.
  (b) In what ways do Sources B and C differ in what they say about the reasons behind the Marshall Plan? (4)
  (c) Referring to the sources, and using your own knowledge, how would you explain these differences? (5)

Study Source D.
  d) What is the attitude of the cartoonist towards the European Recovery Plan? Explain your answer. (4)

Study Source A and look again at the other sources.
  (e) Source A is a political speech. Does this make it any more or less reliable than the other sources for understanding the reasons for United States aid to Europe? Explain your answer fully. (4)

ULEAC

13 International relations, 1964–95 – the road to détente

This topic is covered in Chapter 16.
  (a) Study the passage below and then answer questions i) to v) which follow.
  'Huge sums of money have been spent since 1945 in producing weapons, a large proportion because of the Cold War. In the 1970s people spoke of détente but, by 1980, 450 000 million dollars a year was still being spent. Military leaders said nuclear weapons have been a deterrent. In 1962 an American journalist calculated that, since 1946, 863 international disarmament meetings have been held, involving 1700 hours and 18 million words, but with little success.'
  (i) Write a sentence to explain the meaning of the term 'détente'. (2)
  (ii) Write a sentence to explain the meaning of the term 'deterrent'. (2)
  (ii) Write one or two sentences to explain which types of weapons were mainly discussed at disarmament meetings. (3)
  (iv) Write one or two sentences to explain how space exploration has made the problem of nuclear warfare even worse. (3)
  (v) Write a paragraph to explain the importance of the Helsinki Conference (1973–5) in improving international relations. (5)
  (b) Essay questions.
  EITHER
  (i) What progress was made in the field of arms control between 1946 and 1980? (15)
  OR
  (ii) Why was it so difficult to achieve disarmament in the period 1946 to 1980? (15)

ULEAC

14 Three International case studies

See Chapter 17 for Questions.

15 Russia 1953–95

This topic is covered in Chapter 18.

(a) Study the table below and then answer Questions (i) to (v) which follow.

1976-1980	Target percentage increase in production	Actual percentage increase in production
Heavy industry	38–42	26
Consumer goods	30–42	21
Agriculture	14–17	9

A table showing what the Tenth Five Year Plan aimed to achieve and what was actually achieved.

(i) Write a sentence explaining the term 'Consumer Goods'. (2)
(ii) Write a sentence explaining the term 'Five Year Plan'. (2)
(iii) In the past the Soviet Union has often paid more attention to heavy industry than to consumer goods. Write one or two sentences explaining why this has been the case. (3)
(iv) Write one or two sentences explaining why the Five Year Plans have often failed to meet their targets. (3)
(v) Write a paragraph explaining why Soviet agriculture remained a problem in the 1970's. (5)

(b) This is an essay question. How did Nikita Khrushchev gain power in the 1950's? What were the reasons for his fall from power in 1964? (15)

ULEAC

16 Eastern Europe, 1945–95

This topic is covered in Chapter 19.
Study Sources A, B, C and D which are about the USSR's relations with Eastern Europe, and then answer questions a) to e) which follow.

Source A. Adapted from N. R. MacMahon, *The Hungarian Revolution*, published in 1969

'After the death of Stalin some things began to change. Khrushchev began to talk with the Yugoslavs, who had never followed Stalin's methods. Khrushchev blamed Soviet problems on Stalin. The Secret Police (NKVD) were abolished. This relaxation led to riots in Poland where Gomulka, a popular Polish Communist, was brought to power. Then there were a similar rising in Hungary. A government was formed by Imre Nagy which included some non-Communists. Nagy promised free elections in Hungary and even talked of leaving the Warsaw Pact.'

Source B. A cartoon from a British magazine; 31 October 1956

KHRUSHCHEV
(USSR)

Source C. Quoted in D. Pyrce-Jones, *The Hungarian Revolution*, published in 1969

'As I moved deeper into the city (Budapest), every street was smashed. Hardly a stretch of tramcar rails was left intact . . . Hundreds of yards of paving stones had been torn up, the streets were littered with burnt-out cars. Even before I reached the Duna Hotel, I counted the remains of at least forty tanks . . . at the corner of Stalin Avenue . . . two monster Russian T54 tanks lumbered past, dragging bodies behind them, a warming to all Hungarians of what happened to fighters . . .'

Source D: A photograph showing a huge statute of Stalin being pulled down in Budapest, capital of Hungary, 1956

(a) Study Source A.
    According to Source A, how did the death of Stalin change the situation in Eastern Europe? (3)
(b) Study Sources A and B.
    In what ways does the information in Source A help you to understand Source B? Explain your answer. (4)
(c) Study Sources C and D.
    To what extent does Source D support the evidence of the eye-witnesses in Source C? (4)
(d) Study Sources B and D.
    'Source D is more useful to someone studying the events in Eastern Europe in the 1950s than is Source B.' Do you agree? Give reasons for your answer. (4)
(e) Use your own knowledge to explain why Khrushchev ordered Soviet troops and tanks into Hungary in 1956. (5)

ULEAC

17 The USA 1945–95

This topic is covered in Chapter 21.

The USA 1945–95

Look carefully at Sources A to E which refer to Civil Rights issues in the USA. Then answer all the questions.

Source A. A photograph showing housing for Blacks in Harlem, New York City, in the late 1970s.

Source B. Two photographs showing Black protests in the 1950s and 1960s.
    (i) Two opponents of segregation sit in the whites-only part of a bus in Birmingham, Alabama, 1956.

    (ii) Martin Luther King at the Washington Civil Rights demonstration, August 1963.

Source C. A British newspaper report about the Central High School, Little Rock, Arkansas, published on 5 September 1987.

'Thirty years to the day after Governor Orval Faubus provoked the Eisenhower Government at Little Rock, black and white students stood together outside the Central High School. "This school's great," said a black youth. "Race ain't nothing to worry about here." A white youngster nearby said, "People have got used to the idea that they've got to go to school together." I could see, however, that black and white students keep to their own 'territory' in the school-yard. Furthermore, I learned that still another plan to stop segregation came into force this week.'

Source D. Statistics collected at the time and published by the US government

Unemployment (shown as a % of working population)

Date	All workers	Black workers
1958	6.8	12.6
1961	6.7	12.4
1964	5.2	9.6
1967	3.8	7.4
1970	4.9	8.2

Figures for 1974 showing deaths per 100,000 from certain causes.

	Whites	Blacks
Tuberculosis	1.3	4.1
Infancy diseases	11.3	29.0

Source E. Race relations in the USA in the 1970s and 1980s.

   (i) A newspaper photograph of a Ku Klux Klan rally in Little Rock, Arkansas, 1979.

   (ii) A US newspaper report published on 16 August 1985.

WHITE HOUSE PLANS CIVIL RIGHTS U TURN

'Rules concerning equal rights in employment which were made by President Lyndon Johnson are to be abolished, making higher black unemployment likely.'

(a) Look at source A.

In what ways does the photograph indicate that Harlem was a poor area of New York? (2)

(b) Look at source B **ii**.

Why did Martin Luther King lead this demonstration to Washington in 1963? (2)

(c) Read source D.

How would these statistics be useful to an historian of race relations in the USA? Explain your answer. (6)

(d) Look at sources **Ei** and **Eii**.

Which of these sources gives the more reliable account of race relations in the USA? Explain your answer. (8)

(e) Look at *all* the sources.

'The Civil Rights protests of the 1950s and 1960s achieved nothing for the Blacks of the USA.' Do these sources show this view to be true? Explain your answer fully. (12)

MEG

18 South Africa 1945–95

This topic is covered in Chapter 23.

Study Sources A, B and C, which refer to the origins of apartheid, and answer questions a) to e) which follow.

Source A. Adapted from a speech by the leader of the Nationalist Party, Dr Malan, during the 1948 election campaign

'Will the European race in the future be able to maintain its rule, its purity, and its civilization? Or will it float along until it vanishes for ever, without honour, in the black sea of South Africa's non-European population? If the European can save itself, then can it do so without oppression? Can it do so in consideration of the non-European's natural right to a proper living? Can Europeans respect non-Europeans' right to their own development in accordance with their own requirements and capabilities? Will the all-destroying Communist cancer be checked, or will it be allowed to undermine our freedom, our religion, our own South African nationhood and our European existence?'

Source B. Adapted from a letter written in 1952 from Dr Malan to the African National Congress

'The road to peace and goodwill lies in the acceptance of the fact that separate population groups exist. Each group should have the opportunity of developing its ambitions and abilities in its own area or within its own community. It should be clearly understood that the government is not prepared to grant the Bantu political equality with the European community. It is, however, only too willing to encourage Bantu initiative, Bantu services, and Bantu administration within the Bantu community, and to allow the Bantu people full scope to fulfil their potential.'

Source C. Adapted from a letter written in 1952 from the African National Congress to Dr Malan

'We refer to the campaign of mass action which the ANC intends to launch. As a defenceless and voteless people, we have explored other channels without success. The African people are left with no alternative but to set out on the campaign referred to. It is our firm intention to conduct this campaign in a peaceful manner. Any disturbances, if they must occur, will not be of our making.'

Source D. Adapted from a speech by P W Botha, Prime Minister of South Africa, 1980

'We are moving in a changing world, we must adapt otherwise we shall die . . . The moment you start oppressing people . . . they fight back . . . We must acknowledge people's rights and . . . give to others in a spirit of justice what we demand for ourselves. A white monopoly of power is impossible in the Africa of today . . . A division of power between all racial groups is needed . . . Apartheid is a recipe for permanent conflict.'

(a) Study source A. In what ways does this source show the policies of apartheid adopted by Nationalist governments in South Africa? (4)

(b) Study source B. Is source B a reliable source of information about Bantu attitudes towards the policies of the South African government? Explain your answer. (4)

(c) Both sources A and B express strong opinions. In view of this, how useful are they to someone studying South African history? Give reasons for your answer, referring to the sources. (4)

(d) Study source C. How useful is this source as evidence of the part played by black Africans in the government of South Africa? (3)

(e) Study sources C and D. Do sources C and D indicate that there had been a major change since the 1950s in the racial policies pursued within South Africa by the South African government? Explain your answer. (5)

ULEAC

19 The Middle East, 1914–95

This topic is covered in Chapter 24.

(a) Study this map, which shows the United Nations' proposed partition of the British mandate of Palestine, and then answer questions i) to v) which follow.

(i)   Write a sentence to explain the term 'British mandate'. (2)

(ii) Write a sentence to explain the term 'Zionist'. (2)

(iii) Write one or two sentences to explain why Britain wanted to leave Palestine in 1948. (3)

(iv) Write a paragraph to explain why war broke out in Palestine between the Arabs and the Jews in 1948. (4)

(v) Write a paragraph to explain why Arab forces were defeated in the conflict of 1948–49   (4)

(b) Essay question

What were the causes of the Arab-Israeli war of 1967? Why were the Israeli forces successful in this conflict?   (15)

ULEAC

20 The Suez Crisis: a case study

See Chapter 25 for Questions.

Answers to examination questions

You should read the sections on 'Taking the Examination' and 'Advice and guidance on types of exam question' on pages 4–7. Note that you can build your marks from a mere 1 or 2 (far too simple or vague an answer) up to the highest possible mark (for a further answer). In the suggestions in the following pages we have tried to show how you might get the highest possible mark.

1 International Relations

Testing Assessment Objectives 1–2.

(a) (i) Fear/anger at Russia's gains at San Stefano; perceived need to break up 'Big Bulgaria'; Bismarck's fear of Austro-Russian war.

(ii) Bulgaria split into three parts: one returned to Turkey, the others were denied the right to unite; Russian influence lessened; Britain got Cyprus (to guard against Russian approach to Mediterranean); Austria given 'control' of Bosnia-Herzegovina; independence for Rumania, Montenegro and Serbia (angered by Austrian control of Bosnia-Herzegovina); contributed to crisis which led to war, 1914.

(iii) Austria had lost power in Germany (1866) and Italy (1866 and 1870) and wanted to re-assert Great Power status by grabbing land in the Balkans; in 1885 she had occupied Bosnia-Herzegovina; now, 1908, she formally annexed them. Austria was aware of Serb ambitions, which included the takeover of Bosnia-Herzegovina, as well as bring Slavs in Hungary into an enlarged Serbia; she wanted the chance to have a 'showdown' with Serbia – which she got in 1914.

(iv) The anexation was made possible by: a revolt in Turkey, which indicated that even more of the Balkans would come up for grabs; by Russia's agreement to the annexation in return for an Austrian promise to back Russian claims for ex-Turkish land which would allow her access via the Dardanelles to the sea. Serbia was angered by the annexation and, after two Balkan League Wars (1912–13) was even more determined to take Bosnia-Herzegovina from Austria. Russia was angered by the 'betrayal' by Austria, which refused to honour the Dardanelles promise, and backed Serb enmity towards Austria.

(v) Start with an analytical account of events in the Balkans from 28 June (murder of Archduke by a Serb) through 23 July (Austria's demands on Serbia, made with German support), 24 July (Serb acceptance of most demands, but request for time to consider others – rejected by Austria 25 July when Russia said she would start mobilisation), 28 July (Austria declared war on Serbia), and 30 July – Russia began mobilisation and refused Germans demand to call it off on

1 August when Germany declared war on Russia, and then (3 August) on France, Russia's ally.

An analytical explanation of other factors involved – France-German rivalry since 1870–71; Anglo-German rivalry; colonial clashes; German invasion of Belgium involves Britain in war.

(b) Essay question

(i) To prevent France gaining revenge for the Treaty of 1871, which required the isolation of France and Bismarck's 'control' of the other Powers. 'Control' was achieved by the Dreikairserßund and Reinsurance Treaty which prevented the Franco-Russian alliance and the danger of war on two fronts, by the Triple Alliance which prevented a Franco-Italian alliance, by deliberately avoiding colonial clashes with Britain, France and Italy. Bismarck also 'controlled' France by encouraging her colonial expansion which both distracted attention from the need for revenge and involved her in clashes with Britain and Italy.

(ii) In one, deep sense there was little change; both Bismarck and the Kaiser wanted Germany to be the leading Power. However, Bismarck thought he'd attained that by the defeat of France, and after 1871 by diplomacy. The Kaiser was more aggressive and less inclined to diplomacy. He refused to renew the Reinsurance Treaty and alienated Russia; he adopted a series of anti-British policies (Naval Laws; Kruger Telegram) and tactics (Moroccan crises 1905–11) which pushed Britain into the Entente and military/naval talks with France.

(iii) Analysis and explanation of Naval Laws; Kruger telegram; Morrocan crises; colonial expansion. Similar treatment of British alarm at each of these issues and of growing threat from German industrial expansion and tariff policy (which lessened British trade and led to increased unemployment).

2 First World War

Testing Assessment Objective 3.

(a) Heavy shelling since 3 July 1917; destruction of drainage system; heavy rain (see Sources D (i) and D (ii)).

(b) Take advantages from the Source; e.g. 'exhausted men struggling through mud'; Germans were 'dry men' who had 'machine guns'.

(c) Haig had been responsible for the slaughter on the Somme (1 July – 19 November 1916). In June 1917 he told the War Cabinet of his plan for a new Somme-like 'great push' around Ypres. It is possible to see bias in his account in:

(i) his description of the politicians as 'pessimistic' as compared with his own optimism of success within 'six months';

(ii) his rejection of Prime Minister Lloyd George's idea of the 'decisive moment';

(iii) his determination to stick to his notion of a war of attrition, aimed at bringing Germany to 'total exhaustion' whatever the cost.

Very modern studies of Haig's politics claim that his policy was the right one, and that Germany was fatally weakened by the new offensive, which he launched on 31 July (see Source E for a German opinion). So it is possible to claim that Haig's account is less biased than might be thought at first.

(d) Source D (ii) may be seen as:

(i) a piece of encouraging propaganda by a wily politician who knew better (see Source A);

(ii) encouraging support for a commander being criticised by his own generals (Source B) and by public opinion alarmed at the heavy losses;

(iii) ignoring the fact that the enemy had not been 'driven ... back': only in the final action (late November) did the Canadians take the village of Passchendaele (from which the battle gets its name), and this was only six miles north-east of Ypres. So much for so little.

Source E, written long after the battle, explains why the Allies 'had been able to achieve so little', but also shows how badly the Germans had been affected

('used up German strength'; 'losses ... could no longer be replaced'; bad conditions 'led to rapid wearing out of the German troops').
Overall, Source E is a more reliable view of the battle.

(e) The marks awarded for this sub-question show that the answer has to be an extended piece of writing. The sources show that Lloyd George's view was partially true:

(i) the attackers were hampered by the conditions (use Source B, D (i), E and C for narrative description and effects of the conditions);

(ii) little was gained (Source E) by 'exhausted men .../against/machine guns/ (Source D).

However, modern historians tend more to the view expressed by the German historians (Source E), which shows that the Germans had suffered as much as, and maybe more, than the Allies ('used up German strength'. 'Losses ... could no longer be replaced', while the Allies were 'greater in number', which would be even truer with the arrival of fresh US troops). With the Germans suffering from the conditions and the fighting ('a rapid wearing out ...'), Haig's modern supporters claim that this battle laid the foundations for the victories of 1918.

3 Peacemaking 1919–23

Question (a) tests Assessment Objective 3, and questions (b) and (c) test Assessment Objectives 1–2.

(a) Use the source, and refer to the use of words and phrases such as 'victors' who 'presented the treaty to the German delegation', with 'no discussion' allowed by Germans, who were 'treated like prisoners. . .' and who, on 28 June were 'cowed and pale' as they signed.

(b) Spell out in detail the changes made in both Versailles (with Germany) and Trianon (with Austria-Hungary). Note German losses to France, Belgium and Poland (the Polish corridor). Note the effect of self-determination in the creation of Yugoslavia and Czechoslovakia, and the independence given to (enlarged) Poland. Draw attention to both gainers and losers.

(c) Draw attention to the terms of the Treaty, and show why they led to German anger. Go further than merely saying 'they were too harsh', 'Germans felt humiliated', 'reparations were too high' etc.
Refer to the following:
- Germany was almost defenceless because of military restrictions;
- while loss of Alsace-Lorraine was expected (it had been French before 1871), the loss of part of Prussia to Poland, and the subsequent splitting of Germany was resented;
- German hopes that a Treaty would be based on the 14 Points (although they had rejected such a proposal earlier in 1918) led to claims that they were 'betrayed' by the allies;
- many Germans believed that their army had not been beaten, but that their leaders had sought peace because of the restless political situation in Germany, where people were suffering from starvation (because of the naval blockade), and the country was suffering from political agitation (partly due to left-wingers' hopes for a Bolshevik-style revolution).

4 The League of Nations

(a) This tests Assessment Objective 3.
First you have to use the features appearing in the cartoon: e.g. it was designed by

President Wilson; its main members included Belgium, France, England and Italy; the USA was meant to be the keystone in the structure of the League.

Then you have to interpret what the cartoonist is saying: e.g. that the League is weaker because of the gap in the middle; that the USA is unwilling to join – shown by 'Uncle Sam' sitting to one side.

(b) This tests Assessment Objectives 1–2.

The League was an attempt to move away from the old power politics which had led to war in the past. Its supporters hoped that it would solve international disputes by peaceful negotiations and that it would deter potential aggressors by means of economic and, if necessary, military sanctions.

As the various Treaties were signed, and as statesmen came face to face with new (and old) problems, the members of the League set up a variety of Commission and agencies to deal with them: e.g. Drugs, World Health, Refugees; Minorities; Mandates and Disarmament.

5 Russia 1914–53

Testing Assessment Objectives 1–3.

(a) Destruction and dislocation caused by war (1914–17); loss of land and industries to Germans in Treaty of Brest-Litovsk; dislocation of civil war (1918–1921).

(b) To a committed Bolshevik, like Kopelev in 1927 (Source B (ii), the NEP was 'a retreat', and 'the recovery of capitalism' which Lenin had adopted reluctantly while preparing for 'a new attack' (Source A). So, to steal from the 'awful' NEP men (Source B (ii) might be seen as a young Bolshevik's idea of 'attack' and not as a sin.

(c) Lenin called Bukharin 'the darling of the Party'. Like Lenin (Source A) and Bolsheviks like Kopelev (Source B (ii)) he knew that the NEP had been forced on Lenin by the state of Russian industry (Source E and Source A) and that, after this retreat, there would come another 'attack' on capitalism. Bukharin, a leading Bolshevik thinker, knew that capitalism (encouraged by the NEP) could not co-exist with Marxist-Leninism. However, in this source, he was using his position and influence to win Party support for Lenin's change of direction, promising a dream world (' … endless and beautiful').

(d) If you knew nothing about the NEP, then the illustrations (Sources D (i) and D (ii) would mean nothing to you. Note, too, that the graph (Source E) may be a suspect source;

(i) the 'Russian sources' may have been falsified by the Bolshevik Government: as Mark Twain wrote, 'There are three kinds of lies: lies, damned lies and statistics'.

(ii) the British historian may have misinterpreted the Russian statistics. But, assuming that the graph (Source E) is an honest illustration of the truth, then it does show how, under the NEP, Russian industry and agriculture recovered.

The illustrations may be best seen as propaganda. In Bolshevik Russia, as in all dictatorships, the Government ensured that films (Source D (i) and other media (Source D (ii)) and art forms, were dedicated to the glorification of the Government.

(e) Note the high marks awarded for this sub-question. The question you have to ask is 'Why was the NEP abandoned in 1927?'. First, say why the NEP was introduced (Sources A, B (i) and E). Then, note that Trotsky (Lenin's closest ally) called for the end of the NEP in 1924 and demanded a war on the peasants. Stalin used this anti-Leninism to get Trotsky sacked from his post as Commissar for War (1925). However, the NEP was attacked by other leading Bolsheviks (Source C) including the big city bosses who saw the peasants prosper while industrial workers suffered. In 1926 Trotsky, Zinoviev and Kamenev united to demand the end of the NEP: Stalin's henchmen in the Party Congress denounced all three. Within a year, Stalin had come to see that, with the NEP, there would never be a Communist State and that, indeed, under the NEP, capitalism, particularly among farmers, would flourish. This led him to introduce the first of a series of Five Year Plans for industry and for the collectivisation (State control) of farming. He meant to transform Russia (Source B (i)) not by the NEP which had been glorified (Sources D (i) and D (ii)), but by means of State ownership and control.

Essay question

(i) Relevant subject content: Stalin's position in the Communist Party during Lenin's last years (and explain the importance of the position of the General Secretary); Lenin's creation of a dictatorship and anti-opposition secret police (CHEKA); Stalin's struggle for power with Trotsky – differences of political philosophy as well as of personalities; the use of, and later defeat of, Kamenev and Zinoviev; the removal of opposition inside the Party (purges); the persecution of other groups opposed to his policies, e.g. kulaks and the Church.

Note the corresponding influence of a personal dictatorship, and link your answer to Khrushchev's denunciation of Stalin at the 20th Party Congress.

(ii) Relevant subject content: The nature of Tsarist rule before the War (autocratic; a weak Duma; industrial weaknesses; Stolypin's agricultural reforms; varied opposition groups). Reasons for entry into the War (Pan-Slavism; anti-Austrian expansion in Balkans). Impact of War on Russia (military defeats; German invasion; food shortages; dislocation on at home, particularly in winter 1916–17). Failure of Nicholas to reverse disaster by his intervention at front. Increasing power of Rasputin over political system. February/March Revolution and the abdication.

Note: Was Tsarism doomed to fail, with the War merely hastening the process?

6 China, 1914–49

Testing Assessment Objectives 1–2 (Question a) and Assessment Objective 3 (Questions b–d).

(a) *Causes:* Chiang's determination to wipe out Communism, shown in Shanghai (1927) and attacks on Mao's soviets in Hunan and, later, Kiangsi; reasons for his failure. Chiang's fourth anti-Mao campaign (1932–34) by air and land; encirclement of Mao's forces. Mao decides to found a new soviet in north or north-west.

Effects: constant attacks ('so many battles', Source A) on Mao's forces (Source C); non-Communist Chinese patriots angered by Chiang's refusal to fight Japanese, in control of much of northern China, and his refusal to accept Mao's plea that 'Chinese out not to fight Chinese', but rather should unite against the Japanese. Chinese peasants became sympathetic to communism 'in many provinces' (Source C) partly because of the behaviour of Mao's forces (did not rob, rape or pillage, but paid for what they wanted – unlike Chiang's forces), and because of reforms brought in by Communists against landlords, moneylenders etc. The 'fruit … crop in the future' (Source C) was a correct prophecy: in time the peasants proved to be 'the water' in which the communist 'fish' would flourish.

(b) *Use of sources.* Difficulties mentioned in source – lack of written 'documents'; need to rely on 'memory' which may be faulty ('only too human') as shown by General Pen's 'mistake'. The final sentences show how 'tidying up', often by people who were not there, became a propaganda exercise and created the mouth of the Long March.

(c) *Use of sources.* Use key words from each source as the basis for your answer. *Source B:* mountain; fogs; winds; rain; hailstorm; breathe; cold; chasms; froze. *Source C:* bombing; big forces; distance.

(d) *Use and interpretation.* Taken by itself, Source D might well be merely a photograph of an expedition into some mountains. Used along with the other sources (and with your own knowledge) it confirms part of what you know – snow, mountains, heavy loads etc. So it is of value – but not as valuable, perhaps, as source B. Note, too, that it is at least possible that the photograph may have been 'staged' to create an idea of difficulties, which would make it even less valuable.

7 Germany 1919–39

Questions (a)–(c) test Assessment Objectives 1–2; question (d) tests Assessment Objectives 1, 2 and 3.

(a) German nationalists were angered by French/Belgian occupation of the Ruhr and by the decision of the new Chancellor (Stresemann) to negotiate the reparations issue with the Allies. This reminded them, again, of the hated Treaty of Versailles. The occupation had been a main factor in the massive rise in the rate of inflation which destroyed the savings of the old middle class. The Weimar Government was weak (too many parties, too many anti-Weimar groups) and seemed unable to cope.

(b) Stresemann established a new Mark which helped industry and trade; he got the French/Belgians to leave the Ruhr, and negotiated a reduction in reparations. In 1925 Germany was an equal partner in the Locarno Treaties, and in 1926 admitted to the League. Stresemann got huge loans from US banks which helped German industry to recover; unemployment fell, living standards rose and extremist parties became less popular.

(c) Few Germans really supported the Weimar Government, in spite of Stresemann's successes. Nationalists, industrialists, Communists and ex-soldiers would have preferred some other form of government. Stresemann's success depended on US loans. With the Wall Street Crash of October 1929 (just after Stresemann's death), US banks recalled the loans: many German banks were forced to close, industrialists had less money and were forced to shut down factories so that unemployment shot up. This was the opportunity for extremists – Communists and Nazis – to offer Germans a new form of government.

(d) The figures show that Nazis became popular as unemployment increased. However, note that there were similar rises in unemployment in the USA, Britain and France without an extremist Party gaining so much popularity. So there must have been reasons for the growth of the Nazis other than the rise in unemployment, e.g. anger about the 1919 Treaty (among nationalists, ex-soldiers and others), fear of Communism (with Russia not far away), Germany's lack of experience of democracy, the financial support given to Hitler by industrialists and others, which allowed him to employ strong-arm gangs to harass and bully opponents and voters.
   So the statistics are of some use, but perhaps not of great use.

8 USA 1919–39

Question (c) tests Assessment Objectives 1–2; the other questions test Assessment Objective 3.

(a) That the Government should spend billions of dollars through the 'Alphabet Agencies' and so stimulate the economy.

(b) Source A illustrates the 'circulation of money'. Roosevelt's New Deal proposed government funding for a variety of 'agencies' (see question (c) below) which would 'prime the pump' (Source B) of the economy. The agencies would employ a wide variety of millions of people previously unemployed. Once they got their 'more pay' they would 'demand' more goods and so increase employment in 'industry', leading to more jobs, spending, demand, and so on up the right-hand side of the chart. In a perfect world, the Government would get back the money spent from the 'more taxes'.

(c) There were many agencies whose initials allowed the use of the term 'alphabet'. In Chapter 9 you can find the full titles of FERA, CCC, CWA, AAA, NIRA, ITVA, WPA which, with the 1935 Social Security Act, were the backbone of the New Deal. They were partially successful: millions of people got jobs (if only temporary); labour relations were improved (although many firms resisted the formation of unions in their factories); the banking system recovered. However, while unemployment fell up to 1937, it rose again after that, suggesting that the New Deal was only partially successful.

(d) Use the details of the cartoon, which shows Roosevelt pouring 'money-water', provided by the struggling 'taxpayer', into a 'pump' in the hope that this will 'make it work'. The cartoonist suggests that many 'leaks' led to a waste of 'money-water', seen pouring out in a '16 Billion spent' overflow-waste. Very little water is coming from the 'pump' into the bucket underneath the tap. The cartoonist was 'against' the New Deal. The author of Source C ('businessman'), like the cartoonist, thought that the New Deal was 'wasting billions of dollars'.

(f) The businessman thought that 'giving welfare' would make people become dependent on such help and make it less necessary for them to try to find work and look after themselves. He would allow people to go hungry (and homeless and without help when sick or old) if they did not have, from their own efforts, enough money.

(g) By 'everyone' the reporter meant influential Republican politicians, businessmen (Source C), many newspaper owners and their employees (Source B) and, generally, the rich. In the Presidential election of November 1936, Roosevelt won a greater majority than he had won in 1932, winning every state except Maine and Vermont. Clearly 'everyman' the voter had different opinions to those of the reporter's 'everyone'.

9 International Relations, 1919–39

All the questions test Assessment Objectives 1 and 2, and (b) also tests Assessment Objective 3.

(a) Increased the size of the army and introduced conscription; rearmed and built tanks and large guns; created an air force and navy; occupied the Rhineland, 1936; occupied Austria in the Anschluss, 1938; forced Britain and France to allow the break up of Czechoslovakia, autumn 1938.

(b) Perhaps it does: it shows people giving the Nazi salute and two women crying (for joy?), *but* was the photograph 'staged' by a Nazi photographer? Were the people forced to salute? Why are the men in the background not joining in? Were the women crying out of sadness? So, the source does not necessarily support the view expressed.

(c) First deal with 'September 1938' and the Munich agreement – the encouragement previously given by Hitler to the Sudeten Germans (in land taken from Germany by the Versailles Treaty), Chamberlain's visits to Hitler, Mussolini's support for his fellow-dictator, French unwillingness to go to war in defence of Sudetenland, and the cession to Germany of Sudetenland. Chamberlain's hope that this appeasement would mean 'peace in our time' after Hitler and signed the Agreement.

Then deal with March 1939 when Hitler invaded Bohemia, allowed Hungary to take Ruthenia and so ended the existence of Czechoslovakia. Chamberlain, particularly, felt betrayed: most people now saw that Hitler could not be 'appeased', but would have to be halted by force.

Finally, the Danzig issue. The creation of the Polish corridor (to give Poland an outlet to the sea) had split East Prussia off from the rest of Germany, while the former German port of Danzig was made an internationally-governed city. Hitler wanted to take the corridor and so reunite East Prussia with Germany. This would involve him in a war with Poland to whom Britain and France (already an ally of Poland) gave guarantees that, if invaded, she would get British and French support.

Hitler's invasion of Poland (1 September 1939) drew France and Britain into war (3 September 1939).

10 The Second World War, 1939–45

Testing Assessment Objective 1–2.

(a) (i) On 26 July 1945 at Potsdam, the Allies issued their ultimatum, or *statement of terms for ending the war* with Japan, warning that failure to accept the terms would involve 'utter destruction': the Japanese ignored the ultimatum and the warning.

(ii) 'Kamikaze' is a Japanese term (literally 'divine wind') used to describe the volunteer suicide pilots of the Japanese Imperial Navy, who guided their explosive-packed aircraft into enemy ships in the last year of the War, when Allied forces were closing in on the Japanese homeland.

(iii) Stalin only declared war on Japan on 8–9 August 1945, two days after the dropping of the first atomic bomb (Hiroshima) and as the second bomb was about to be dropped (Nagasaki). He did so because: he knew that his forces would not have to fight for very long; he wanted to get control of Manchuria (to hand on to Mao's Chinese Communists) and part, at least of Korea; he wanted to extend Russian influence into the Pacific.

(iv) The reconquest of Japanese-held islands in the Pacific saw bitter fighting and many casualties for US forces: the taking of Iwo Jima led to 20,000 US deaths: Okinawa cost 40,000 US lives. In planning for the invasion of mainland Japan, the Allies took account of 2 million dedicated Japanese soldiers and 5000 kamikaze pilots (see (ii) above), and feared that millions of Allied men would be killed. President Truman and his advisers hoped that the destruction caused by the atomic bomb would force Japan to surrender, so that millions of Allied lives would be saved.

(v) The small military clique which controlled Japanese policy (and the Emperor) were unwilling to accept the Allied terms for surrender: the occupation of Japan by Allied forces; the disarming of Japan and the destruction of all War potential; and the deposing of the military from power. Only on 10 August (after the bombing of Nagasaki) did the Emperor make a historic broadcast in which he appealed for terms of surrender and the war ended on 15 August 1945.

(b) Essay question

(i) Main points to be developed: Japan had been at war with China since 1937 and her well-trained army was able to take advantage of the French defeat in Europe to take over French Indo-China (July 1941). The militarists who controlled the Japanese Government had long planned the conquest of Asia (and India and Europe) and, in December 1941 ordered the destruction of the US fleet at Pearl Harbour. At the same time they attacked US bases in the Philippines, British colonies in Burma, Malaya, Singapore and Hong Kong, and the Dutch colonies in modern Indonesia. The USA was not prepared for war and her armies were forced to surrender the Philippines: the British were already under great pressure in Europe and had little capacity to spare to fight the Japanese, whose armies travelled quickly (often on bicycles) along routes prepared by pre-war Japanese settlers in the invaded countries, and were better supported from the air than were the badly armed, and poorly led British and US forces.

(ii) First agree with the statement.

Once the USA entered the war (December 1941) she quickly built new munitions factories and adapted existing factories for munitions production. She developed new, better-built and better-armed ships, planes and tanks in large numbers, and supplied the needs of both the British and Russians. She sent men to fight in North Africa and Europe.

Then point out (and disagree with the statement):

• Britain's role – Battle of Britain; Battle of the Atlantic; scientific developments, including radar;

• Hitler's mistakes in invading Russia, in declaring war on the USA in support of Japan, and the problem he had in holding down the conquered countries of Europe where resistance movements made their contribution to German difficulties and ultimate defeat.

Finally, agree that, probably, the USA role was 'the main reason'.

11 The United Nations

Questions (a)–(e) test Assessment Objective 3; (f) and (g) test Assessment Objectives 1–3.

(a) Truman was President of the USA in 1950.

(b) Refer to the sources: the League had 'died' because of failure to 'exercise' power against 'aggression' by Japan, Italy and Germany in the 1930s. A major weakness of the League had been that the USA was not a member. In the 1940s Roosevelt had been a main agent in the formation of the UNO, Truman was determined to use US/UNO power to stop aggression by Russian-backed North Korea.

(c) Use the source: reasons given in the source were:

(i) 'to meet force with force …'. The 'attack on Korea', if left unchallenged, would have shown Stalin that aggression could succeed – as it had done for the dictators in the 1930s. Stalin had threatened to use force in Berlin (1948–9) and had been deterred by the Allied show of force there.

(ii) To uphold the notion of 'collective security' which the League had failed to uphold in the 1930s. Truman (Source A) was determined that the UNO should play a powerful and active role in world affairs, and exercise its 'authority'.

(d) The views expressed in the sources agree on: the need for vigorous action by the UN; the leadership of the USA – shown by Truman in Source A and expressed by a member of his cabinet in Source B; showing a major difference between the League (dead in Source A because of inaction and, by implication, US isolationism) and UNO, which would uphold 'collective security' which the League had only talked about.

Source A, however, has nothing to offer concerning the nature of 'the operation' which is dealt with in the last two sentences of Source B. On this, then, the sources differ but, obviously, do not disagree.

(e) Use the source by picking out words which show 'bias', e.g. fraud, imperialist, puppet.

. In spite of this 'bias' the source is useful in giving us some part of the account of the events of 1950–53:

• the Security Council voted for 'intervention';
• the USSR was absent from the Council (see (f);
• the USA led the military action;
• UN/US forces defeated the invaders and went into North Korea (see Source D);
• the Chinese became involved.

You might note that this account fails to mention important issues, e.g. that North Korea invaded the South and started the crisis, that Truman dismissed MacArthur. In spite of these and other omissions, disagree with the statement.

(f) The Chinese seat on the Security Council was occupied by a delegate from Chiang Kai-Shek's government, which had been defeated by Mao's forces and had fled to Taiwan (Formosa). The Council refused to allow a Mao-appointed delegate to replace Chiang's man: Russia protested and, in protest, absented herself from Council meetings in 1950.

(g) The left-hand map shows the extent of North Korean success in 1950. The UN/US forces might have done a 'Dunkirk' and fled from Pusan to Japan, and Korea would have become a Communist state.

The right-hand map shows:

• the extent of the UN/US success after the Inchon landings, with US troops at the Chinese border (the Yalu River);

- the extent of Chinese success, with part of South Korea occupied by Chinese Communist forces;
- the expulsion of these forces across the 38th parallel – the border between North and South Korea.

Was the action a success? Yes, in that South Korea did not go Communist, and that the US forces (from many nations) had upheld the authority of the UN (you should use the idea of Source B here). However, by getting the Chinese involved (which they were not in 1950), the US had created problems for the future. Overall, the action may be seen as a success.

12 International Relations 1945–64

Testing Assessment Objective 3.

(a) Use the source:
- para. 1 shows belief in democracy, freedom, liberty;
- para. 2 shows opposition to dictatorship with terror, control, fixed elections and suppression;
- para. 3 shows how far the USA had come since the isolationism of the 1930s. Now willing to help free peoples by 'mainly' non-military means – implying willingness to use force if necessary.

(b) They differ in:
   (i) *Scope*. Source A expresses a humanitarian attitude (against 'hunger … chaos') and looks for the economic revival 'in the world'.
       Source C agrees with Source B on 'economic breakdown', but refers only to 'Europe', while Source A refers to 'the world'.
   (ii) *Attitude*. Source C implies that 'fear of communism' was a factor, while Source B specifically says that the 'policy is directed not against any country or doctrine …'.

(c) The difference in *scope* can be explained by the fact that, by 1965 (Source C), the Plan applied only to Europe and not to 'the world' (Source B). The difference in attitude can be explained by the fact that by 1965 (Source C) the Plan applied only in 'most of the free countries in Europe' (Source C). Stalin, led by his henchman Zhdanov, had rejected the Plan for the USSR itself, and forced Polish and Czech Communist governments to reverse earlier decisions to accept Marshall's offer of help: he had already forced most of the other satellites to reject the offer – only Tito in Yugoslavia refused to obey and, having accepted the Plan, was ejected from the Cominform.

(d) The cartoonist approved of the 'angelic' Marshall blowing a gentle wind, labelled 'ERP' to help drive the European 'windmill' to activate not merely food production (as suggested), and so overcome 'hunger' (Source B), but industry generally, in a 'revival of the economy' (Source B), and so avoid 'economic breakdown' (Source C). The Plan required united action by countries wishing to take advantage of the Plan. This unity (a step on the road to the integration in Western Europe) would ensure that war between the participating states was less likely in the future.

(e) Sources B and D have no obvious, or even implied, political content. Source C implies that US aid was 'inspired' partly by 'fear of Communism' in poverty-stricken Europe.

Source A is an expression of support for democracy (para. 1) and of opposition to Communism (para. 2), and that support/opposition would be shown by 'mainly', although not entirely, 'economic and financial aid' (para. 3).

As an explanation of US aid to Europe, Source A is the most valuable of the sources, although it has nothing to say about Europe's poverty-stricken condition, which is dealt with in Sources B, C and D.

13 International relations 1964–95

Testing Assessment Objectives 1–2.

(a) (i) Détente means a lessening of tensions between hostile powers (see the Glossary also).

(ii) A deterrent is a means of dissuading or hindering an opponent from taking hostile action for fear of forceful retaliation.

(iii) A proposed reduction in 'troops and arms in Central Europe' made in 1974 concentrated on:
- nuclear missiles – intercontinental, long-range and intermediate-range;
- conventional weapons – including tanks and aircraft;
- numbers of men and women in the forces.

Later talks involved B-1 bombers, Stealth aircraft, neutron bombs and Trident nuclear submarines.

(iv) Increasingly, power rockets used in space exploration led to more powerfully propelled nuclear missiles; the increasing number of satellites stationed in space increased suspicion about spying; the USA had tried to develop a Strategic Defense Initiative ('Star Wars') to use weapons based in space to shoot down missiles. These weapons, if developed, might also be used in attack.

(v) The Conference met in a favourable climate: USA/USSR had signed SALT 1 (May 1972) and were holding further disarmament talks; West Germany had signed treaties with the USSR and Poland; the Vietnam War had ended (1973). Thirty-three European states (including Russia) and the USA and Canada agreed to: recognise Russia's control over Eastern Europe; give up West Germany's claim to be the 'only German state', which led to the first international recognition of the state of East Germany. Russia agreed to allow outside inspection of her record on human rights, and in return was allowed to buy US wheat.

(b) Essay questions

(i) Main points to develop; there was no agreement 1946–63; the Test Ban Treaty, 1963, signed by the USA, USSR and Britain, banned the testing of nuclear weapons in the atmosphere, in outer space or under water, but allowed underground testing. More than 90 countries had signed the Treaty by 1965, but France and China refused to sign and continued testing nuclear weapons in the atmosphere; the Nuclear Non-Proliferation Treaty was signed by the USA, USSR, Britain and over 100 other countries. It aimed to limit the spread of nuclear weapons, and countries which had them agreed not to help others to get the means of producing them, while those who did not have them agreed not to try to get those means; the Strategic Arms Limitations Talks (SALT) were held between the USA and USSR to try to limit their stock of nuclear weapons and to slow down the arms race. In SALT 1 (signed 1972) a limit was placed on the number of intercontinental nuclear weapons. SALT 2 was agreed in 1979, but was doomed by western anger at the Russian refusal to allow on-site inspection and at the invasion of Afghanistan.

(ii) Main points to develop: Russia was suspicious of the West because of past history (invasions in 1914 and 1941, intervention against the Bolsheviks in 1918–21, the appeasement of Hitler, especially at Munich, 1938). Russia saw the USA as anti-Communist (the Marshall Plan, Truman Doctrine and formation of NATO) with the refusal to recognise East Germany (until 1975) as a sign of that attitude. The western powers had their suspicions and fears – of an aggressive Communism (with the promise of 'world revolution'), the takeover of Eastern Europe, Berlin in 1948–9 and 1961, support for colonial rebels in the Dutch East Indies and Malaysia, and for the North Koreans in 1950–53. Fears were increased by the size of the forces of the Warsaw Pact countries, the attempt to base missiles in Cuba (1962), and the Russian support for the anti-US forces in Vietnam, and for anti-western rebels in various parts of Africa (Eritrea, Angola, Mozambique).

14 Three International case studies

The Berlin Wall, 1961–89

Testing Assessment Objective 3.

(a) It proves that the East German Government *thought* it had good reasons. Quote from the source: 'activities … against the GDR', 'centre for spying', 'smuggle … agents into the GDR', 'sabotage'. It shows also that the Government *thought* that the Wall would 'stop all this activity'. The accusations about anti-Government activity were probably all true. So, from the GDR Government's point of view, there were good reasons for building the Wall. What the source overlooks (conveniently) is the major reason for the building of the Wall – the economic effects of the flight from the country of skilled workers (Source C) and the hope that the Wall would somehow hide the attractive Western life-style from the East Germans.

(b) Use the source: it shows delegates from the USA, USSR and Britain negotiating the terms of what became the Test Ban Treaty of 1963. It suggests that the Berlin crisis was a time-bomb waiting to explode (the fuse already lit), and which would both end these negotiations and, maybe, bring these states to war (Source E). It is useful as evidence of the awareness of the depth of the crisis at the time the Wall was built built.

(c) Use Source D: it shows some of the obstacles in the way of anyone trying to escape to the West (where a civilian walks freely). List the obstacles – wall; barriers on top of wall; wire; concrete 'teeth' to stop lorries/cars getting near the Wall. It cannot show the mines which were planted in the area immediately to the east of the Wall, nor does it show the armed guards who both patrolled the eastern area and/or were stationed in look-out posts from which potential escapers were shot. So Source D does support Mann's claim.

(d) Both Sources C and E were written long after the 1961 Crisis. There is no evidence to suggest that the author of Source E was wiser or better informed than the author of Source C, in spite of his advantage of greater hindsight. Use the sources to show that they agreed on the flight of people, and on the likely economic effects of that flight. The main difference between the sources lies in the final line of Source E, but there is no evidence that the collapse of the GDR would have led to war: indeed, when the Wall did come down, it led to a greater sense of peace. Disagree with the statement.

(e) The Introduction suggests that the building of the Wall was part of the argument about 'Berlin', and less serious than 'the most serious dispute … of 1948–9'. Source B suggests that the building of the Wall was itself a threat to peace (the ticking bomb labelled 'Berlin').

Sources C and E point to the number of East Germans who 'escaped' to the West. Since the Wall was meant to prevent this movement (Sources A and D) this increased the bitterness of potential escapers, and led to increased internal antagonism to the GDR Government, which was forced to become even more repressive which, in turn, angered the West German Government and the western Allies, and did not 'make for peace'. Source E, on the other hand, does imply that the Wall contributed 'to peace' (Source A) by suggesting that a continuation of the 'rush of people' would have led to 'the collapse of the East German state [and] brought the two Superpowers into violent collision'.

In (d) we have shown that there was no evidence offered for this conclusion drawn by the author of Source E. So, the evidence from the Introduction and other sources does not support the East German claim.

The Cuban Crisis, 1962

Questions (a) and (b) test Assessment Objective 3; (c) tests Assessment Objectives 1, 2 and 3.

(a) No one source can ever fully explain a complex situation. The source does help to explain Kennedy's opposition: the range of missiles based so close to the USA; the effect on so many major US cities if attacked by nuclear missiles. But Kennedy's opposition had deeper roots which are not dealt with in the source: long-term US suspicion of Russian policy (in Eastern Europe, Korea, Berlin 1948–9 and 1961).

(b) Note the differences in origin (one is American, one is Russian) so that, not surprisingly, they reach different conclusions (both claiming a victory for their side) because they express different intentions behind the actions of their countries (the USA wanted to get the Russian missile bases off the island of Cuba; the Russians claimed they wanted to prevent a second invasion by the USA – recall the Bay of Pigs). The Russians also claimed that they wanted the USA to know what it was like to be 'surrounded … with military bases and threatened with nuclear weapons' as the USSR was by missiles, based in Turkey in particular. Note, too, the existence of the hot-line between Washington and Moscow which allowed talks to take place between the Statesmen.

(c) Describe the source – both men sitting on missiles while they arm wrestle, both with their fingers on the button which would set the missiles off. Explain the source: the arm wrestle represents the struggle for power between two politicians and their countries; the fingers on buttons represent the real danger of nuclear war which would have destroyed both the USA and the USSR. Then link the explanations with the events of the Cuban crisis. Finally, draw a conclusion from the source: were they really prepared to go to war? You might add that here we have an example of brinkmanship.

Vietnam

When 'using your own knowledge', Assessment Objectives 1–2 are being tested: when using or commenting on 'sources', Assessment Objective 3 is being tested. So, before tackling the question, study the sources carefully and critically.

(a) (i) Use details from the sources: 'to prevent … Communist influence' 'to assist them … to resist Communism' 'to help them contribute … free world'. 'The threat to the free nations …' 'to take over South Vietnam and Laos', 'to defend their freedom'.

Your own knowledge should provide: US dislike/fear of North Vietnam before and after Geneva Settlement, 1954; the Domino Theory; Kennedy's aid to Diem; Johnson and the Tonkin incident; Viet Cong attacks on US troops in Saigon.

(b) Comment on the sources: they come from Vietnamese sources and so are biased; the artist of C clearly supports the Communists, while D is by the founder of the Vietminh, the anti-French (until 1954) and anti-US Communist governing body of North Vietnam.

They both show that there was opposition to the USA, *but* many in North Vietnam were anti-Communist (and some fled to the South), while many more in South Vietnam were opposed to Communism.

Use your own knowledge to show that opposition to the USA grew over time, partly because of dislike of 'foreign' influence, but mainly because of reaction against US tactics – intensive bombing, use of chemical warfare.

(c) Comment on the sources: F is evidence of growth of US 'youth culture' in the age of 'flower power' and widespread use of drugs. G (and many TV programmes) brought the reality of war to US citizens at home. Both F and G may be seen as unreliable – were they stage-managed? Was student protest widespread? (Answer 'Yes', but this isn't clear from merely one picture). Both F and G were examples of the propaganda put out by anti-war liberals who tended to have great influence in the media.

Source E is an example of hindsight reporting and use of statistics. Its reliability depends on the value of the sources used to compile the graph, and the bias of the author. It may well be reliable, and itself be a reflection of the influence of the media and its use of pictorial propaganda (F and G).

(d) Use the source. Does it 'explain how and why', or does it merely say, in effect, that the war ended? Was it true that a major reason for seeking peace was because of 'the Presidential election', or were there economic reasons (inflation, weakening of the dollar), international reasons (anti-war protests in most countries) and domestic pressures (from increasing numbers of young people (F) and old opposed to the horrors, the waste and the ineffectiveness of US tactics and strategies)? Was it 'peace was at hand' which gained Nixon his 'landslide', or was he helped by the weakness of the too liberal policies of a weak Democratic candidate?

Note, too, that with this issue, as with all important historic issues, there are bound to be different interpretations presented (in hindsight) by authors with their own inevitable bias.

(e) Use the following guide.

(i) The Communists could never hope for equality with the US in terms of weapons or size of forces: mention bombers, artillery, helicopter gunships, chemicals. Hence the absence of large-scale battles.

(ii) In guerrilla warfare, relatively small groups make attacks on bases, supply lines, buildings, important individuals in 'hit and run' attacks, after which they often fade away into the general population ('swimming like fish in the water' wrote Mao), which made it almost impossible for US forces to distinguish between hostile and friendly Vietnamese.

US reaction was to increase its bombing and use of chemical warfare – which led, over time, to the growth of opposition even among anti-Communist Vietnamese, and so increased the influence of the Communists.

The increase in US activity had harmful effects on the US economy, led to increased opposition in the USA and in the rest of the world. The failure of the US (illustrated by the Tet offensive on the US headquarters in Saigon) forced Nixon to begin to consider ending the war. 'Might' clearly was not, in US terms, 'right'.

15 Russia, 1953–95

Testing (mainly) Assessment Objectives 1 and 2.

(a) (i) Goods bought by ordinary people ('consumers') for their own use, e.g. cars, TVs, clothes, furniture; different to 'industrial goods' such as machinery, plant and buildings (used to produce other goods).

(ii) Starting in 1928, Stalin began the system by which, every five years, a Moscow-based planning commission laid down details of what every factory/farm/mine etc, was to produce during the next five years. Interrupted by the war, the planning system was resumed in peacetime.

(iii) In 1928, Russia was relatively a backward country due to lack of investment in industrial goods (see i) above) in the nineteenth century, the losses of 1914–18, the effects of the Civil War: Stalin wanted Russia to become a model Communist state, her output as great as that of the USA, able to produce military goods to guard Russia from invasion, and able to help other states to modernise. After 1945, Russia had also to make up for the heavy losses suffered during 1941–45. All this meant that materials and labour had to be devoted to producing industrial goods, so little was left for consumer goods.

(iv) Over ambitious; dishonest and corrupt local controllers; failure of transport systems (even in 1987, half the farming output rotted while waiting to be taken to markets); lazy, drunk and poorly-motivated workers, lack of modern machinery and fertilisers (in 1980, 40 million Russian farm workers produced less than 4 million US farmers). Khrushchev's plan to use 'Virgin Lands' in Siberia failed as valuable topsoil was blown away, leading to the creation of 'dustbowls'.

(b) Essay question

1950s: Stalin's death, 1953; triumvirate in charge (Prime Minister Malenkov, Deputy PM Bulganin and Khrushchev combined to sack Malenkov; 1957 Bulganin and Army tried to sack Khrushchev, attempt failed and 1958 Khrushchev became Prime Minister as well as Party Secretary, with Marshall Zhukov ensuring he had Army support.

1964: Party leaders feared Khrushchev developing Stalinistic 'cult of personality', and angered by his attempts to change organisation of Party; Army leaders angered by Cuban policy and failure of Berlin policy to get western powers to recognise East Germany (and Khrushchev's sacking of his supporter Zhukov lessened his influence with Army leaders); many Russians ashamed of his 'boorish' behaviour when abroad; failure of his 'Virgin Lands' plan and failure to produce more consumer goods; his quarrel with Mao in China. While on holiday, he was sacked by Party bosses and on return failed in attempt to regain power.

16 Eastern Europe, 1945–95

Testing Assessment Objectives 1 and 2 (question (e)) and 3.

(a) Use the source: Khrushchev's relations with Yugoslavia which had broken with Stalin over Marshall Aid, his attack on Stalin's memory and policies, and the abolition of the NKVD all created a climate in which other critics felt encouraged to act – in Poland and Hungary in particular.

(b) Interpret the source. The Yugoslav 'bear' has escaped Russian control (see Source A) and stands tall at the top of the cartoon; the Polish 'bear' has begun to step off his platform, while the Hungarian bear has begun to slip away (a reminder that Nagy went further than Gomulka in his opposition to Russian control – see Source A).

So, Source A helps our understanding of Source B, but only in Source B do we get an indication that Khrushchev was going to try (and succeed) in getting Poland and Hungary back into line.

(c) Source D shows only one relatively small scene: it may not have been true of (Source C) as a whole. It may have been staged by a cameraman (or indeed, taken on its own, might merely show a serious traffic accident). However, in Source D we can see 'paving stones' (Source C), a street 'littered with burnt-out cars', 'tramcar rails' torn up (Source C). Although we do not see 'Russian tanks' (Source C), we do get the impression of unrest. So, Source D helps to support Source C.

(d) Compare and interpret the sources. Source D may be said to have limited value (see (c) above), but may be valuable to someone who knows something of the events of 1956 as they affected Budapest. Clearly it cannot tell us anything about 'the events in Eastern Europe' as a whole, and we know that there were no such scenes in most other satellite states. Source B may be seen merely as western propaganda (it comes from a British source). However, to someone who knows something of 'the events in Eastern Europe', it is useful as showing Russia as the controlling power, the submissiveness of some states (Albania etc), and the different nature of unrest in Poland and Hungary (see Source A), with Yugoslavia seen as freed from Russian control. So, disagree with comment.

(e) The uprising in Hungary was more serious than that in Poland, where Gomulka did not share power with non-Communists, nor break with Russia over the Warsaw Pact. In Hungary, Nagy (Source A), got the Russians to withdraw their forces, gave freedom to press and other media, allowed non-Communist parties to be formed, and offered the promise of 'free elections'. Most seriously, he said that Hungary would withdraw from the Warsaw Pact and owe no allegiance to Russia. Khrushchev then ordered the attack.

17 The USA, 1945–95

Testing Assessment Objectives 3 (questions a, c, d and e) and 1–2 (questions b and e particularly).

(a) Use details from the source. Conditions of clapped out car (tyres, windows), of housing (windows, scraps of furniture coming out) and of littered street. But was it a staged photograph? Doubtful.

(b) King was leader of Civil Rights Movement calling for equal rights for black people in politics, law and social life: peaceful campaigning in face of brutal hostility made little progress. Need for government legislation, hence the march to Kennedy's Washington (which led to the Civil Rights Act, 1964).

(c) Interpret and explain source. *Useful:* black unemployment twice level of white, showing need for reform in education, laws against bias by employers and white unions – note slight improvement in figures for 1970. Death rate among blacks three times as high as among whites, showing higher level of poverty and poor housing among blacks (Source A), lower incomes leading to poorer diet; less medical care for blacks than whites.

(d) Interpret and evaluate the sources. Source E(i) taken in Little Rock: for Little Rock, 1957, see Source C and use quote from there. By 1979, Civil Rights legislation working (voting rights, job opportunities, education reforms (Source E(II). The Klan (Source E(i)) long-term violent enemy of blacks (and Jews, Catholics and other minorities). Poster suggests it may have lost ground, but in 1979 was 'rising again', supported by angry and bigoted whites. However, E(i) might be merely a propaganda photograph showing only a small and decreasing minority, anxious to win attention.

Source E(ii) was written during Reagan's presidency during which some of the Civil Rights legislation of 1964–8 was to be 'abolished', so lessening the chances of further improvements in, for example, job opportunities (see 1967 and 1970 in Source D). E(ii) is an indication of official policy and, because of the effects of the changed policy, it is a more reliable source of race relations than E(i).

(e) Too strong to say 'nothing'. E(ii) shows Johnson's 'equal rights in employment' laws which had helped blacks for 20 years: similar legislation has helped black voters so that, even in the southern states, (including Alabama – E(ii) there were many black mayors and councillors and Congressmen. Source C suggests some lessening of bigotry among white children – maybe reluctantly ('got used to the idea ...'), but also suggests black/white separateness ('in the school yard') and the onset of fresh anti-black legislation. Source E(i) suggests, at worst, a growth in the Klan and, even at best, that some whites wanted the Klan to 'rise again'. The poor housing conditions of the 1970s (Source A) and the higher-than-white rate of black unemployment (Source D) indicate that, at that time, many blacks were still a depressed class. So, 'absolutely nothing' is too strong a verdict. Something (much?) had been done for some (few?) blacks, but little had been done for the many.

18 South Africa 1945–95

Testing mainly Assessment Objective 3.

(a) Use and interpret the source which shows: the aim (sentence 1); fears (sentence 2); the claim that it can be done peacefully (sentence 3) and that 'non-Europeans' would get their 'natural rights'; fear of Communism (final sentence). The source also brings out the idea of separate development for blacks and whites – but not how this was to be achieved, and that the whites would be supreme – but not the nature of the laws needed to attain this, or of police, prisons, punishments that would be needed. So, limited on *nature* of policies, but useful on *reasons* for policies.

(b) Use and interpret the source. Possible to infer that leaders of 'the Bantu people' wanted 'political equality', although this is not stated clearly. Shows policy of separate development of 'the Bantu initiative ... administration ...', but does not show that Bantu leaders were opposed to this notion of life 'within the Bantu community'. It does suggest the idea of separate homelands, but does not show that ANC leaders opposed this idea. The final line is a lie: the Bantu people would not be allowed to 'fulfil their potential', and the ANC leaders showed in their other protests that their people were victimised in terms of housing, education, social services etc. Only partly useful.

(c) Use the sources. Source A helps understand the origins of apartheid policy (white fears of 'black sea' and of future of white 'civilisation'). Source B shows black opposition to 'separate' development, and shows main areas in which apartheid laws would be applied – 'groups' foretell Homelands and Group Areas Act; the final line draws attention to future education and housing Laws. Very useful, although both have their limitations, as explained in (a) and (b).

(d) Use the source. Blacks were 'voteless' and so unable to influence politicians through the ballot box. Hence, having 'explored … without success' they plan 'peaceful' anti-apartheid campaigns.

(e) There had been no change in policy between 1952 (Source C) and 1980 (Source D): in spite of 'peaceful' campaigns (Source C) and, as these failed, more violent terrorism, there was still 'a white monopoly of power'. Source D does show that there was a major change in government thinking because of the 'changing world', in which all other African states had gained independence, with some acting as supporters of violent ANC campaigns. Outside South Africa the Anti-Apartheid Movement had isolated the country by trade boycotts, investment withdrawal, sports and cultural boycotts, all of which encouraged the oppressed to 'fight back' so that, unless whites 'acknowledge people's rights …' and an end to 'white monopoly of power' the country faced damaging and 'permanent conflict'. So, the sources do not show any change in racial policies, but Source D indicates that change was on the way.

19 The Middle East

Testing Assessment Objectives 1 and 2.

(a) (i) Refer to Treaty of Sèvres, 1920, when parts of the former Turkish Empire were handed to Britain and France as Mandates (see Glossary). Britain had Palestine as one of the Mandates.

(ii) For definition see Glossary.

(iii) Britain was unable to afford to keep the large forces needed to stop riots by Arabs and Jews and inter-communal fighting (see also withdrawal from Greece and the need for the Truman Doctrine).

The Labour Government was opposed to colonialism (see withdrawal from India at this time).

(iv) May 1948: UNO took Mandate back from Britain and proposed to divide Palestine between Jews and Arabs (refer to map); Israel declared its existence as an independent state, and was recognised by the USA and others; the Arab states rejected the idea of division and refused to recognise Israel; forces from five Arab states invaded the new state.

(v) Each Arab state had its own ambitions, and there was no unity in the campaign; the Jews could concentrate on defeating first one, then the other. Arab armies were badly led, while Jewish forces were commanded by men who had served in the British army or had led anti-Arab campaigns in Palestine before 1948. Arab soldiers (as opposed to their heads of state) had less determination than did the Israelis, who either had to fight or face extermination.

(b) Essay question
Main points to be developed: uneasy peace after Suez War, 1956; UN peacekeeping force along Israeli-Egyptian border and in Gulf of Aqaba. Nasser (with Syria as partner in United Arab Republic) wanted to extend his influence over other Arab states, and approved anti-Western activities in Lebanon, Iraq, Aden and the Yemen. In Spring 1967, there was increased PLO terrorism and Syrian shelling of Israel from the Golan Heights. Nasser's claim to be the dominant Arab leader was now challenged by Syria, Iraq and Saudi Arabia, so he needed to act in order to win wider Arab approval. On 4 June 1967 Egypt and Jordan signed a military pact. Nasser demanded withdrawal of UN peacekeeping forces. On 5 June 1967 Israel, fearing a war whenever Nasser felt ready, launched its pre-emptive strike against Egypt, Syria and Jordan: all surrendered by 11 June 1967.

20 The Suez Crisis: a Case Study

Testing Assessment Objective 3.

(a) (i) Use the details from the sources. Source A (by a British Cabinet Minister of the time) notes the 'withdrawal of aid' promised by the USA and Britain to help Nasser build 'the Aswan Dam' which was meant to help provide electricity for industry and domestic users, and to help irrigate farmlands. This 'insult' led to the nationalisation of the Canal (Source B). Nasser meant to use canal income to finance the Dam. Source C (from a British source) shows British claims that Nasser had torn up at least two international treaties – the 'Suez Canal Treaty' of 1888 (and had done so 'with no discussion with … parties to the Treaty', Source D), and the UN-arranged 'Treaty on Israeli shipping', which provided for Israeli shipping to use the Gulf of Aqaba – and that he used 'Cairo Radio' to make 'anti-British broadcasts' attacking British involvement in the Middle East in general. Source D (by a leading spokesman for the Labour Opposition) supports Eden's anti-Nasser attitude. Eden (and Morrison) saw Nasser ('a pocket dictator) as a smaller ('pocket') version of Hitler and Mussolini, whose aggressive policies had not been halted in the 1930s and had made them as popular as Nasser was with the Egyptians (Source B). Source D infers that Nasser had to be stopped, while Source C gives evidence of reasons for Britain's decision to use force.

(ii) However, the sources do not *fully* explain the outbreak of war. They do not mention French anger at Nasser's aid to Algerian rebels, the Israeli determination to get freedom for their shipping and to stop Egyptian-backed terrorist attacks on Israel, or the failure of repeated international efforts to get Nasser to agree to some form of international control of the Canal.

(b) Indeed, confusion reigned. Source E shows Eisenhower and Dulles at odds over 'force', with Dulles 'suddenly changing his views' at critical times, having misled the British and French in the meantime. Source F shows that a British Cabinet Committee had a simplistic view of an attack on Egypt, which ignored the probable reactions by other Arab states, Eisenhower's opposition (especially once the Presidential election campaign opened), the known hostility of the large Afro-Asian bloc in the UN (Source K), and the certain opposition from Russia (Source J). Source G allowed the British to believe that they had US support for the use of force ('other means for the assertion of their rights'), although, on the next day, Eisenhower opposed 'war' (Source H). Note, too, that in 1954 Eden had negotiated the withdrawal of British troops from bases along the Canal which had been made ineffective by constant terrorist attacks. How did he mean to control Egypt if the attack on the Canal had succeeded? Total occupation?

(c) No. The cartoons are very valuable pieces of evidence. Use them in your answer. Source C was an expression of widespread British anger at Nasser (with Source D giving the Labour view) and of Israeli hostility over the 'shipping' position. However, the cartoonist does not show that Nasser was legally entitled to nationalise the Company (as the International Court later agreed), nor does it show anything of the 'insult' (Source A) over the Aswan Dam aid.

Source K is even more useful. It shows the attitude of the UN (representing the international community), it shows that the military adventure had failed, and that Nasser was even more popular with Arabs than ever before. In the background, Russia is shown as savagely repressing the Hungarian rising, freer to get on with this since world attention was focussed on the Suez problem.

Answers to quick questions

Chapter 1 Russia, 1900–1914
1 1H; 2F; 3E; 4C; 5J; 6B; 7D; 8A; 9G.
2 (i) Social Democratic Labour Party;
   (ii) Social Revolutionary Party.
3 (i) Bolsheviks;
   (ii) Mensheviks.
4 Father Gapon.

Chapter 2 International Relations, 1870–1914
1 Alsace and Lorraine.
2 (i) Germany & Austria-Hungary;
   (ii) France and Russia.
3 (i) Bosnia and Herzegovina;
   (ii) Serbia.
4 Germany, Austria-Hungary, Russia.
5 (i) France;
   (ii) Russia.
6 (i) London;
   (ii) Bucharest.
7 Agadir.
8 A: Mediterranean;
   B: North Sea.
9 Russia refused to call off mobilisation.
10 The invasion of Belgium and refusal to withdraw.

Chapter 3 The First World War
1 (a) Haig;
   (b) Pétain;
   (c) Scheer;
   (d) Lawrence;
   (e) Wilson;
   (f) Hamilton;
   (g) Foch;
   (h) Russia;
   (i) Salonika;
   (j) Lusitania
   (k) Dardanelles.
2 (a) Cambrai;
   (b) Jutland;
   (c) Falkland Islands.

Chapter 4 Peacemaking, 1919–1923
1 The Saar coalfields.
2 France to control the coalfields for 5 years; the League to govern the region after 1919.
3 Alsace and Lorraine.
4 To be returned to France.
5 Rhineland to be demilitarised; Germany not to have any forces or fortifications in the territory.
6 Czechoslovakia.
7 Austria-Hungary.
8 Austria.
9 Not to be allowed to unite with Germany.
10 (i) Poland;
   (ii) East Prussia;
   (iii) Danzig.
11 Germany, Russia and Austria-Hungary.
12 Germany.
13 Danzig named a 'Free City' governed by the League.
14 West Prussia was given to Poland to provide a 'corridor to the sea'.

Chapter 5 The League of Nations
1 Wilson.
2 The 14 Points.
3 Geneva.
4 The Assembly and Council.
5 (i) International Labour Organisation;
   (ii) System of government for the former colonies of the defeated Powers.
6 Economic and military.
7 (i) USA;
   (ii) Germany;
   (iii) Russia.
8 Manchuria, 1931.
9 Disarmament

Chapter 6 Russia, 1917–1953

1. (i) The last Tsar;
   (ii) Wife (Tsarina) of Nicholas II;
   (iii) 'Monk' adviser to Tsarina and 'healer' of her son Alexis.
2. Provisional Government led by Lvov.
3. Land, Peace, Bread and Freedom.
4. By armed rising led by Trotsky.
5. Lenin's secret police.
6. New Economic Policy.
7. Trotsky.
8. Coal, steel, electricity, railways, construction.
9. Agriculture.
10. Successor to Cheka.

Chapter 7 China, 1911–1949

1. Manchu.
2. (i) Nanking;
   (ii) Peking.
3. The Boxers.
4. Kuo Min Tang: Nationalism; democracy; people's livelihood.
5. 1921.
6. Chiang Kai-shek.
7. (i) Kiangsi;
   (ii) Yenan.
8. (i) 1931;
   (ii) 1937.
9. Peking; October 1949.
10. Formosa (Taiwan).

Chapter 8 Germany 1918–1939

1. Weimar.
2. (i) Communist enemies of Weimar;
   (ii) right-wing opponents of Weimar.
3. Led to rapid inflation.
4. Stresemann.
5. Munich; 1923;
6. *Mein Kampf.*
7. The pure-bred Germans.
8. Hindenburg.
9. The Enabling Act, 1933.
10. The SA.
11. Propaganda.

Chapter 9 The USA 1919–1939

1. Ford.
2. Hire purchase.
3. Agriculture.
4. 1929.
5. Chicago.
6. Hoover.
7. The Wall Street Crash.
8. (i) Civilian Conservation Corps;
   (ii) National Recovery Administration;
   (iii) Agricultural Adjustment Act;
   (iv) Tennessee Valley Authority.
9. Isolationist.

Chapter 10 International Relations, 1919–1939

1. France and Great Britain.
2. Dawes and Young.
3. 1925.
4. Great Britain, France, Germany, Italy, Belgium.
5. It guaranteed the Franco-German border.
6. 1931; Lytton.
7. 1939.
8. (i) Hoare;
   (ii) Laval.
9. He sent in troops to occupy the demilitarised zone.
10. Great Britain, France, Italy.

Chapter 11 India, 1900–49

1. 1885.
2. Hindu.
3. (i) Morley;
   (ii) Minto.
4. Ultimate self-government.
5. A day of strike, prayer and fasting.
6. Sikhs.
7. The government's monopoly of the salt trade.
8. The passing of the Government of India Act.
9. Muslims.
10. Because of his 'Quit India' campaign.
11. Mountbatten.

Chapter 12 The Second World War, 1939–1945

1. Poland.
2. The Maginot Line.
3. April 1940.
4. Vichy.
5. The invasions of
   (i) Britain;
   (ii) Russia;
   (iii) Europe.
6. (i) Al Alamein;
   (ii) Stalingrad;
   (iii) Coral Sea and Midway Island.
7. (i) An artificial harbour towed to France;
   (ii) The Pipe Line Under The Ocean.

8 (i) von Paulus;   9 Hiroshima.
   (ii) Zhukov.   10 1 May 1945.

Chapter 13 The British Home Front

1914–18
1 (i) Rupert Brooke;
  (ii) Owen; Sassoon; Graves; Thomas.
2 (i) Asquith;
  (ii) Lloyd George.
3 Lloyd George.
4 1916.
5 Zeppelins and Gothas.
6 To increase food production.

1939–45
1 (i) Air Raid Precautions;
  (ii) Defence of the Realm Act.
2 (i) September 1938;
  (ii) September 1939.
3 Ernest Bevin.
4 Lord Beaverbrook.
5 Petrol was rationed.
6 (i) Lancaster and Halifax;
  (ii) Liberators and Fortresses.
7 Beveridge.

Chapter 14 The United Nations Organisation

1 1941–45.
2 Roosevelt and Churchill.
3 1942.
4 Yalta.
5 Warsaw Pact and NATO.
6 Five.
7 Children, refugees.
8 1950–53.
9 1956.
10 The League of Nations.

Chapter 15 International Relations, 1945–64

1 Yalta and Potsdam.
2 Stalin.
3 1949.
4 Fulton, Missouri, USA.
5 Truman; Marshall.
6 Greece.
7 North Atlantic Treaty Organisation.
8 The Warsaw Pact.
9 Built the Berlin Wall.
10 (i) Indo-China/Vietnam;
  (ii) France, Britain, the USA, USSR and China.
11 Eisenhower.

Chapter 16 Towards détente, 1964–95

1 (i) Brezhnev;
  (ii) Gorbachev;
  (iii) Yeltsin.
2 (i) Angola and Ethiopia;
  (ii) Syria and Iraq.
3 Because of Warsaw Pact's superiority in conventional forces.
4 Mutual Assured Destruction.
5 China and USSR.
6 Strategic Arms Limitation Talks.
7 (i) Increased trade and western investment;
  (ii) Easing of tension and improvement in Russia's policies on human rights.
8 (i) Carter;
  (ii) Reagan;
  (iii) Bush.
9 Strategic Defence Initiative.
10 Tehran.

Chapter 18 Russia 1953–95

1 Khrushchev.
2 The 20th Party Congress.
3 Yes.
4 The West.
5 Brezhnev.
6 Old men.
7 1985.
8 Perestroika and Glasnost.
9 Boris Yeltsin.
10. The CIS.

Chapter 19 Eastern Europe, 1945–95

1 Poland, Rumania, Hungary, Bulgaria.
2 Albania and Yugoslavia.
3 Tito.
4 Masaryk and Benes.
5 (i) Gottwald;
  (ii) Gomulka.
6 (i) Nagy;
  (ii) Kadar.
7 (i) Budapest;
  (ii) Prague.
8 Dubcek.
9 Solidarity.
10 Jaruzelski.

Chapter 20 Western European integration

1 OEEC, ECSC, Benelux Union.
2 Messina.
3 1957.
4 1961 and 1967.
5 The European Commission.
6 Fifteen.
7 The Maastricht Treaty.
8 The Single European Act.
9 Common Agricultural Policy.
10 The Council of Ministers.

Chapter 21 The USA 1945–95

1 Roosevelt and Truman.
2 Joseph McCarthy.
3 The Ku Klux Klan.
4 Martin Luther King.
5 JF Kennedy and LB Johnson.
6 Stokey Carmichael and Malcom `X'.
7 Nixon.
8 Presley and Dylan.
9 The Vietnam War.
10 The Hippie Movement.

Chapter 22 China 1945–95

1 Japan.
2 Land.
3 They were collectivised.
4 1958.
5 Mao.
6 Deng and Hu Yaobang.
7 Tiananmen Square.
8 The USSR.
9 1971.
10 Tibet.

Chapter 23 South Africa 1945–95

1 1948.
2 The Dutch Reformed Church.
3 Dr Malan.
4 (i) 1950.
   (ii) 1959.
(iii) 1950.
(iv) 1950.
6 Presidents Botha and de Klerk.
7 Nelson Mandela.
8 April 1994.

Chapter 24 The Middle East

1 May 1948.
2 Ben Gurion.
3 The West Bank.
4 Nasser.
5 Aswan.
6 The Golan Heights.
7 (i) Organisation of Petroleum
       Exporting Countries;
   (ii) Palestine Liberation Organisation.
8 September 1970.
9 Munich, 1972.
10 Egypt, Syria, Jordan, Iraq and Saudi Arabia.
11 Uganda.
12 Sadat, Begin and Carter.
13 1982.
14 Intifadah.
15 Rabin and Peres; Yasser Arafat.

Abbreviations and Glossary

ABM Anti-ballistic missile. A ballistic missile is first powered by some explosive or fuel, then depends only on gravity. ABMs are meant to shoot these down.

abdicate (to) To give up some office or power. Nicolas II (Unit 6) and Edward VIII of Britain gave up their thrones.

amnesty The granting of forgiveness, a pardon, usually to political offenders.

anarchy A country without effective government, or the political and social disorder following from the inability of government to control things.

ANC The African National Congress, a predominantly black organization opposed to the whites-only policies of the South African government (see apartheid).

annexation The taking of territory, often without any right.

ANZAC The Australian and New Zealand Army Corps (1914–18). ANZAC Day, 25 April, commemorates the landing of the Corps in Gallipoli in 1915.

ANZUS The Australian, New Zealand and United States Pact signed in 1951.

apartheid The South African system for separating the races.

appeasement Reaching agreement by negotiating with and conciliation of a potential aggressor. In the late 1930s it came to be identified with giving way to Hitler.

arbitration The settlement of disputes through the verdict of someone not involved in the dispute.

armistice An agreement to end fighting so that negotiations for a peace treaty can take place.

autarky The plan for economic self-sufficiency in Germany in the late 1930s. Nazi Germany wanted to be economically independent.

authoritarian The opposite of 'liberal'. An authoritarian government imposes strict discipline and represses opposition (see totalitarianism).

autocracy Rule by one person, a dictatorship (see dictatorship).

Bolsheviks Those members of the Russian Social Democratic Party who believed that a Marxist revolution would be brought about only by a small, dedicated organization. They were led by Lenin. The name comes from the Russian word for the majority which Lenin and his followers had after a debate in 1903.

BOSS The Bureau of State Security, the South African force mainly used to crush anti-apartheid opposition.

bourgeoisie A French word used to describe the middle classes, the capitalist owners of industry.

boycott (to) To unite to refuse to deal with someone or some nation; to refuse to handle someone's goods.

caste The term applied to the 2000 divisions of Hindu society in India. There are four main divisions: priests, rulers and warriors, traders and farmers, and artisans. Those outside these divisions are called Untouchables. Caste is hereditary and the members of each caste are equal and united in religion. Caste largely determines occupation. It is an exclusive system, with little contact with those outside the caste.

centre Political parties of the centre are neither extreme socialists nor extremely conservative (i.e. the right). They have middle-of-the-road policies.

Cheka Lenin's secret police, the name coming from the Russian initials for Extraordinary Commission.

CIA The Central Intelligence Agency (USA).

co-existence A state of international relations in which rivals (such as the USA and USSR) tolerate one another. Neither seeks to bring down the other by force (a 'hot war'), although dislike remains. When the dislike becomes very strong the world may have a period of 'cold war' – see below.

cold war Such a 'war' is fought by various 'peaceful' weapons – such as propaganda, economic sanctions, aid (even military) to opponents of the rival régime. The rivals (since 1945 the USA and USSR) have stopped short of military confrontation although they have supported rivals in various 'local' wars as in Korea and Vietnam.

colonialism The policy of obtaining and maintaining colonies; opponents of this policy use the word to argue that the colonial (or occupying) power exploits backward or weak people for its own economic benefit.

collectivisation The policy of joining small farms into one large holding. Stalin implemented this policy to destroy the bourgeois (see bourgeoisie) kulaks.

Comecon The Council for Mutual Economic Assistance.

Cominform The Communist Information Bureau.

concordat An agreement, usually between the Church and State.

Congress A meeting of delegates. In the USA it is the national legislative body (or Parliament); in India the name was used by Indian politicians campaigning against British colonialism (see above). They were, by using the word, claiming to be the Indian 'Parliament' even though they had no power.

constitution The principles by which a country is governed. In many countries there is a written constitution which expresses these principles.

containment The building of alliances in an effort to frighten an enemy and prevent its expansion.

convoy A number of merchant ships sailing together under the escort of warships.

coup d'état A violent or illegal change of government; the seizure of power by a non-elected group, or by an individual (see putsch).

covenant An agreement setting out the aims and rules (of the League of Nations).

Czech Legion While they were being evacuated from eastern Russia along the Trans-Siberian Railway in 1918, Czech prisoners-of-war overpowered their guards and began a private march to Moscow. They were halted by Trotsky's Red Army outside Kazan. The plight of this Legion was the official reason for the various foreign interventions in the Russian Civil War.

democracy (from demos, the Greek word for 'the people') Rule by the people; a system of government which allows the mass of the people (the electorate) to have some control over their rules; a system which tolerates minority views.

DMZ A demilitarized zone as in the Rhineland after 1919 and in Korea after 1953 and such as was proposed by various people for Central Europe in the 1960s.

depression A fall or reduction in the amount of industrial and trading activity such as followed (a) the First World War, (b) the Wall Street Crash, 1929 and (c) the rise in oil prices after 1973.

desegregation The ending of segregation.

détente The easing of strained relations between rival States. It is part of the policy of co-existence.

dictatorship Rule by one person who has usually gained power by a coup d'état and who suppresses democracy (see above) in his or her totalitarian state (see totalitarianism).

diktat The imposition of severe terms by a victor on a defeated nation. Often used of the Treaty of Versailles – by Germans.

distressed areas Those areas of Britain which suffered severe unemployment during the depression (see above) during the inter-war period.

dole The amount of money paid weekly by the State to unemployed workers.

Dominion A term used to describe the first self-governing (and therefore independent) parts of the British Empire – Australia, Canada, New Zealand and South Africa. Dominion status was defined in 1926 and in the Statute of Westminster, 1931. Dominions were free from British control but retained a connection with the British Throne.

Duma Originally this described the Russian elected town councils. It was more commonly used in the 19th century by liberals as the title of their proposed Russian Council of State – or Parliament.

EEC The European Economic Community, or Common Market.

EFTA The European Free Trade Association.

emancipation The setting free of people – from slavery (in the USA) or serfdom (in Russia) or from legal disabilities (such as women suffered).

entente A friendly understanding between people in which they settle their past differences. The Entente Cordiale between Britain and France, 1904, was followed by an Anglo-Russian Entente in 1907.

FAO The Food and Agricultural Organization (of the United Nations).

federal This is used to describe the system of government in which several states form a unity (or union) but remain independent in internal affairs. It is also used to describe the policy of supporting a central government as opposed to those who favour government by separate states or provinces. Australia, Canada, West Germany and the USA have federal systems of government.

FLN The initials of the French words for the National Liberation Front (of Algeria).

franchise The right to vote (see suffrage).

Führer The German word for leader, taken by Hitler in 1934.

GDR The German Federal Republic (East Germany).

GPU The Russian initials for the State Political Department, once the name for the Russian secret police, later the OGPU.

guerrilla A fighter engaged in irregular warfare, usually as a member of an organization resisting the government. Guerrilla warfare describes the methods used by resistance movements who use hit-and-run tactics and sabotage. Urban guerrillas refers to groups operating in towns. Guerrilla is a Spanish word and was first used to describe fighters resisting Napoleon's rule in Spain.

humanitarian Someone campaigning for some humane purpose or welfare.

ICBM Intercontinental ballistic missiles (see ABM above).

immigrants People who come to live, as permanent residents, in a foreign country.

imperialism The extension of the power of one country over other (usually backward) countries. Dollar imperialism is a term used by critics to describe the process by which the US government and US firms gain control of the economy of a country.

Russian imperialism is used to describe the extension of Russian control of Eastern Europe and, more recently, Afghanistan.

indemnity Usually used to describe a sum of money, a sort of fine, forced out of one country by another after a war (see reparations).

independence The freedom granted to former colonies when the colonial power gives up control. Independence movements are organizations campaigning for independence. They often use guerrilla tactics (see above) when the colonialist power refuses to accept their demands (see FLN).

inflation A general increase of prices and a fall in the purchasing value of money. It usually results from an increase in the quantity of currency, as in Germany in 1923. It may also be the result of increased raw material prices, as with oil after 1973.

integration The merging together of peoples of different races into one society; the integration in US schools refers to the attempts to abolish segregated schools (see below) so that black and white children attended the same school.

investment The spending of money on stocks and shares; the spending of money by individuals or governments on various projects. Such spending creates employment, but may lead to inflation (see above).

isolationism The policy of staying out of involvement in the affairs of other countries. It is particularly used to refer to US foreign policy after 1920.

Izvestia One of the two official Soviet newspapers. It means 'news'. See also *Pravda*.

KGB The Russian 'secret branch', as the secret police was known after Stalin's death. (See MVD below.)

Lebensraum (living space) Territory which Germans (particularly the Nazis) claimed was necessary for natural development. Such territory was often rich in natural resources.

Mandates Areas of the German and Turkish colonial empires which were placed under the control of powers named by the League of Nations so that they could be prepared for independence (see independence).

manifesto The publicly stated policy (usually in writing) of an organization, usually of a political party.

MBFR Mutual and Balanced Force Reduction.

mediate (to) To intervene, or form the connecting link, between two rival groups in the hope of bringing them to agreement (see arbitration).

Mig The Russian air design team of Mikoyan and Gurevich.

ministerial responsibility The responsibility of government ministers to parliament, where ministers have to answer for their actions. In many countries this is regarded as an essential part of democracy (see democracy). It does not exist in an autocracy (see autocracy or dictatorship).

MIRV Multiple Independently-targeted Re-entry Vehicle, a ballistic missile.

MVD The initials of the Russian secret police when it changed from being the NKVD and before it became the KGB.

NASA National Aeronautics and Space Administration (USA).

nation The people of a country under one government.

nationalism Patriotic feeling; pride in one's own country. It may take the form of a campaign for independence in a colonial country. It may lead to a campaign to make one's nation united and strong. It may lead to a desire to make one's country supreme over others.

nationalization The taking over of the ownership of private property, e.g. the nationalization of the coal industry made it the property of the nation instead of the property of private mine owners.

NATO The North Atlantic Treaty Organization.

NEP The New Economic Policy developed by Lenin and ended by Stalin.

NKVD The name of the Russian secret police during its most notorious period under Stalin's direction (see MVD above).

NLF The National Liberation Front, a title used by nationalists fighting a guerrilla war (see guerrilla) in (a) Aden and (b) Vietnam.

OEEC The Organization for European Economic Co-operation.

OGPU The Central State Political Department, the name of the Russian secret police which succeeded the Cheka (see Cheka).

OPEC The Organization of Petroleum Exporting Countries.

pacifism The belief that all war is wrong. Pacifists refuse to take an active part in fighting during a war.

pact An agreement or treaty.

Pan-Slavism A belief that the whole (*pan* = Greek for 'all') Slavonic peoples should work together; they shared a common (orthodox) religion and common enemies (Austria and Turkey).

partisan A word used in the Second World War to describe anti-German guerrillas (see guerrilla), particularly Yugoslavia, Italy and France.

panzer German armoured troops.

plebiscite A vote of all the people in a given area on a particular issue. In 1935 the people of the Saar voted in a plebiscite to be re-united with Germany.

PLO The Palestine Liberation Organization which engaged in guerrilla war against Israel.

pogrom The organized massacre of a minority group, especially of Jews in Russia (from the Russian word for 'destroy').

police state A state in which a secret police supervises the people's activities.

Politburo The small group of leaders who controlled Soviet policy-making. It took charge of the Communist Party of the Soviet Union when its Central Committee was not in session.

Pravda Another official Soviet newspaper. It means 'Truth'. (See *Izvestia*, 'News'.) Russians joked that they get plenty of Izvestia but not much Pravda in their newspapers.

proletariat Wage-earners who have no property and depend on their daily labour for their subsistence. Marxists use it to describe the working masses who, they say, are kept down by the bourgeoisie (see bourgeoisie).

propaganda A word used by critics of attempts to spread a certain doctrine or belief; the means of spreading a belief. It comes from the Latin *propagare* (meaning to multiply plants by layering).

prohibition This usually refers to the attempt to ban the manufacture and sale of alcoholic drink in the USA between 1920 and 1933.

protection A system of tariffs to protect home industries against foreign imports. It is the opposite of free trade.

protectorate A country which is controlled and/or developed by a stronger country. Some mandated territories (see Mandates) became known as protectorates.

puppet (state) A country which claims to be independent but which is actually controlled by a greater power (see satellite).

purge (to) To get rid of 'undesirable' people in the army or state; particularly applied to Stalin's policy in the 1930s.

putsch From the Swiss word for 'blow'. A German attempt at a coup d'état; particularly applied to Hitler's attempt to seize power in 1923.

race People of common descent, perhaps of a distinctive ethnic group. People of different races may be found in one nation (see nation) as in the USA and South Africa.

radical From the Latin word for root. Someone who campaigns for major reforms and changes.

reactionary Someone opposed to change who may, even, want to 'turn back the clock' and undo past reforms.

referendum A vote on a single issue (see plebiscite).

Reichstag The Lower (or popularly-elected) House of the German Parliament.

reparations Compensation for injury or damages imposed by the victorious country and paid by the conquered. They were similar to an indemnity (see indemnity) but were a compensation rather than a fine.

republic A state without a monarchy, that has a president as the head of state.

revisionism (a) The demand for change of some treaty such as the Treaty of Versailles. (b) More recently it has been used about communists who seek to 'revise' Marx's teachings. It is most often used, by those who think that a violent revolution is essential, as an attack on revisionists who think that communism can be achieved by peaceful means. Mao Tse-tung denounced Khrushchev as a revisionist; China is now ruled by such revisionists.

SALT The Strategic Arms Limitation Talks.

SAM Surface-to-Air Missiles.

sanctions Penalties or methods used to put pressure on nations committing what others condemn as illegal actions. Economic sanctions involve restrictions on trade. Military sanctions involve entering into war.

satellite (a) A country, seemingly independent, but in reality controlled by a greater power (see puppet). (b) One of the artificial bodies sent into orbit around the earth or other planet.

SD Social Democrat.

secession A separation or breaking away of one part of a union (of states or races). The Southern States wanted to break away from the Federal United States; Biafra wanted to break away from Nigeria.

segregation A separation, usually imposed, of different groups of people. (See apartheid, desegregation and integration.)

Senate The Upper House of the US Congress.

socialism A political and social theory which argues that the community as a whole should own and control the means of production (see nationalization), distribution and exchange. In its extreme form it is Marxist.

soviet A council or committee elected in a district of Russia. In 1905 and 1917 soviets were formed by revolutionaries. (See USSR.)

SR Social Revolutionary.

suffrage The right to vote (see franchise).

SWAPO The South West African People's Organization which campaigned for the independence (see independence) of the mandated territory which was formerly German South West Africa.

tariffs Taxes on imports. (See protection.)

totalitarianism A system of government which does not allow a rival to the ruling party. Nazi Germany and Soviet Russia are examples of totalitarian régimes.

tribalism Loyalty to the tribe rather than to the nation (see nation), a feature of some independent African states.

TVA The Tennessee Valley Authority (USA).

U-2 The Lockheed spy-plane (USA).

UDI A Unilateral Declaration of Independence by a country claiming independence (see independence) without the permission of the colonial power (e.g. Rhodesia, 1965).

ultimatum A final proposal or statement of terms, the rejection of which by the opposition (party or nation) leads to a break in friendly relations and may lead to war.

USSR The Union of Soviet Socialist Republics. (See soviet, socialist and republic.)

UNICEF The United Nations International Children's Emergency Fund.

UNO The United Nations Organization.

UNRRA United Nations Relief and Rehabilitation Administration.

Untouchables Those who are outside the Indian caste system (see caste). They do the most menial jobs and are the most underprivileged.

V1; V2 From the initial of the German *Vergeltungswaffen*; reprisal weapons. V1 was a flying bomb (or 'doodle bug'); V2 was a supersonic rocket.

VSO Voluntary Service Overseas.

veto The right to reject a law or proposal. Such a power is possessed by rulers, presidents, some Upper Houses of Parliament and by the permanent members of the Security Council of the UNO (see above). Every member of the League of Nations had such a veto.

Watergate This complex of buildings contained the headquarters of the Democratic Party during the Presidential election in 1971. Republican burglars broke in and the subsequent scandals surrounding this break-in led to the resignation and imprisonment of the Vice-President, Spiro Agnew, and the resignation of the President, Richard Nixon.

WHO The World Health Organization.

welfare state A state with comprehensive social services and social security systems in health and education and against sickness, unemployment and old age.

ZAPU The Zimbabwe African People's Union which led to the guerrilla war (see guerrilla) by African nationalists (see nationalism) trying to overthrow the whites-only government which had declared UDI (see UDI).

Zionist A supporter of the colonization of Palestine by the Jews. The World Zionist Organization was founded in 1897.

Index

Abyssinia 71–2
Adenauer, Konrad 130
Afghanistan 108, 109
Africa
    European colonisation 21–2
    mandated territories 34
    South 148–52
    World War II campaigns 83–4
African National Congress (ANC) 149–51
air warfare 27, 82, 83, 90, 91
Albania 23, 83, 125
Amritsar 77, 79
apartheid 148–50
appeasement 73
Arabs 28, 35, 153–9
Arafat, Yasser 155, 156, 157–8
arms race 106
Aswan Dam 155, 160
Atlantic Charter 95
Austria 20–2, 23, 34–5, 72–3

Balfour, A.J. 36, 153
Balkans 20–1, 22, 23, 28, 34, 83
Battle of the Atlantic 82–3
Battle of Britain 82
Battle of the Coral Sea 85
Battle of El Alamein 83–4
Battle of Midway Island 85
Battle of Stalingrad 84
battles
    World War I 27, 28, 29, 30
    World War II 82–6
Begin, Menachem 157–8
Belgium 24
Ben Gurion, David 154
Benes, Edward 73–4
Berlin airlift 102–3
Berlin Wall 111–14
Bevin, Ernest 91
Bismarck, Otto von 22
Blitz 92
blitzkrieg 81–2, 84
Bolsheviks 16, 43, 44
Bosnia 23
Boxer uprising 51
Brezhnev, Leonid 104, 106, 107–8, 121–2
Brownshirts (SA) 60, 61
Bulganin, Nikolai 103, 120
Bulgaria 20, 83, 84, 125
Bush, George 109, 139

Cadets (Russia) 17–18
Carter, Jimmy 107, 138–9
caste system 80
Castro, Fidel 114
Chamberlain, Neville 73–4, 81

Chiang Kai-shek 53–6, 86
China 51–7, 141–7
Chou En-lai 53, 55, 142, 143, 145
Churchill, Winston S. 81, 86–7, 95, 101, 130
civil rights, USA 136–8
Clinton, Bill 139
Cold War 101–9
Cominform 102, 125
Commonwealth of Independent States (CIS) 123
communism
    China 53, 54–6, 141–6
    Eastern Europe 102, 122, 125–8
    Germany 58, 59, 60, 61
    Russia 16, 44, 45–7, 120–3
    USA 65, 136
Congo 97
Congress Party, India 76, 77, 78, 79
convoys, wartime 29, 82
Corfu 40–1
Covenant, League of Nations 38
Cuban crisis (1962) 114–16
Cultural Revolution (China) 143–4
Czechoslovakia 73–4, 125, 126, 127

Danzig (Gdansk) 33, 40, 74
Dardanelles 23, 28
Dawes Plan 59
de Gaulle, Charles 131
De Klerk, F.W. 151
Deng Xiaoping 144, 145–6
Depression, USA 66
détente 107
disarmament 41
dissidents 107–8, 126–7
Domino Theory 116
Dubcek, Alexander 127
Dulles, John Foster 116, 160
Duma 17–18, 43
Dunkirk 81–2

Eden, Anthony 73, 160
Egypt 23, 83, 153–7
Eisenhower, Dwight D. 84, 97, 103–4, 136, 160
entente
    Anglo-French (Entente Cordiale) 23
    Anglo-Russian 23
Europe
    Eastern 125–8
    Western, integration 129–34
European Coal and Steel Community (ECSC) 130
European Community 131–2
European Economic Community (EEC) 130–1
    Britain and 132–3
European Union 132
examinations 1–2
    answering questions 5–6

coursework 2–4
    questions and answers 165–206
    revision 4–5
    syllabuses 8–14
    types of question 6–7

Food and Agricultural Organisation (FAO) 98
Formosa (Taiwan) 56

Gandhi (Mahatma) 77–8, 79
Gaza Strip 154, 155
GCSE *see* examinations
Geneva, conferences 103, 116
Germany
    1870–1914 20–4
    1918–39 58–63
    World War I 26–31
    effects of Treaty of Versailles 33–4, 58
    World War II 81–7
    after World War II 102–3, 104
Germany, East 126
Gestapo 61
glasnost 122
Goebbels, Joseph 60, 61
Goering, Herman 61
Golan Heights 156–7
Gomulka, Wladislaw 125, 126, 127
Gorbachev, Mikhail 108–9, 122–3
Great Leap Forward (1958) 142, 143
Greece 83, 102
Grenada 108
guerillas 102, 114, 116, 125

Hammarskjold, Dag 96, 97
Heath, Edward 131
Helsinki Agreement 107
Hitler, Adolf 60–3, 72–4, 86
Ho Chi-minh 116
Hungary 74, 83, 84, 125, 126

India 76–80
inflation, Germany 59
International Court of Justice 96
International Labour Organisation (ILO) 39–40,
    97
International Monetary Fund (IMF) 98
Iran 108
Iraq 35–6, 98, 153, 154, 155, 156
iron curtain 101, 102
isolationism, USA 68
Israel 154–9
Italy 35, 71–2, 83

Japan 7, 16, 53, 55, 71, 85–6
Jews
    Arabs and 153–9
    homeland for 36, 153
    Nazi persecution of 62
    in Russia 107
Jinnah, M. Ali 78, 79

Johnson, Lyndon B. 116, 137–8
Jordan 35–6, 154, 156

Kennedy, John F. 104, 114, 116, 137
Kerensky, Alexander 44
King, Martin Luther 137, 138
Korea 97, 103
Kosygin, Alexsei 104, 121
Khrushchev, Nikita 48, 111, 114, 120–1, 126,
    144
Ku Klux Klan 65, 136–7
kulaks 18, 47
Kuo Min Tang (KMT) 52, 54, 55

Laval, Pierre 71–2
Lawrence, T.E. (Lawrence of Arabia) 28, 35
League of Nations 38–42, 70–3
Lebanon 35–6, 153, 155, 157–8
Lenin, V.I. 16, 44–6
Libya 83, 108
Liu Shao-chi 142, 143–4
Lloyd George, David 33, 89, 90
Long March 55
Ludendorff, Erich 30, 58, 60

MacArthur, General George D. 97, 136
McCarthy, Senator Joseph 136
MacMillan, Harold 131, 160
Maginot Line 81
Manchuria 56, 71
mandates
    Africa 34
    Middle East 36, 153
Mandela, Nelson 150–1
Mao Tse-tung 53–6, 141–5
Marshall Plan 102
marxism 16, 102
Mensheviks 16
Mesopotamia *see* Iraq
Middle East 153–9
    mandated territories 36, 153
    World War I 28, 30, 35–6
    World War II 83
Monnet, Jean 130
Morocco 23
Mountbatten, Earl Louis 79
Mulberry Harbour 86
Munich 59, 74
Mussolini, Benito 71, 72–3, 83, 85
Mutual Assured Destruction (MAD) 106

Nagy, Imry 126
Nasser, Gamel 155–6, 160–1
Nazi Party 60–3
Nazi-Soviet Pact 74
Nehru, Jawaharlal 78–9
New Deal 67–8
New Economic Policy (NEP) 45
Nicholas II, tsar 15–18, 43
Nixon, Richard 106–7, 117, 138, 144

North Atlantic Treaty Organisation (NATO) 95, 103
nuclear weapons/missiles 106

October Manifesto (1905) 17
OEEC 129–30
oil 153, 157
OPEC 153, 157

Pakistan 78, 79–80
Palestine 35–6, 153–4
Palestinian Liberation Organisation (PLO) 155–8
Pearl Harbour 85
perestroika 122
Pétain, Marshall 82
plebiscites 73
Poland 35, 74, 81, 84, 125, 126, 127–8
Potsdam 87, 101
prohibition 65
purges, Stalinist Russia 46

Rabin, Itzhak 158
radar 82, 83
Rasputin, G. 43
Reagan, Ronald 108–9, 139
Reichstag 58, 60, 61
reparations 34, 59
revolutions
    China (1911) 52
    Germany (1918–22) 58–9
    Russia (1917) 43–4
Rhineland 33–4, 73
Roosevelt, Franklin Delano 67–8, 86–7, 95, 135
Ruhr 59
Rumania 20, 83, 84, 125
Russia
    1900–1914 15–19
    1914–53 43–9
    World War I 26, 28
    World War II 47–8, 84
    Cold War 101–9
    1953–95 120–4

SA 60, 61
Saar 33
Sadat, Anwar 156, 157
SALT treaties 107–8
sanctions 38, 70, 71, 96, 98, 108
Saudi Arabia 154, 156
Schlieffen Plan 26
Schumann, Robert 130
sea warfare 29, 82–3, 85
secret police
    Germany (Gestapo; SS) 61
    Russia (CHEKA; NKVD) 45, 46, 49, 120
Security Council 96
Serbia 20–1, 23–4
Simon Commission 78
Sinai 156
Solidarity 127

South Africa 148–52
SS 61
Stalin, Josef 46–9, 86–7, 102–3, 120, 125–6
Stolypin, P. 17, 18
Strategic Defence Initiative (SDI; Star Wars) 108–9
Stresa Front 73
Streseman, Gustav 59
submarines 29, 82–3, 90
Sudetenland 73, 74
Suez 97, 153, 160–3
summit meetings
    allied leaders (1941–5) 86–7
    since 1945 103–4, 108–9
Sun Yat-sen 52, 53
Syria 35–6, 153, 154, 155–8

Taiwan (Formosa) 56
tariffs 68, 131
Thatcher, Margaret 131, 133
Tiananmen Square 146
Tito, J. Broz 102, 125
treaties
    Brest Litovsk (1918) 44–5
    Bucharest (1913) 23
    Frankfurt (1871) 20
    Lausanne (1923) 35–6
    Locarno (1925) 59, 70
    London (1839) 24
    Maastricht (1993) 132
    NATO (1949) 103
    Nazi-Soviet (1939) 74
    Reinsurance (1878) 22
    Rome (1956) 130
    St Germain (1919) 34–5
    Sèvres (1920) 35–6
    Strategic Arms Limitation (1970s) 107–8
    Versailles (1919) 33–4, 58, 70, 72
Trotsky, Leon 16, 17, 44, 45, 46
Truman, Harry S. 87, 97, 101, 102, 135–6
Turkey 28, 35

U-boats 29, 82–3, 90
United Nations Organisation 95–100
United States of America
    World War I 29
    1919–39 64–9
    World War II 85–6, 135
    Cold War 101–9
    1945–97 135–40
USSR *see* Russia

Vietcong 116–17
Vietnam 103, 116–19

Walesa, Lech 127–8
Wall Street crash (1929) 66
wars
    Arab-Israeli 154, 155, 156–7
    Balkan League (1912–13) 23
    Chinese Civil War 56

Chinese-Japanese 55
Franco-Prussian (1870–71) 20
Gulf 98
Korean (1950–3) 97, 103
Russian Civil War (1918–22) 45
Russian-Japanese (1904) 16
Russian-Turkish (1877–78) 20
Vietnam 116–19, 138, 139
Yugoslavian civil war 98
see also World War I; World War II
Warsaw Pact 95, 103
Washington Naval Conferences (1921–2) 68
Weimar Republic 58–60
William (Wilhelm) II, Kaiser 22–3, 30
Wilson, Woodrow 30, 32–3
women and war 89, 91
World Health Organisation (WHO) 98
World War I 26–31

background 20–3
British home front 88–90
outbreak 23–4
peace treaties 30, 32–6
World War II 81–7
background 72–4
British home front 90–3

Yalta 86–7, 95
Yeltsin, Boris 109, 123
Yemen 155, 156
Young Plan 59
youth culture 139
Yuan Shih k'ai 52–3
Yugoslavia 83, 98, 102, 125

Zhdanov, Andrei 102
Zinoviev, Grigoriy 46